From *Unit History, 639th AAA AW Battalion*

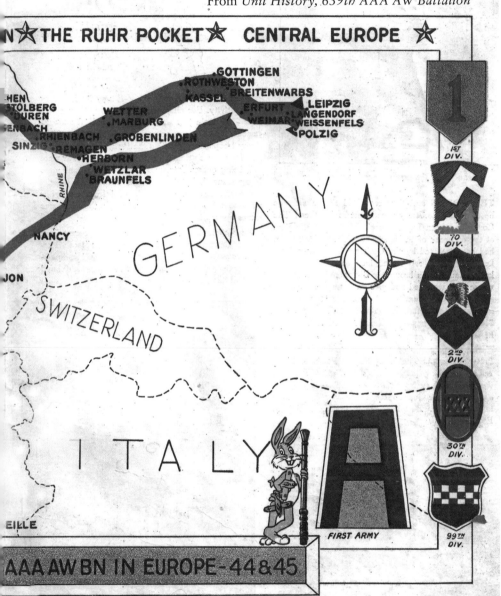

Here's My Heart

A LEGACY OF
LOVE AND WAR

Leigh W. Callan

RM
RiverMont
PRESS

Here's My Heart: A Legacy of Love and War

Copyright © 2015 by Leigh W. Callan

All Rights Reserved. No part of this publication may be reproduced, stored in a retrieval system or transmitted, in any form or by any means—electronic, mechanical, photocopying, recording or otherwise—without prior written permission from the publisher, except for the inclusion of brief quotations in a review.

For information about this title or to order other books and/or electronic media, contact the publisher:
RiverMont Press, LLC
3 Central Plaza, #166
Rome, Georgia 30161-3233
Web address: www.rivermontpress.com

To contact the author:
E-mail: lwcallan@rivermontpress.com

Library of Congress Control Number: 2015950984
ISBN: 978-0-9967381-7-0

Printed in the United States of America

Cover and Interior design: 1106 Design, Phoenix, AZ

Ah, love, let us be true

To one another! for the world which seems

To lie before us like a land of dreams,

So various, so beautiful, so new,

Hath really neither joy, nor love, nor light,

Nor certitude, nor help for pain,

And here we are, as on a darkling plain

Swept with confused alarms of struggle and flight,

Where ignorant armies clash by night.

—Matthew Arnold
"Dover Beach" (1867)

To loved ones separated by miles and duty:

*May you stay connected for all time through the written word,
allowing your story to touch generations of family yet to come.*

Contents

Part I: The Stateside Story

Of Love, Marriage and Combat Readiness
Letters from November 26, 1942, through October 5, 1944

Part II: The Overseas Story: England–Belgium–Germany
Of Deployment, Combat and Victory
Letters from October 5, 1944, through June 11, 1945

Part III: The Overseas Story: Southern France
Of Post-Combat Assignments and the Agonizing Wait for
    Passage Home
Letters from June 19, 1945, through November 15, 1945

Contents

Foreword

Many things define a person. Looking at remnants of my father's life, I found much material to sort through, including letters, scrapbooks, souvenirs, photographs and Dad's unpublished written memoir. In prioritizing and collating the material, I have come to know my father, Doyle Kennedy Whittenburg, in ways I did not while he was alive. What began three years after his death as a compilation for family posterity has revealed far-reaching truths.

These things defined him:

> His own father died in 1928 when Dad was eleven; his mother was left to raise five children through the Great Depression. She raised them well. He loved, respected and honored her throughout his life.

> He was a lieutenant during World War II (WWII) serving in the European Theater of Operations (ETO). His antiaircraft artillery (AA or AAA) unit earned three battle stars, one each for the Ardennes Campaign, the Battle of the Bulge, and defense of the bridgehead at Remagen in the Rhineland Campaign.

> He processed the significance of his role in world history for the rest of his life, telling his war stories over and over again.

He loved a woman completely and steadfastly for 63 years. He gave her emotional and physical support in caring for their children and home. Few women have been loved the way he loved her.

He supported his three children in every endeavor and was immensely proud of his family and his home. He was generous of spirit if not of material things.

He was an ardent observer of nature and, having much insight about even the smallest of events happening around him, always eagerly shared his observations. His guidance fostered in us the same curiosity, steering us toward our careers.

The majority of my father's story is told in his own words through his letters to my mother during the war years. Therein is a comprehensive story representing any US soldier training for combat duty in any era and every war. It is the timeless story of a soldier falling in love and then having doubts about wartime marriage. It is the story of overcoming fear to do unimaginable duty while maintaining a love connection through words on paper. A story of love and survival both, it is a guide for coping with separation under extreme circumstances. The backdrop is WWII, but this story—so very intimate and personal—is about the soldier and his lady, not the war.

The events that occurred during the war years led to important transitions in this soldier's psyche—classic coming-of-age conversions. Self-doubt led to self-confidence. A loner became a lover and loyal life-mate. Prejudices developed and then abated. Patriotism and resulting heroism grew from his deep love and caring for his people back home.

His experiences in Europe impacted my father so much that he wrote several chapters about them for a memoir some forty years after the fact. I am amazed by how much specific information he accurately remembered. The details revealed by letters and memoir about his circumstances, environment and human experience provided a roadmap for my brother and me. We followed our father's track, sleeping where he slept, praying where he prayed, bathing where he bathed and meeting people he met and remembered for the rest of his life.

My mother's voice and presence in the story is strong. Indeed, it is her story as much as my father's, although in the early stages of this project, her presence was largely inferred through his responses to her letters. None of her letters survived, because he was unable to keep them during the hazards of war. Now past her ninth decade, she has actively participated in this project by sharing her own memories. I am fortunate to have her by my side to answer questions and make clarifying comments. On my request, she has written her own memoir chapters from the home front perspective, helping to complete and greatly enriching the narrative as a whole.

This project was initially intended for family only, but I gradually came to realize the material could be of value to others interested in reading about firsthand experience from WWII and to those in current service as they cope with separation from loved ones. Much can be discovered about social adjustments in a wartime culture by reading Dad's in-the-moment observations and opinions, which offer free access to the daily mindset of this citizen soldier and the opportunity to experience the highs and lows of his journey as if by his side.

One thing I know. On the fifth day of transcribing his words sixty some-odd years after they were written, I fell in love with this young man who became my father. And I understood why my parents' marriage lasted for sixty-two years, "until death do us part."

EDITORIAL CHOICES

This book focuses on my father's words from wartime letters and a subsequent memoir. A prologue from his childhood memoir sets the stage and a short epilogue of postwar events completes the story. I have relied on two US Army publications to validate or complete certain descriptions of military activities: *Unit History of the 639th AAA AW Battalion* and more specifically *Battery D History* of that battalion, both written by the participating soldiers and produced by the army following V-E Day for distribution to troops in the units. Dad's copies are frayed and dog-eared from repeated use as references through the years. Certain events are supported by online histories of other army units; excerpts are cited in place. Detailed background information about the Battle of the Bulge can be found in Hugh M. Cole's *The Ardennes: Battle of the Bulge* provided online by the US Army Center of Military History.

My own comments and explanations are interspersed and include the powerful encounters I experienced in 2010 while physically retracing my father's footsteps along the route of the 639th through England, Belgium and Germany.

Letters are chronologically arranged unless otherwise noted. During the stateside correspondence, Dad rarely dated his letters. Mom dated them when she received them, and if she received more than one at once, she dated them by context. In Europe, he dated them as written, but one letter may have taken a day or two to complete.

The early letters are complete, but repetitive content is omitted from subsequent letters. Many are only represented by a sentence or two of the original, and some are excluded altogether. At my mother's request, I have omitted very personal material written as this young couple faced typical struggles with passion and anxiety during an unpredictable future.

The sections written in my own words are italicized, with the exception of short bracketed editorial corrections and explanations. Quotations from supporting sources occurring within my italicized commentary appear in plain font. Parenthetical phrases are Dad's own.

I have chosen to correct my father's errors in spelling and mechanics in order to make the content flow well. (Once he promised he wouldn't take my mother for "granite," and later he called her "deer.") Understandably, he often misspelled foreign words. Most of these I have caught and corrected. A few remain a mystery. Some abbreviations that Dad used to save valuable space on Victory mail (or V-mail) are herein written in full. His references to "the Army" are left capitalized since that important entity is very much a character in this story, as is, in one instance, "Home." Dad's most consistent inconsistency is using lowercase "army" for general adjective use, such as "an army camp," but using uppercase "Army" for the subject of a verb as in "The Army thinks it needs me." I prefer to retain his pattern.

Dad only capitalized pet names for Juby if they were at the beginning of a sentence, and he rarely set them off by commas. The words "sweet" and "honey" flowed from his pen as easily as breath from his body. I have chosen to leave these names in lowercase within a sentence as they occur throughout the letters, but I have altered punctuation where necessary. Grammar, syntax and technical details (run-on sentences, misplaced modifiers, dates, time references, military titles, etc.) have been selectively corrected and regularized with the goal of preserving the "sound" of my father's own voice. In rare cases, I have preserved irregularities—such as variances in reporting time of day, where the alternation between systems (e.g., nine o'clock and 0900) reveals the divide he straddles between army and civilian life.

ACKNOWLEDGMENTS

I owe many people a debt of gratitude for encouragement, patience, reassurance and participation in the development of this work. The project was actually Dad's idea at the outset. Through the years he would say to me, "You know, we have all of my letters." He knew they were important and wanted me to work with them, so he deserves the credit for initiating the work. After all, the majority of the text originates with him. Mom has contributed clarifying information and continued support. Indeed, it was her diligence that preserved bits and pieces of the story all along, providing a strong foundation from which to launch this venture.

The first people to read an early draft other than family members were Laurence W. Marvin, professor of history at Berry College and author of *The Occitan War: A Military and Political History of the Albigensian Crusade, 1209–1218,* and Cheryl Fitzner, retired Spanish teacher, history buff, traveler and hiking buddy. Both made valuable comments that helped further the project. Longtime friends Trish and John Dunaway continually prodded me to persevere and introduced me to Gayle Wurst, an editor and literary agent at Princeton International Agency of the Arts, who is specialized in military history. Her editorial advice was invaluable as I continued to massage the material into a reader-worthy product. Among other things, she taught me that good editorial changes clarify but do not change the truth. Darlene Ulseth Callan, retired educator, was my constant consultant on writing mechanics, helping make sense from nonsense. Dan Roper, editor and publisher of *Georgia BackRoads,* gave me lessons about the publishing world. Aviation expert Colin Heaton interpreted photographs and combat records of the 639th AAA AW Battalion. Renate Corbin graciously shared her memories of childhood in Nazi Germany as well as her experiences on V-E Day. Many other friends, acquaintances and family members patiently listened to me when all of my conversation seemed stuck in the 1940s.

Guide extraordinaire Michael Baert shepherded my brother and me across Belgium and Germany, allowing Dad's words and descriptions to become very real to us. He introduced us to the surviving members of the Jamar family who deserve thanks for welcoming us with open arms and sharing their memories of those historic days. Lastly, my utmost appreciation goes to my brother, Neal Kennedy (Ken) Whittenburg, who shared the mission and the emotion as we walked Dad's path side by side, and to our sister, Jan Greene, who kept our mother calm while we were gone so far away.

THE PHOTOGRAPHS

The exchange of photographs is as crucial to this story as the exchange of what Dad called "word pictures." At first, he belittled the idea of trading "likenesses," saying it only would make him miss his loved ones more. Eventually he relented and ended up begging for snapshots, was thankful to get them and shared many of his own after learning photography by trial and error.

Mom created scrapbooks with the photographs and other mementos such as postcards and news articles that Dad sent her. She included many photographs of herself in pinup poses that she had sent to Dad. I scanned them all, improved the quality where I could and chose some to illustrate the text. All photographs and illustrations that are not otherwise credited are from this Whittenburg Family Collection. Some of these, such as the photographs of stateside training and those taken in Europe before V-E Day, were given to Dad by his fellow soldiers.

Late in his combat service, when Dad acquired cameras and equipment and taught himself photography, he sent many more negatives and prints home. In so doing, he documented history. Some important examples are included here, despite their poor quality. Also included are my own photographs of souvenirs Dad was so proud to send home as well as photographs from my "In His Footsteps" tour of 2010, paired with photographs from scrapbooks to produce a "then and now" comparison.

Preface

*M*y dad, Doyle K. Whittenburg, lived eleven days past his 89th birthday and just a few weeks short of the 62nd anniversary of his marriage to Mom. While we were growing up, he was a Sunday School teacher. He would take us with him on Sunday, and we would attend our separate classes. We rarely stayed for worship services, confusing me somewhat since I thought worship was what we were studying for. Instead he would take us to his mother's house for an hour visit with Grandmother Whittenburg and Aunt Eleanor. There I would read the "Quotable Quotes," "Humor in Uniform" and "Laughter Is the Best Medicine" parts of Reader's Digest *and enjoy photographs in* Life Magazine *and* Norman Rockwell's art on the cover of Saturday Evening Post. At noon we would return home for Mom's Sunday dinner: home-fried chicken (Col. Sanders was not yet selling Kentucky-fried, or Mom would have surely bought it!) and the typical trimmings—mashed potatoes and gravy, fried okra and squash in summer and dried beans in winter, and biscuits always.

I realized later that Sunday was Mom's morning to sleep late, have some quiet time and enjoy putting a meal on the table. During the week, she was a working mom and had to rush us all out the door fortified with some milk and a Pillsbury cinnamon bun (the kind that is packaged in a tube that you whack on the side of the counter to open). In the evenings she would come home from her

hard day at work to hear us chime in unison, "What's for supper?"
She would go straight to the kitchen and start whatever quick-fix
meal she could. I remember many Swanson frozen foods and/or
canned items. But we were well fed. When Dad came home, he
would always walk to the stove where she was working and give
her a strong embrace and a long romantic kiss.

Saturdays were spent doing household chores under her direc-
tion. It appeared to us that we had that typical family portrayed in
the highly popular television series Father Knows Best *(1954–1960)*
and Leave It to Beaver *(1957–1963). It is through transcribing his*
early letters and later memoir that I learned where the foundation
for our own It's a Wonderful Life *came from.*

Through the years, Dad became continually more talkative
about his war experiences. He connected every aspect of daily
living to something he remembered from those amazing events
of the 1940s. We tired of hearing the repeated stories, but always
appreciated their power and thought his flair for the dramatic
greatly embellished the telling.

A year before Dad's death, an episode of pulmonary distress
landed him in the hospital on powerful medication. He began hal-
lucinating. I had elected to stay through the night with him. He
never slept. The hallucinations were so real that he mustered great
strength from somewhere and kept trying to get out of bed and go
"to another room" or "home" or someplace he was imagining. To
protect him from himself, he had to be restrained. That was the
worst night of my life, to see him trying to chew the restraints off,
to have him beg me to remove them. A few days later, I watched
him stare out of the hospital window viewing an intersection busy
with traffic. In the distance, a part of Lavender Mountain was
visible. It was a clear day. He kept remarking about the snow on
the mountain. There was no snow. Suddenly he became agitated
because he visualized a plane crashing into the mountain. He said
he saw the smoke rise. After reading his letters, I now assume

that this particular hallucination was a flashback to an incident he witnessed and described fully in his memoir.

As I focus on his written word from beginning to end, he speaks to me anew, and I at last begin to hear him.

Prologue

Before War, There Was Poverty

From Doyle K. Whittenburg's unpublished memoir [written during the 1990s, excerpts from "Depression Work," "The Worst Years" and "The Opposite Sex"]:

The Depression that followed the 1929 stock market crash caught everyone by surprise. I look back on those days and realize that the higher up the financial ladder a person was at the time, the harder he hit bottom. My father died in 1928, leaving my mother to raise five children alone. This gave us a head start on learning how to overcome poverty.

My family ate well compared to others, since we depended on home gardens and bartering instead of using money. There was very little waste in our family. Scraps from the table were fed to a hog that would be slaughtered in the fall or early winter. The weather had to be cold or the meat would spoil. Neighbors would come to help during a hog killing, and it was a great festive time. It called for a lot of work, but it was fun.

Selling garden produce in season or nosegays of sweet pea blossoms and violets tied with sewing thread would bring in a dollar

1

each day. These items could be placed for sale near the cash register at a drug store uptown. The boys in the family earned money from neighbors by working in gardens or cutting and splitting wood. We trapped and shot rabbits in the winter months. A live rabbit would bring 25 cents on the community market; one killed with a 22 cal. rifle, fifteen cents; one killed by shotgun, ten cents. Bird shot left in the rabbit broke teeth.

For several years Mama took in travelers. A small sign in the front yard said "Tourist Home." Her price was $1.00 for one and $1.50 for two people including use of the family bath. Breakfast was extra. (One of the original bed and breakfast enterprises!) She moved all of us into the back of the house—three rooms and a screened-in back porch for six people. This left two rooms to rent out. She could accommodate five people, maybe six with the right relationship. It was amazing how many nights we had guests. This was before the days of motor hotels. It got to the point that repeat customers started showing up from up north. Most were headed for Florida looking for work. They had heard that Florida was building, so they were on their way, hoping.

Mama was a resourceful business woman. She insisted on her guests parking their cars just over and down an incline in the driveway by the side of the house. This was a precaution to prevent them from pushing their car out to the street before it was started, sneaking away without paying. She allowed three couples to stay and not pay, but with a promise that when they got their feet on the ground they would send the money. In all three cases the money came within three months.

Mama crocheted doilies, tablecloths and armchair protectors and created cloth dolls dressed up in clown suits. She made a display in a showcase she bought somewhere for $2.00 and placed it in the back part of the hall separating the two rooms she rented. Neighbor women brought in their handicrafts including beautiful handmade quilts. They paid Mama a percentage of the sale on the items sold on consignment. This venture brought considerable income to the home coffers.

While Mama was running the hotel and doing for five children, she was a case aide for WPA [Works Progress Administration, a New Deal agency providing work and support for families during the Great Depression]. There were a great many men out of work. At the time very few women worked out of the home. Some

Mama Whittenburg surrounded by her children, circa 1929

Will is tallest at left and Doyle is in front of Will.
Mary is tallest at right. Eleanor and Jack are in front of Mama.
They named this picture "Tobacco Road."

department stores would use them as seamstresses to make hats and alter clothing. Men would leave their families reluctantly to go to another town or state to find work, hoping to send for their families later. Many of the men would come to our back door and offer to do some work for a meal. If there was something to do in the way of work, Mama would have him to do it. Then she would have the man come in the kitchen, and she would feed him whatever was left from the previous meal. She would sit down and talk to the man about his troubles. Everyone back then was in the same boat, searching for a way to exist. When a black man came to the door, she treated him the same way, except she sat with him on the back steps while he ate and they talked. This separation of races was the custom years ago.

The years 1929 through 1934 were the absolute worst years of my life, when I was aged 12–16. Money was very short at home. We did not have too much in the way of clothing. Enough warm clothing was especially a problem. We were taught to look after our clothes. Our best clothes were saved for school days and Sundays. The women in the family were very good at patching, mending and re-fitting hand-me-downs. We hardly ever wore shoes in the summertime. We saved our money to buy school shoes. What one had to wear to school influenced the psychological attitude of the wearer. Peer pressure was in every classroom. One guy wore a different pair of pants, a different shirt and sweater each day, and had three pairs of shoes. Another girl or two had just as many changes of dresses, skirts, blouses and shoes. Even some of their lunches we considered high-quality cuisine. I just couldn't compete, I thought. It was a most miserable time.

I was in love with dozens of girls during those years. Not one of them ever knew it. I was afraid that if I displayed any signs at all of caring, the girl at the time might let me catch her or she would tell me to take a hike. The former possibility was frightening because, if she had accepted my admiration, it would have called for money

4

that I didn't have. I didn't even have a bicycle. Back then a one-dollar bill would have paid for two show tickets, two hamburgers, and two cokes. Cokes were five cents. I didn't have a dollar bill. On the other hand, if the girl in question refused my admiration, it would have humiliated me. There was no romance from age 13 to 19. There were too many fears; also a sense of morality generated from having two sisters prevented me from pursuing opportunities.

After graduation from high school, I tried every food place in town for employment—Triangle, Poss's, Troy's, Toonerville Trolley and others to no avail. The year I graduated, there were many men with families who needed work. That was why it was so difficult for a teenager to find employment. One summer I worked at O'Neill's Manufacturing Company for 25 cents per day. I also worked as a gardener-laborer, digging grass and weeds from flower beds. I worked about three months at this. I finally had to hire out to Mr. R. S. Kennard, a merchandise broker on Third Avenue uptown. I worked for him for nine months without pay. He said that he could not pay me a salary, but I could work for experience, which I sorely needed. I did his books under his direction; I unloaded freight cars loaded with potatoes, sugar, salt, flour and other things. All these items were packed in 100-pound bags. We sold sugar on the sly to the Armuchee moonshiners. I never did learn just how the transactions were carried out. Couldn't be much sold to one customer. The revenuers would check the sales record and know who might be operating a still. I could see a lot of talking over in warehouse corners. I didn't know the people, so I couldn't put it together. I always thought that it was cash payment for some of the shipment.

I grew up in a church with very little ceremonial ritual. I remember preachers that shouted out hell-and-damnation sermons, plump mamas holding babies, three to five children sitting along the church bench (the smallest one closest to Mama) and maybe a daddy at the other end of the bench, but not often. I remember an awful lot of sweating, including the preacher. Hand fans moved so rapidly back and forth that they almost whistled like the wind. Windows were opened on both sides of the church in an attempt to create a cross draft. Man was it hot! Clouds of dust stirred up by drivers outside would eventually pass through the church windows. Most roads were not paved, so the dry clay would easily turn into dust. The draft through the church windows would pull the dust into the church. When the congregation emerged, their faces and hands would be coated with a thin layer of mud. It was the reverse in the winter. There were wood stoves, cracks in the doors, cracks in the floor and broken windows which had not been repaired during the summer.

In those days mamas, mostly, taught the children right from wrong, directed them to do duties around home and helped with schoolwork. Daddies usually were struggling to make enough money at the plant or on the farm or maybe some of both to feed and clothe the family. My mother's teachings prevented me from doing improper things. I guess that you would call it proper upbringing. I had a fear of embarrassing my mother. She had taught me right from wrong.

Doyle had special love and respect for his mother, widowed in 1928 and left to raise her five children during the Great Depression. Here is a note from her Garden Club when he first went into service:

August 18, 1941

Dear Mrs. Whittenburg:

The Istalena Garden Club members wish to send you a few words of encouragement, since you, along with thousands of other mothers, have given a boy to service to Uncle Sam.

Often a woman is responsible for events by whose crash and splendor she herself is obscured. Often too, she shapes the career of husband, brother or son.

A man succeeds and reaps the honors of public applause when, in truth, a quiet little woman has made it all possible—by her test and encouragement has held him to his best, has had faith in him when his own faith has languished, has cheered him with the unfailing assurance, "You can, you must, you will."

Sincerely, Mrs. Mark Horton, Secretary

Call to Arms—Dating a Soldier

Doyle eventually took a job with J. C. Penney's Department Store in retail sales. He was transferred to Lake City, Florida, for two years, then to Ft. Payne, Alabama, where he was drafted on August 12, 1941, at the age of 24. Entering at Ft. MacPherson in Atlanta, he was assigned to Ft. Eustis, a large US Army Transportation Center in Virginia used during WWII for basic training of the Coastal Artillery. Training in an antiaircraft unit, he was promoted from buck private to corporal on November 28, 1941, then to sergeant on August 24, 1942.

The Unit History of the 639th AAA AW Battalion *(hereafter cited as* Unit History, 639th BN) *documents the activation of the 514th Coast Artillery Regiment in March of 1942, which in January 1943 was split into three separate battalions: the 217th Gun Battalion, the 363rd Searchlight Battalion and the 639th Coast Artillery (AA) Battalion. As the 639th, the battalion continued a role as School Troops until August 1943.*

The Battery D History, 639th AAA AW Battalion *(hereafter cited as* Battery D History, 639th BN) *further details the training program. Suffering a shortage of actual 37mm guns, battery members built wooden guns to use in practice:* "It was a very common sight to see the men simulating lowering and raising the gun, hearing them call off their numbers and take imaginary posts at the gun" *[Battery D*

Recruits at Ft. Eustis, Virginia, training with a WWI machine gun.
Doyle is seated at left.

History, 639th BN]. Months later, 37mm and 40mm guns were acquired and rotated for training.

In the same month Doyle was drafted, he stopped by his brother Will's workplace. Juby (nee Ruby Jewel) Baugh, age 19, was Will's secretary. For the next year, every time that Doyle was expected home on furlough, Will asked Juby to get him dates. She did. In the fall of 1942, unable to procure Doyle a date as usual, she said, "I guess you're stuck with me." Will thought she was too young to date a soldier even if it was his brother, so he arranged dinner dates at his house where he and his bride, Anne, could chaperone the pair.

The furloughs were few and far between, and Doyle and Juby struck up a correspondence while he was at Ft. Eustis. She wrote him first. Not until his third letter did he get the spelling of her nickname right.

Part I

The Stateside Story

Of Love, Marriage and Combat Readiness

November 26, 1942, through October 5, 1944

Chapter 1

Early Courtship

Ft. Eustis, Virginia

November 26, 1942

Dear Jubee,

Cute, I calls it, and mighty sweet of you to think of writing to me. What you say that you and me make our friendship an alliance of perfect frankness? In writing letters we won't try to weigh words but will write just what comes into our minds. A friendship isn't a friendship if the two concerned have to handle each other with gloves on. Understand, don't you?

You asked me how the Army is. Well, the Army is OK, but it is very hard to leave family and friends and come back to it. But when I got back, I learned that I might get seven more days leave about January 1st. Oh, if I do I will be very, very happy. If I come to Rome again soon, you must find time for a date or two with me. Is it a bargain? I was told that from now on every cadreman here would be made to take a seven-day furlough every three months. If this is true, I don't know whether I want to leave Ft. Eustis or not.

Did you have a good time at the party? I bet you did. You are the type to have a good time regardless of where you are. A very good trait, my sweet.

A little bit of advice—don't let Will get you down with his kidding. He really likes to joke with others. You and I will just have a private friendship. He will be kidding both of us. Let him have his fun. When you and I were together, you were always saying, "Talk to me." Well, I hope as you read this you can imagine that I am there, just talking. That's the way I felt when I read your letter. It was just like having a chat with you. I enjoyed it so much. Well, baby, keep your chin up and I'll be seeing you soon. I hope.

Good night, Doyle

P.S. Forgive the informality of this, the first letter. But you must remember our Alliance. (I hope you join the Alliance.) Remember the rule of it. No formality. D.

December 8, 1942

Dear Jube,

Well, I am back in the groove. I am again back to the spot of being a tough Army Sergeant. I have made only two of the new recruits cry so far, however. My trip home softened me up a little bit, but now that I am back in the swing of things I have no feelings of pity for any of the recruits. So much for my other self. I will now delve into my more civilized self, or in other words, how I am when I am at Home. I only have pleasant memories of my swell trip to Rome. You contributed, I think, more than your share in making my furlough a very wonderful and enjoyable one. I am sitting here now watching the snow come down in blinding flurries and thinking of the wonderful Indian summer weather that you all, including me, enjoyed while I was there. The snow is very wet and forming slush about three inches deep. There are no signs of it abating. It is

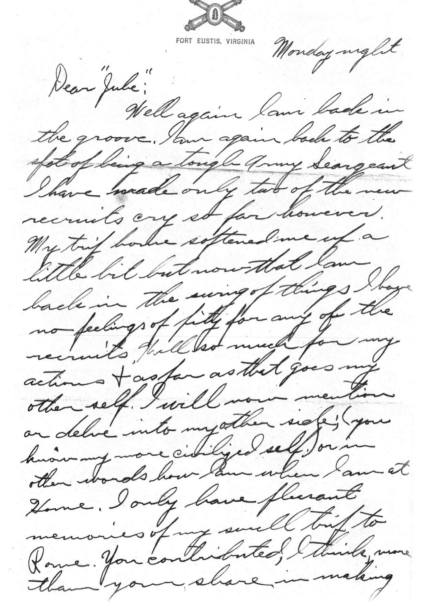

FORT EUSTIS, VIRGINIA

Monday night

Dear "Julie":

Well again I am back in the groove. I am again back to the spot of being a tough Army Seargeant. I have made only two of the new recruits cry so far however. My trip home softened me up a little bit but now that I am back in the swing of things I have no feelings of pitty for any of the recruits, thrill so much for my actions & as far as that goes my other self. I will now mention or delve into my other side; (you know my more civilized self) or in other words how I am when I am at Home. I only have pleasant memories of my small trip to Rome. You contributed, I think, more than your share in making

Original

15

beautiful now, but we are in for some miserable slopping around. The weather here is such a lousy contrast to the weather I so liked in "dea' ole" Georgia.

You mentioned bowling in your epistle. I would be delighted to bowl with you sometime. I always did like to play games with experts because they always give me a few good pointers. To me, one who bowls a score of one hundred is an expert. We'll try it together some time. Maybe someday I'll have the opportunity to get you on a tennis court. That's where I have done most of my courting.

Juby bowling

Gad! But it is snowing "cats and dogs" if there is such a phrase for snow. It is coming down so hard you can't see over fifty feet from the window. If it turns cold, we'll probably have a "White Christmas," speaking literally. Speaking in terms of spirit, though, it won't be so white. We might not be with our families and girlfriends in body, but remember this: we can send our thoughts and spirits winging their way on lacy clouds to any place we want them to go. You can be sure that at Christmastime we think only of our family and friends. Last Christmas was the tough one for the men that didn't get home. You remember we had just gone into the war and everything was in reverse. But now things are beginning to shape for the better. So it will be much whiter this year. Don't you agree with me? You never thought that soldiers thought and felt like this, did you? I am only speaking what they all feel.

I'll be thinking of you and awaiting a word or two from you.

Be sweet, Doyle

December 21, 1942

Dear Juby,

Now that Christmas is so near, all I think of is home and you and my friends there in Rome, but I don't know when I will get another leave. Oh well, why should I feel sorry for myself? Who the hell am I? I am only one in millions. I should be thankful that I am as close to home as I am.

I wish you were near. I would take great delight in wallowing you in the lovely ten-inch snow we have here. No kidding, don't you just love to fight and roll in snow? Snowmen and battles with snow balls? Also, sledding and a big bonfire to roast hotdogs and marshmallows. Yes, we did all this last night; but you know it wasn't half the fun it was when we could share our fun and delight with the opposite sex. Yes, we miss our girlfriends to the utmost. We are looking forward to the time when we can play in that carefree manner again. I will stop by saying again, please smile and don't be depressed. Do it for me, will you? Thanks!   Good night, Doyle

January 7, 1943 [after a leave]

Dear Juby,

So "solly" my sweet, about this chat on scratch paper. You see the PX [Post Exchange] was out of stationery tonight and so am I. Anyway, it makes no difference what one writes on. The main thing is the thoughts therein. And speaking of thoughts, my thoughts keep drifting back to you. Thoughts of the swell time I had while I was with you. Hmm! Just think, I wasted three days of my leave thinking you were out each night raising hell and having a good time. You have to admit that you gave me, let us say, a bum steer by handing me that line about the champagne that a boyfriend gave you. Men are blind as bats anyway, and I guess women are too, because you should have seen that I wanted a date with you the worst ever. *[Juby had a chance meeting with a friend at a soda shop on Broad Street downtown. At a booth in the back, he showed her a flask of champagne and asked her if she wanted a taste. After a sip, she was not impressed and declined any more. She told this to Doyle in a letter as a minor incident. He imagined a more significant tryst.]*

I wish you could have been with me today. I went with the battery to Williamsburg to look over this very historical town. The Rockefeller Foundation has rebuilt Williamsburg to its eighteenth-century status. If you like antiques such as guns, furniture, glassware, etc., you would have been in heaven at Williamsburg. Everything there is many years old. The women that took us through the beautiful sights were dressed in long eighteenth-century frocks, and the men were dressed in the knickers, patent pumps and ruffled shirts of that period. We saw the pillory and stocks, the dungeons of the jail, or "gaol" as it was spelled then, and the Governor's Palace. I took a ride through town in the horse-drawn "hack" shepherded by a Negro "slave" dressed in period dress. I sat in a church pew where Washington, Jefferson, Clay, Henry and many more of our forefathers did. Every business house in town is built on this eighteenth-century plan of architecture. It looks just like a sleepy colonial town except for the students in William and Mary College. They dress in the ultramodern fashion, but the buildings of the college are the old type. I saw some beautiful girls over there today. And something to interest you maybe—I also saw some handsome men.

We are going to the rifle range day after tomorrow. This event is something I always dread. It used to be a lot of fun but not anymore since responsibility has started piling up. It is quite some job to look after sixty-seven men. We will be at the range Saturday, Monday and Tuesday. May Allah help me. About four weeks from now we are going on a week's maneuver to Virginia Beach. Before the war started, it was a famous summer resort. Now it has been taken over by the Army. I am looking forward to some pleasant evenings when we do go.

The thing I am really looking forward to is a visit to dear old Rome, Georgia, sometime in the near future: you, the family and other friends. Ah! It will be swell.   Good night, Doyle

January 11, 1943

Dear Juby,

I haven't heard from you since I wrote my last letter. I want to talk to you so bad. Again snow is falling. Huge flakes of it. I do wish you were here to help me enjoy the silent melancholy. Maybe it's not melancholy at all. I think you know the feeling that goes with the steady downfall of big, beautiful snowflakes. It is hard to explain. It is between thrilling and depressing. It's a wonderful feeling, but deep down inside you have a yearning for the events and people that you love.

Besides the desire to write to you, I wanted to ask you if you knew a girl that lives at Beech Street. She is about thirty years old. Find out all you can about her. I think that I can tell you, if you know her, something that will tickle you to death. This world we live in is so small, I have found. You're curious, aren't you?

One of the boys here has asked me to go to the movies. There is so little to do that I guess that I had better tag along. I wish you could go with us. Until next time I will be thinking of you.

Good evening, Doyle

January 17, 1943

Dear Juby,

First I will try to answer the deluge of questions you cast upon me in your last letter. By the way, I had rather hear more about you and what you do than read a lot of questions pertaining to me and my welfare.

I. Yes, I do like you. What the hell would I be writing to you for if I didn't?

II. About the dame on Beech Street. No, I didn't meet up with her. A friend of mine here (a corporal) sent his name and description into one of these lonely-heart or get-acquainted clubs. Last week he got a letter from this girl. She told him since she was 30 years old and he was only 28, she wasn't writing for herself but for another girl who was only 23. Also, she would appreciate it very much if he wouldn't tell the younger girl where she got his address. We have so much fun getting the letters from the poor girls. John has had three letters from Georgia girls and four from Tennessee. You see, John is married and he has more fun with his wife when he gets a letter. I hope this answers question number two.

III. You asked when I will be home. God only knows. Maybe you are hoping with me that it will be in February. More information later.

IV. I did get to Washington over a weekend. I had a most wonderful time. I spent most of the weekend in a hotel room drinking. Do you blame me? If I had gotten out, I would have been picked up by an MP [Military Police], so I can't tell you much about the city of Washington. Once during my drunk I felt, or at least thought, that I was the President himself. What fun we had.

V. No, I haven't been to New York. We have been so busy with the training here that I just haven't felt like I could rightly take a pass for three days. But maybe I can go up soon.

VI. You asked, "Would you like to come home?" Ha! My sweet, you can answer that one. Then you asked what's stopping me. Well, only a few simple ARs [Army Regulations]. Believe me baby, if I could, I would be on my way now.

VII. Now comes the last and the jackpot question. You asked if you could have one of my pictures. I might as well be frank. So here 'tis and also the reason why. No, you can't. You see, my mother dragged me into the studio to have the picture made. It may seem childish to you, but I don't like to have my picture made and especially displayed on tables and dressers and such. I think I shall write to the photographer about using the picture in his window. Mama had three pictures made, one for each member of the family. So you will have to be content without one. I hope you will understand. If you get angry, let me know exactly how you feel. I like to talk to someone that's mad. They say things they otherwise wouldn't say.

21

Well, you expressed your hopes that you would see me walk in some fine morning. I can say this: you can't possibly hope any more than I do. I hope I have answered all of the questions in the question box. Give Brother Will my love and best wishes. Tell him that he might write sometime if he finds time in the hub-bub of business. Be as sweet as you were on your porch that night until I return, honey.   Always thinking of you, Doyle

January 25, 1943

Hello Sweet,

I am now down at #2 Guard House. Don't be alarmed, I am not a prisoner. I am the Sergeant of the Guard. We have five prisoners in now. Quite a few less than we usually have here. I came on duty today at twelve o'clock and will be relieved tomorrow at twelve o'clock.

I went to the dentist twice this last week. The captain who did the work for me was really swell. He is an old bachelor and really is a lot of fun. He filled five cavities for me. He was really smooth and didn't hurt me once. His female assistant was rather smooth, too. Wheeeee. Oh boy! You know we get free medical aid in addition to our meager salary. But this is enough about me for a while.

I haven't heard from you since I refused to let you have the picture. But again I say, "Please try to see it my way." My feelings about photographs might seem childish to you, but nevertheless, that's the way I feel. So don't get too, too angry with me. I have a surprise for you. That's all I can say about it now. But keep it in mind, will you?

You know what got me started on this letter? No? I was sitting here listening to the radio, and all at once the orchestra started playing "Why Don't You Fall in Love with Me?" I just had to write you then. It's funny! I always connect a girl with some lovely piece of music. There are so many tunes that bring back to my memory a girl that I have gone with during my days of courting. Music and romance go hand in hand anyway. You know, "A Melody Is Like a Pretty Girl" or vice-versa.

Always thinking and dreaming of you, Doyle

February 1, 1943

Dear J.B.,

It seems like years since I have seen you. You know one thing, my sweet? Never has a girl been on my mind like you have. I went to a movie tonight. It was *Casablanca*. When Ingrid Bergman and Humphrey Bogart went into their love scenes, it made me think of my last visit home. You and I could teach them a few things. That's just between you and me, sweet.

Now! You seem to be worried about the picture episode. I had Will get the picture and if he hadn't gotten it for you, I would have gotten it myself when I came home.

I don't care for pictures because I can't bear to look at the image of someone I care for. It makes my heart ache if I can't be with them. I haven't got even a snapshot of any member of my family. If I can't be with them, I certainly don't want anything around to remind me about them. Do you follow me?

Please don't worry about the letter that you wrote. I enjoyed it. It was so long. You know I read all of your letters five or six times and sometimes I read them more. It makes me feel that I have been with you. It was nice to hear that you like to sew and cook. You will make some man a wonderful wife. It's too bad that I am destined to be a bachelor. I like to be on the move too well to be a married man. The *Wild Geese* always seem to call me. I'll probably have to eat these words someday, however.

Sergeant Doyle K. Whittenburg
The picture that was in the photographer's window

Again, I hope to see you in the near future. I will let you know by the end of the week whether or not I will be able to leave the first of next week.　　　　Always thinking of you, Doyle

February 15, 1943 [after a leave]

Dearest Juby,

I have already started missing you, my sweet. I arrived this afternoon at about four o'clock. I made wonderful connections. Only had to wait one hour in Richmond. Well honey, I just wanted you to know that I arrived safely and I want you to be my Gal-entine always.　　　　Yours always, Doyle

February 21, 1943 (#2 Guard House)

Dearest Juby,

Forgive me dea' for not writing to you three or four times this last week. But it's better that I didn't because I have been feeling very depressed. I don't know whether it's because I met and got to know you and then had to leave you or not—but I think that is the main reason. We have been working very, very hard here in camp since I have returned. We have been going on 18-mile hikes and running the obstacle course at night. There is one bright spot in it all—I have a wonderful chance to go to Camp Davis for OCS [Officer Candidate School].

The tune (our tune) "Why Don't You Fall in Love with Me?" by Fitch Bandwagon is being played now. Damn! Sweet, you haunt me.

I don't know whether you like poetry, but I am enclosing a poem that expresses my feelings completely. The "things I want to tell you" will take me an eternity to say. Oh, if I only knew that your answer to me would be "I knew—for it was so with me," I would be very happy. Really, don't you think the poem is lovely?

RELEASE

I think if I should have to go before
The things I want to tell you have been said,
I could not lie at peace—eternally—
But must awake and seek your face instead.

And then if you would smile into my eyes
And say, "I knew—for it was so with me"—
My happy dust would mingle with the earth
As laughing rivers run into the sea.

[Enclosed clipping, source unknown]

25

I found this poem, attributed to Nena Gray, in the April 3, 1944 edition of the Camden News, *Camden, Arkansas. Clearly the poem was circulating in 1943 when Doyle sent Juby the unidentified clipping.*

February 21, 1943, continued

I live and live over and over again our wonderful nights together. They are only memories now, but such wonderful memories. I think we do rather nicely in love scenes, don't you? When you mentioned all the people looking at us at the station, to tell you the truth, I didn't realize that there was anyone there but us. That was the first time I have ever kissed a girl in public and not felt a little embarrassed. You have brought about a great many "firsts" in my life, my sweet.

Oh yes, I am not an inmate in #2 Guard House. I am Sergeant of the Guard. Or did you notice at the top of this letter? Well honey, the Officer of the Day just came in so I must stop and talk to him for a while. Keep your fingers crossed for me in regard to the OCS plans. I'll let you know how I come out in my next letter.

All my love to you, Doyle

February 23, 1943

Dear Juby,

It was only last night that I was talking to you, but I was sitting here and all I could think of was the wonderful time you gave me while I was home. I just had to get out my scratch pad and talk to you some more. Now it's OK for you to date or even marry some boy there if you will be happy, but filling dates with my married brother is just too much for me to take. I have already written to him about it. The next step will be to write his wife. Don't think that I am a tattletale, but you see I must stand up for my rights. Ha! Ha! Write and tell me what he wanted, will you? I am glad to hear that you have found one day of your work enjoyable, if it is payday. *[Will took Juby on a lunch errand to pick out flowers for Anne. Juby mentioned the impending meeting in a letter to Doyle.]*

About the boyfriend that has returned. There is your chance to start your family of two boys and one girl that you spoke of. You are at just the right age to start a family. Of course, if I am correct (I think I am), you will find that he will be rather independent since there is a shortage of men. I don't blame him, however. If I was on the outside, I would have a long list of girlfriends. Or maybe I am being a little bit conceited. Well, I did all right when I was a civilian, even if it was a thousand years ago. You helped in a big way make me forget that I was a soldier while I was home.

I slept for a while this afternoon and then got up and went to the barber shop. As you already know, I was on guard last night. And the Sergeant of the Guard gets the afternoon off after he is relieved, explaining the reason why I could sleep this afternoon. By the way, I missed a twenty-mile hike today too. Am I very lucky or am I?

I miss you so much and am already thinking about my next trip home. When, I don't know, but someday we will be together again.   All my love, Doyle

March 1, 1943

Dearest Juby,

Hello, my sweet. I start school in the morning. I don't know yet what I am up against, but I know one thing. I certainly can take anything that they dish out. I am now living in a tent. I will be here about seven weeks and then I go to Camp Davis, North Carolina. I will be there fifteen weeks. So to answer your question about when I will be home, it will probably be in about five months. If I get a commission, I will be given a ten-day leave. It will be worth working hard those five months just to be able to see you. I am going to be forced to stop dreaming about you, however. I can't have two kinds of figures in my head at once. You know—your figure and the figures of algebra and trigonometry. However, just to think of you in my spare time will be an inspiration to me. It's funny how I became so attached to you in the short time I have known you.   Always loving you, Doyle

March 8, 1943

Dearest Juby,

Gee honey, when I get a letter from you it's just like words from an angel. You don't know what your letters mean to me. Really, they are a message from heaven. I get down in the dumps, so to speak, and when I hear from you I spring back into the sunshine of memories. Ah baby, you are everything to me. Never did I think I would say this to any girl but here I am, saying it to you.

You mentioned something about meeting me halfway sometime. Baby, this is out because I am so busy here, and I will be for about six more weeks, and then I will be going to Camp Davis for thirteen weeks. It will be busier down there than here. So please be patient until I get my commission, and then I will be home for ten days. It will be heavenly, won't it? I am going to have trouble getting through because I have never had trigonometry; nevertheless, I am going to do my best. That's why I have warned you that you might not hear from me as often as you have in the past. Let us meet each other in our thoughts at nine o'clock each night. What do you say? Even if you are in some other guy's arms, think of me for a minute, will you? I try, and I find it hard, very hard to forget you when I am studying and having class. I have to do it or I won't get what I want. I want to become a commissioned officer so bad, and I will. You know they say that one can have anything one really wants. I have some studying to do now. Remember that my heart goes with this short note. Please be careful with my heart—don't break it beyond repair. I'll be thinking of you as much as possible.   I love you dearest, Doyle

28

March 9, 1943 (just 24 hours since I talked to you)

Dearest Juby,

I am sitting on my bunk in tent #215 (my tent) writing to the sweetest gal I have ever known. I am by myself, and when I started thinking, I thought of you the first thing. It doesn't seem exactly right that things are as they are, but who are we to beef about the present situation? You and I are just small fish in this scheme.

I went to a movie last night, *Random Harvest*. For goodness sake, if you get a chance to see it, do so. It is a most wonderful love story. Someday I am going to show you a most wonderful time. Just you see, honey. Oh, I miss you so much! Your letters are welcome epistles. I got two today and two Saturday. I don't see how you can keep it up. Some guy will sweep you off your feet pretty soon, and that will be the end of our lovely friendship. You know as well as I do that we have too damned many things against us and they will be for a long time to come. Why, tell me, did all these things have to happen to our generation? Oh hell, there I go feeling sorry for us. Every generation has its trials and tribulations. We have to face it, however, and bravely too. But until worse things happen, we can at least talk and make love to each other, even if it's only with paper and pen. Well honey, if I am not too busy studying tomorrow night I will talk to you some more. Maybe I won't be so depressed tomorrow.   All my love, Doyle

As the lengthy separation makes Doyle's heart grow fonder and needier, his letters become repetitive. Some subsequent letters are omitted and others are condensed, including only the especially romantic segments and descriptions of the daily activities of an officer candidate. Salutations and closings are minimized.

March 15, 1943

I have had one week on algebra and one week on logarithms and right triangles. I made 84 on my algebra, and I don't know yet how I came out on trig. It is a little bit easier to live in tents since I have become accustomed to it. I have just returned from a movie. It was very good, a musical with Don Ameche and Jack Oakie, *Something to Shout About.* The feature song was "You'd Be So Nice To Come Home To." I got a letter from Anne yesterday. She said you had told Will about what I wrote you. Remember when I said I didn't like for you to have dates with my brother? Well, she wrote me and said that I had better keep my gal away from her Willie. Hah! Ah, that Anne is a swell gal. Really a great addition to the Whittenburg clan.

Brother Will and his wife, Anne

March 22, 1943

Today is the first day of spring. You know yourself that in spring a young man's fancy turns to love and stuff. Of course, I didn't feel very much change at the break of spring because I have been thinking of love and stuff for quite a while now. There are five inches of snow on the ground and it is still snowing. Some of the snow just fell on the bunk beside me. It fell through a big slit just above my bunk. Some life I am living here. One bright thing is that I have only one more week to live here. I have been working on my shoes and my brass. My sweet, I will leave you now.

April 16, 1943

I am writing during my chow hour. Oh honey, I miss you so much, but I must keep my mind on my studies. If and when this war is over baby, and if you are willing, we will have so many good times together. Is it a date? You mentioned a date with one of the cadets and you wanted to know if I was jealous. Damn right I am, but still I am glad you had it and hope you have more dates.

You mentioned photographs. I'll have to admit that I am weakening fast. I would like to have a snapshot of you to carry in my wallet. Sometime when you are writing, please enclose one of your likenesses. You're laughing, aren't you? Well you should, since I flatly said that I didn't want a picture of you.

Sweet, I didn't know until now that there was so much to learn. I am up to my neck in figures, theories, formulae, etc. Gosh, I just can't see how I am going to hold everything I am supposed to. Maybe I can though.

Four days ago some WAACs [Women's Auxiliary Army Corps] came to Ft. Eustis. They are really nice. I have a date for tomorrow night with one of them. She is from Staten Island, New York. I am looking forward to a good time, but I know that I will only think of you when I am with her. Think about me, honey, tomorrow night.

I am leaving for Camp Davis tomorrow week. In a way I am glad, but still I hate to leave some of the boys here. But all in all, I think that I am doing the best thing. Please forgive me, baby, for neglecting you.

April 20, 1943

If your letter of the 15th was merely a ruse to get me to write to you, you have succeeded, baby. *[Juby recalls that she wrote an angry letter after being misled by Doyle's sister Eleanor and his sister-in-law Betty, who attempted to break off the relationship.]* I sent you a letter about four days ago. By now you should have it. After you have read it, answer this question. Could I write a letter like that and in the meantime be making plans to marry someone else? Not on your life, sweet. Where my family got the information, I would like to know. I also would like to meet the unlucky girl and find out when the alleged event will take place.

The way I feel now, I will never get married. You have helped make it so because you believe every little thing you hear. Don't you think I spoke frankly enough to you when we were together? When and if I do decide to get married, do you think I would fail to let you know? Not on your life. Honey, I wish that you hadn't written that letter. It was rather foolish, wasn't it? You know me better than that.

After reading this letter, if you still want to send my letters back, don't bother. Just burn them up and call it quits. But you know, seventeen weeks will go by so very fast and then we can be together again. Can't we? Just who have you met that is more interesting than me? Hah!

From Juby's memoir [written in 2009 at age 86, "The Cadet"]:

During on-again, off-again correspondence and courtship with Doyle, I met and dated a US Air Force Cadet stationed at Battey Hospital. [Battey General Hospital in Rome was built in 1943 to service WWII soldiers.] The USO [United Service Organizations] sponsored "get-together" parties and dances on weekends for the military stationed at Battey. My parents didn't think I should go, but one weekend a friend they liked and trusted talked them into letting me go. It was a dance at the Forrest Hotel ballroom, very crowded with military guys and lots of Rome girls. I had a great time. I met Rex, we danced a lot, and he asked me for a date to attend a big military parade and festivities at Battey for the cadets and their families the next weekend. Since Rex did not have any family to come, I went as his guest. I met some of his buddies and their families. It was a great weekend.

When dating, we either had to stay at my parents' house or ride the bus uptown and just walk and talk. Rex came almost every Sunday. He would ride the bus, having to transfer along the way, so we actually had very little time to get to know each other. During this time, Doyle's feelings were off and on, and I was certainly confused about him.

Rex called one night telling me he had fallen in love with me but was shipping out the next day. He said he would write. He did call from somewhere (New York, I think). The next time I heard from him, he was in England before leaving for the combat zone. We corresponded until I had to write him that I had married. The next Christmas I had a card from him wishing me well and asking could I write to him if Mr. Whittenburg wouldn't mind. I never did.

US Air Forces exhibit at a war bond drive

Chapter 2

Becoming an Officer

Camp Davis, North Carolina
Officers Candidate School

May 3, 1943

Dearest Juby,

It is so hard to write very much of interest from an army camp. Even if it is a new camp, the buildings are the same and the routine is the same. I am now at the Post Service Club. There are hundreds of soldiers here. Some are writing and some are around the piano singing; others are in the refreshment room buying drinks, etc. I bet you would like to be here among the boys. Oh boy, would I like for you to be here. I can almost feel you in my arms.

Missing you, Doyle

May 10, 1943

When I think of the fifteen weeks before I can see you again, it seems like an eternity. But if I don't work hard here and do a great deal of studying, I won't get to see you until the war is over. So you see why I just must get a commission out of my schooling here. I stand a very good chance, if comparison has anything to do with it, because I (I'm not bragging) am above the average man here in military learning and experience in handling men. The thing that is going to give me trouble is mathematics. I just yesterday had my quiz on math. I am rather sure I passed it.

Well honey, I will stop by telling you that you are always the leading lady on the stage of my dreams. You are always in the spotlight of my heart. The curtain rises when my weary eyelids close, and the play is over when they open again. During the day I keep saying to myself "Mr. Whittenburg, that was a beautiful leading lady in a most wonderful play you saw last night." Daydreams of you turn into slumber dreams, and slumber dreams back into daydreams; a vicious, but pleasant cycle. Well honey, good day for now and let me hear from you.

May 18, 1943

Good morning, my love. I awoke this morning from a most wonderful dream. You were in my arms and things were so peaceful. I miss you so very much, sweet.

I was picked yesterday out of 600 men to be Battalion Commander. Boy did I get a thrill out of that. Being out in front of all those men and giving them commands. I really strutted around too. I led all the brass hats (officers) through the ranks on their inspection tour. I am an authority on military questions here. The men that I am in school with think there is nothing like me for a soldier. I am rather proud of myself. If I can pass all the courses, I will have no trouble at all. My leadership is excellent. I have no worries when it comes to this. Baby, offer up a word of prayer for me on my academics, will you? I am under a constant mental and physical pressure. I have never had so much on my mind at one time in all my life. But it is good for me.

I would like for you to come up for my graduation, but it will be impossible because of the shortage of lodging and the inefficient transportation. Eleanor has already expressed her desire to come up for the event, but I have refused her because of the above reasons. An army camp is no place for a woman. It would be all right if one could find rooms and could get from the room to camp and back. But here it is worse than at Eustis.

I can't get it into my head that you really mean it when you say you love me because I just can't see how a girl as sweet and lovely as you could fall for a punk like me. I like to hear it though, sweet. Did you have a good time in Atlanta? I bet you did. Have a good time every time you can, but think of me often because maybe our thoughts will meet somewhere in space and will unite. I think we are always together mentally however. We think along the same lines. *[Juby recalls this trip: "We girls spent a lovely weekend browsing and eating. We stayed at the beautiful Winecoff Hotel." The hotel, billed as "absolutely fireproof," burned on December 7, 1946, killing 119 people—the deadliest hotel fire in US history.]*

L-R: Juby, friend "Boots," Juby's sister Frances
and friend Mary Lee in Atlanta

May 31, 1943

I am planning to go into Wilmington next weekend. I am going to get a room in a hotel and some whiskey and pitch a big sloppy drunk just to relieve the pressure. Of course if I can find a girl, I will take her to a movie or sumpin.' Wish me luck, baby. I must do something to relieve the pressure that is building up inside of me. Damn it's terrific. If I can't find some diversion, I will go nuts before the next three months are over.

I just stopped to play some table tennis with one of the boys. I won too. I am scheduled to play some court tennis in the morning. I played last week and beat all comers.

This last week we had a course in aircraft identification and motor transportation. If I passed the tests OK, I finished the first five weeks without a single mark against my name. If I can only get by as easy the next twelve weeks, it will be about the easiest seventeen weeks of my army career. The only tough thing about it is that I have to be on the go all the time. Just as soon as you let down, the officers are all over you. You see, the main training you get here is how to stand up under terrific mental and physical strain. If I don't finish here, I will be shipped to a combat zone. (They are playing "You'll Never Know" on the radio.) When I finish and come home, I will be very proud of myself because it is quite an accomplishment. If I don't finish, I won't let it get me down. I'll still be a good soldier. We have a job to do and it will be done.

June 7, 1943

I stopped for a minute to gaze at the photo you sent me. You are sooo sweet. If you were near, I would crush you in my arms and kiss you until you gasped for breath. Just you wait until this war is over, baby. Then we will go and really do. Honey, it is almost time for lights out now (10:30), so I'll say good night and be sweet, my love.

Juby

June 28, 1943

You suggest that I have too many outside interests. Honey, if I didn't I would go completely nuts. And if I see a lot of girls and still have my love for you, it's a good sign, isn't it? I really don't think you are as jealous as you seem to be. You probably have learned by now that I have a slight bit of suspicion toward women. Forgive me; I can't help it. It must have been born in me. I have tried and tried to overcome it but I haven't yet. I can say that I put more trust in you than any woman I have ever gone with. But even you I doubt at times. The things you said in the two letters of yesterday were just too good to be true. Time will tell. (I am going to stop now and go to the beach. I'll tell you about it when I return.)

I just got back from three hours of play in the sunshine, water and sand. There were about fifty WAACs and about 2,000 soldiers on the beach, which is a part of the camp reservation here. I could have had much more fun if you had been with us. The breakers were rolling in about fifteen or twenty feet high. When they hit you, they knock you over and over. Ah, it was fun. I'll take you to a beach someday. You'll love it. I am a lovely lobster pink; a good start for a tan. I am going to the beach twice every weekend now, and then three weeks before I graduate, I will have the opportunity of swimming and sunbathing every day for an hour. When I come home, I will be quite brown.

I have just returned from study hall after a stop by the Post Service Club. Every time I go there, I come away sick at heart for those poor women who are wives, sisters or mothers of soldiers. Some of them are working in the cafeteria; others are just visiting. Oh gosh, what some women will do for their love. Never would I ask or even permit anyone I loved to go through such hardship as some of those poor girls do. I guess, though, that they are happy. For me, it is much better to know that my loved ones are at home where they are comfortable.

Honey, you just can't realize just how much you help me along. When I receive a letter from you, I become so relaxed. Mine is true love, my sweet.

June 29, 1943

I received your most anxiously awaited letter this morning. Honey, I'll tell you now that I just love to have you write that you love me. I have read the letter five times this afternoon. I have been daydreaming all afternoon about what we will do when I come home. There is only one drawback. I flunked a subject last week. It is a probability that it will set me back, and if it does I will just die. It will mean eight additional weeks before I can come home. Thursday is what they call "Bloody Thursday," when they do most

40

of the setting back and dismissing. If I get by, I will be home in two months and as a lieutenant. So honey, if you have ever offered up a prayer, do so for me, will you? I feel like kicking myself in the pants for failing that exam. If I had taken my time, I could have passed it, but I got careless and failed. I will let you know the verdict just as soon as I know.

You mentioned that Will was to come to North Carolina. I hope that he comes close enough to camp for me to see him. Of course, to see you would put me on top of the world. Honey, the ten days at home will be the happiest days of my life. After those ten days, the Army can send me to Africa, Australia, England, India or anywhere, but I will have the memories of home and you to take with me. They are playing "People Will Say We're in Love" now. They won't be far wrong either, baby.

I am getting into wonderful shape here. They call this the streamlined OCS because all the candidates that finish are so slender. The pace that we follow could do nothing but streamline us. But we are getting hard and tough. The music they are playing now is so beautiful. It calms me so much. I just stop writing to listen and dream of you. Ah! I see such a beautiful vision. You are on a white pedestal in a most gorgeous white dress and I am at the foot of the pedestal with my hands upraised, reaching out for you. Jessica Dragonette is now singing "I Dream of Love." Heavenly.

July 5, 1943

I wish you could have been with me yesterday. The day would have been complete. I spent about four hours at the beach, and did I get a good sunburn! You would so much enjoy riding the huge waves that were coming in. They are so big that you think they are going to cover you up, but all at once they get under you and raise you to their crest and then pass on, leaving you in shallow water. Someday you and I will go to some beach together for a frolic. It's most enjoyable.

The last letter I received from you was the one with the pictures in it. You don't know just how much those pictures mean to me. Now, with ten weeks behind me and only seven more to go, time moves slow, slow, slow. It's so hard to write just what I think of you. I have tried at times, but it is so cold and lacking of passion and love when it is in black and white. Love is something that is intangible. Two people know that it's there, but they can't seem to place their fingers on it. It's inexpressible, don't you think?

Thanks again for the snapshots. All the guys here thought they were wonderful. In fact, some of the boys come to my bunk and ask me to let them see my girl's picture. (You are my girl, aren't you?)

I breezed through last week's work with flying colors. Next week is supposedly the hardest week of the entire course. I must buckle down. Well honey, until next week I will stop by saying I love you.

July 8, 1943

I was sorry to hear that your sister's husband is being shipped abroad. I can't see why I couldn't be sent in his place. He has a wife that he would like to see and be with now and then. Of course, I have a honey that I would like to see and be with too, but it's different when one is married. It is really tough. Your sister is going to suffer more than he is because he will be seeing and doing new things that will occupy his time and mind. The home front army really suffers most, I know.

Last evening we had to turn in a list of size and quantity of clothing that we are going to buy when we become officers. It gave me somewhat of a thrill to think that I can start ordering officer's clothing. Just think, only six more weeks from tomorrow (if nothing happens), I will be a commissioned officer in the Army of the United States. And six weeks from Friday, I will be with you. It's funny; you seem to have grown closer to me than when I was home. Well, they say that absence makes the heart grow fonder. I hope yours has. Has it?

July 19, 1943

"Somebody Loves You (This I Know)." Ah, yes I do. If I hadn't thought of you, I wouldn't have had the inspiration to go through with what I have. I passed my last test just this last Friday. From now on it is practical work, the same thing I was doing when I left Ft. Eustis. So nothing can stop me now. I am really getting excited now. Just think, one more month.

July 27, 1943

Good morning, my sweet. When the eight o'clock bell rang, I was dreaming about you. I cursed the guy that rang the bell because I was in the middle of a long kiss when it rang.

We slept out on the ground Friday night. We had our tents pitched in a swamp, and boy, were the mosquitoes bad. We broke camp at five o'clock in the morning and rolled our packs in the dark. We were back at camp by seven o'clock for breakfast. I wish you had been there in the tent with me. Have you ever slept all night on the ground? No? Well after the first time, it isn't so bad. I am used to it now. To all of us, it was a break. We were off at five o'clock in the afternoon. We all got together and had a song-fest. Well honey, I just started the letter in order to tell you that you are the sweetest and best gal in the world and that I love you tenderly. So now that I have said it, I will cease firing until later in the week.

August 1, 1943

I went to the Clothing Exchange last night and bought my uniform. I got a wonderful fit. When I come home, I will be wearing summer uniform. I want you to see me in my dress uniform, which is considered winter dress. We will arrange for you to see me dressed up.

We go back to classrooms next week and then have three days in the field, which will be rather rugged. But I know I can take it because I will soon be on my way home. Oh happy day!

August 3, 1943

I hope you have recovered completely from your cold. You must be in fine fettle when I get there. We will be staying out until the wee hours of the morning. Do you mind?

It is nice of you to make elaborate plans to entertain me. We are going to have a wonderful time at the barbecue. I am glad that it is to be on Saturday. I might not take you home that night. We will watch the sun come up. It will be nice to say good morning to you. You know, wake you up with a soft caress and a good morning kiss. What would the folks say if I brought you in at eight or nine o'clock? They wouldn't like it, I know. Maybe we better not spend the night together. We'll talk about it when I'm there.

How time does drag at present. I see you everywhere I look. I am certainly glad that most of the academics are over because I can't concentrate on a thing. All I do is daydream now.

August 9, 1943

Starting in the morning, we are to be out in the field for four days and three nights. I am to be first sergeant on the trip. I don't know what is expected of the first sergeant, but I am going to try to take it as it comes.

Three months from now, I will be in an overseas station. I am glad that at long last I am able to get into this war. I realize what I have been doing is important, but I have wanted to do a little fighting for a long time. Now I have my chance. I just stopped long enough to eat chow. We had roast beef, spuds, green butterbeans, lettuce and tomato salad, chocolate milk, etc. The best meal in quite some time.

August 10, 1943

Well honey, you can tell everyone now that I will be a lieutenant. It is a sure thing. I weathered the field problem without any mishap. In fact I had a lot of fun out there. We supplied antiaircraft protection for Seymour Johnson Air Field at Goldsboro. We were camped across the street from some barracks. We used our ingenuity and got permission to use the latrine over there. We had hot water to shower and shave every morning. We raided a farmer's watermelon patch for several nice watermelons. We had plenty of good ice cream. I don't guess you know it, but I am now a civilian! When I take my oath of office, I will be a member of the Army of the United States. I was under Selective Service status. But we can talk of this when I get home. Approximately 24 hours after you read this letter, you will be in my arms.   Be seein' you, Doyle.

In class

Break time in the only shade available

Graduating candidates, Doyle is center, front row
(detail from larger photograph)
OCS class commissioned August 19, 1943

Notice Doyle's wide stance, typical of him in many photos.

PROJECT REPORT: June 5, 2009

I've typed 50 single-spaced pages of direct transcriptions of Dad's (Doyle's) letters to Mom (Juby), written in 1943 as they began a long-distance courtship—I am put in mind of my own courtship via letters during the Vietnam era. There are the same ploys—a word or two to "innocently" invoke jealousy, flirtatious "ha-ha" moments, emphatic statements about remaining unmarried, ridiculously pompous statements ("I don't want any pictures of loved ones.") and false pride juxtaposed with insecurity. And there is neediness, oh the neediness—begging for letters, then saying don't send me letters like that last one. There is parsing of every line and every word; the gut-wrenching pushing away and pulling toward each other, trying to reconcile a budding love with the inevitability of separation at best and tragedy at worst. Wartime letters have a universal urgency, it seems. I've become mesmerized.

Transcribing so many letters is tedious but incredibly heartwarming. Each typing session extends longer than the last because I must know what the next installment of this page-turner reveals. I am truly transported back in time, present when my parents face their own emotional battles while the country as a whole steps up to "The Big One."

Many letters consist of repetitive expressions of love with the soothing rhythm of a transcendental chant. But any new experience or phrase in a letter from home can trigger lyrical description or profound thought. All in all, Dad opens his soul and pours out his heart. Word after word, he shares what he learns as he makes the transition from "not having a clue what to do" to becoming an officer. Page after page, he gives credit to Mom for making a good soldier of him. Five years older than she, he is at times patronizing. Between the conversational sweet talk and occasional condescending outbursts, I learn (as did Mom) what his soldiering days were like. The letters show a man exceptionally open about his feelings—verbally expressive of every thought, good and bad. As ardor grows, he is persistent, genuinely tender and very romantic. I feel in my heart the love that captured my mother's heart so long ago.

For the last 20 or so years of Dad's life, he wanted me to take on this project. I don't feel guilty about waiting until he was gone because, knowing him, he would have called me constantly to ask which letters I'd typed today and what my reaction to them had been. I have been able to essentially isolate myself so that I can fully absorb every nuance. In so doing, I've become emotionally closer to my father than ever before. When I finish this first pass through the stack of letters, I am going to ask Mom particular questions as well as pull together photographs and souvenirs to place with appropriate letters. My hope is to synchronize the whole story of my parents' lives during the dramatic early years of their relationship.

I am typing as I read so I won't be tempted to skip the repetitive parts. I can read his handwriting quite well after having recognized that all his lower case "p's" look exactly like "f's," as in "haffy" for "happy." I want to capture every "I love you" and "I miss you" and "I want to come home." I'll have to make some careful choices later in order to delete redundancy. My typing speed (as fast as I read) is allowing my own errors to creep in. These are fairly easy to spot on rereading, and I'll eventually find and correct all of them. I don't yet know how to handle the punctuation, grammatical errors and awkward sentence structure of the stream-of-consciousness style of the letters. I hope to achieve readability while maintaining the original voice of this soldier, especially as he writes during extreme conditions. I must seek professional guidance from someone not as emotionally invested as I am. My goal is to craft a book that is readable and interesting to others, yet preserves the integrity of the original material—its intimacy and tone—while linking the individual and personal nature of my father's story to its national and even global historical significance.

Chapter 3

The 2nd Lt. and His Lady

The next letters are more about love and the anguish of separation than they are about army life. Some of them are rhythmic love mantras that could have been part of songs sung by the Lettermen group I listened to in the 1960s. Yes, Doyle was Juby's letter man.

August 30, 1943

Dearest Juby,

This is the first time I have written the salutation to a letter to you and know definitely that I mean it. It is rather difficult to write things down. You know—my feelings. Kisses can't be transmitted to paper. If they could, I would send you hundreds and hundreds in this letter. I know I love you kid. (You have noticed I call you this now, haven't you?) I want you and me to keep our love aflame by writing to each other. Honey, I will try to make you continue to care for me. Please, if you ever find that you don't love me, let me know, will you? As long as I think I have a chance I will carry the torch, but if you decide you don't love me, I will try to let the flame die.

I might be sorry someday I didn't marry you while I was there, but I still don't think it would be fair to you since I may not come back. I mentioned marriage above as if I could have if I wanted to, not even considering that maybe you wouldn't want it that way. I have never considered your side of it. You have never mentioned marriage, have you? If our love continues as it is now, we will be married after the war.

I arrived a couple of hours ago, and I am now quartered in barracks down in what we call "Mosquito Hollow." It is raining a slow drizzling rain which gives me much melancholy (if that's the word). It's funny how one can be so happy one day and so down in the dumps the next. That's me now, down in the dumps. But tomorrow maybe I will feel better. If you promise to think of me, I know I can go through anything. I am to go to school for ten days; then I don't know where I will go. Somewhere here on the post, however.

Well kid, I will continue to love you and will be oh so anxious to see and hear from you. All my love, Doyle

September 1, 1943

Forgive me honey for some of the things I did while I was home. I was mad. I will rectify my actions someday if you will permit me. I am sure you will because you are such a fine girl. It's funny how you have grown to mean so much to me. Just like you said one night about my letters: at first it was "Dear Juby," then "Dearest Juby," then "Juby Dearest;" and from "As ever" to "All my love." It's a wonderful progression, isn't it honey? If you hadn't started us off, where would we be today?

September 6, 1943

Honey, if I hadn't received your letters today I would have just died. (Does that sound like love?) When I saw your handwriting, my morale jumped to the sky. You just can't realize what you and your letters do to me. At one time I didn't think we could stay together through correspondence, but now I know, honey, that we can. We have everything to look forward to, haven't we? When the war is over, we can test our love by a little, short courtship you know, to make sure that the war hasn't changed either one of us, and then we can do what we have been waiting for and will wait for. Won't we, dear? Ah, to be home for good will be the happiest moment of my life. Once I wanted, you know, to go to South America, but not anymore. I am going to settle somewhere in Georgia and stay there the remainder of my natural life, "honey chile."

Your letter about swimming, watermelon, etc., made me homesick. Those things are what we are fighting for, my sweet. Ah, I didn't realize until I got in the Army just what America has to offer. You don't want to miss seeing *This Is the Army*. In that picture you can see my viewpoint about wartime marriages. So go see it, my dear.

I wrote Mama and told her to give one of the pictures to Will for you, so the next time you see him he probably will have it for you. Well until later honey, I will stop writing but will continue to think of and love you. *[By this point Juby had gone to work as a secretary at the plant where her father worked, Tubize, a rayon textile plant converted to wartime industry, now making fabric for parachutes.]*

September 7, 1943

Just received your letter of last Friday. Listen honey, don't ever think I could get mad at you. Maybe I didn't make myself clear in that letter. I was apologizing for my actions once or twice while I was home. When I spoke of being mad I meant that I was, well, insane. I didn't mean "mad" in the sense of angry. I was just crazy for you and didn't control myself very well. Do you understand what I am trying to say?

You are so easy to get along with and would be so nice to come home to every night. But honey, that can only be dreamed of at the present time. Eh? Our dreams will keep us oh so close together. We can't be parted now, can we? Our thoughts will meet out there

51

in space somewhere regardless of where I go or where you go, and someday, in some way, we will come together again. Our dreams are going to make the time short too. You know we have a war to win. Thanks to you, I made the grade as a lieutenant. Now I must study to make a good one. I might not keep up this pace of writing three or four letters a week because I will be put in a battery and will have to go to work. But I will guarantee one a week. Tonight I can almost feel you sitting here on the bunk with me. You almost answer me when I write something. It would be nice to know that we could be so happy and to know we wouldn't be torn apart after ten days, wouldn't it? But the war will end and our complete happiness will begin. That day won't be so far away, will it, my sweet? Well honey, continue to be sweet and continue to haunt me because I love it.

September 9, 1943

Oh yes, when you go to see *This Is the Army*, notice in the kitchen scene the cook that is singing in the kitchen quartet. He was the sergeant in charge of battalion shows in my old battalion at Eustis. His name is Sergeant Prost. He is the original voice of Donald Duck. He's quite an entertainer. He only has a very small part in that show.

September 11, 1943

It is harder to get a leave from this place than it is to get a discharge. You asked me when I was going to call you. Well honey, this I can't answer because of the poor facilities we have here for making calls. Sometime when I am in Wilmington I will try to get through to you. It usually takes from two to four hours to get a call through. It is such a short distance from here to Rome, yet it is just the same as thousands of miles as far as communication is concerned.

Anne is correct when she said I "had it bad." She found out through Will. I wrote him a letter telling him about falling for you so I am sure that Anne read the letter. It's a shame that we have fallen for each other under the circumstances. It's really tough. But we did have ten days of happiness, didn't we?

September 13, 1943

Hello, my sweet. How are you today? I hope you are having fun because I am not. I start school again in the morning. It will last about six weeks. I don't know what is in store for me after that. In the Army, one never knows just where he stands.

In one of your letters you mentioned that a thousand or so soldiers were camped on Nix's farm. I didn't like the way you said that. You led me to believe you would like to go out to the farm and spread joy among the boys. Remember there are no strings attached now, but there will be. *[Juby has clarified this remark, explaining that the army rented fields on the farm owned by Hudson Nix, Juby's boss, where soldiers lived in tents. She participated in social events for the soldiers.]* You want me to be jealous—but honey I can't afford to be jealous of you now. If I was I would go nuts. I would imagine everything, and in time I would be forced to go AWOL [Absent Without Official Leave].

Another thing, if you date a lot and still think of me and love me, we have nothing to worry about, do we? When I come home to stay, if you think that you are ready to settle down to a home life, we will certainly do that. But honey, you and I can't truthfully say what we do want. We aren't living in a normal world anymore. We must settle down and let the world settle down before we try anything. *[Parts of this letter are so personal that Juby exercised her right of censorship. The reader must read between the lines as Doyle comments on the obscure subject in the next letter.]*

September 14, 1943

I am still thinking of that letter of yesterday. Boy did I run wild in that letter. I wrote a little of everything, didn't I sweet? I bet you are still trying to figure it out. Or maybe you understood it perfectly. I'll try to boil it down into a few words: I tried to convey to you that I love you and always will and hope that your love for me will last forever and forever. Does that clear it up for you? We have gone over what I wrote a dozen times in letters and when we were together, so I think you know what I mean.

September 16, 1943

I just received a long, long letter from the sweetest, loveliest, most understanding girl (and I love her) that I have ever known. You might know her. She has heavy brunette hair and a most beautiful face with the cutest nose, and her lips are oh so divine. You know, when I kiss her lips, I almost swoon. She's wonderful. She works in personnel at Tubize and lives in the village. I wish I was there now. She said in a letter that she loves me because I treat her so good. I'm sorry that I didn't marry her while I was home last, but maybe it's better I didn't. I think that she and I used our heads. I am going to marry her someday. I hope you think it is a good idea. (Yes, I'm crazy.)

"When I told them how beautiful you are ..." Yes, it's playing. The guy that sleeps by me has a record player. "And I'm the man whose wife someday you'll be ..." [Lyrics from "They Didn't Believe Me," sung by Frank Sinatra.] Oh honey, that's one of our songs. Now it's "I Guess I'll Have to Dream the Rest" [another song sung by Frank Sinatra]. You and I love the same type of music and each other, don't we kid?

There's another song I want you to get if you don't already have it. I don't even know the name of it. The other night I heard it in the PX. It is a vocal by Frankie. When I heard it a lump came in my throat. I could see you, honey, but I couldn't touch you. Gosh it made me lonely. The opening words are all that I heard because I had to get out of the place; it was killing me. I went to my barracks and crawled into bed and I'll have to admit, honey, a tear or two trickled down my cheek. The song is so lovely, but under the circumstances heartbreaking. I want you to go get it as soon as I find out the name.

Honey, I bet every letter you get from me leaves you dizzy trying to figure it out. I just ramble on and on, first one thing and then another and back again. In fact, when I write you I am not responsible at all. It's all your fault. You and you alone have done this to me. You hinted for the first date. Boy am I glad! I love you dearly and will meet you in my dreams to leave you again at Reveille. For us now, honey, it's "From Taps until Reveille."

Chapter 4

To Marry or Not to Marry? That Is the Question

September 18, 1943

Dearest Juby,

Just a few minutes ago I finished a most heavenly letter, my sweet. You mentioned wartime marriages. You said that if a couple had known each other for ages and had weighed the facts it was perfectly OK. Well honey, you know that you and I have only known each other since I have been in the Army. We have been together only on my very short leaves. We haven't really had a test yet. We have been keeping in touch with each other by correspondence. Keeping each other cheered up. But if we were really separated so that we couldn't hear from each other, I wonder if our love would dwindle. Oh I hope that it never does, honey. Let's drop the subject here and now. Why should we worry about the future? For now we will just write each other saying sweet nothings and such.

Write me sometime, Doyle

September 20, 1943

Dreams and your letters are all that I have now and also the satisfaction that you love me. Why did you wait so long to say you would be my wife? I have taken it for granted I guess, but you are right—you never mentioned before wanting to be my wife. Maybe it would have been better if you had never said it. It will be such a long time and such a hard struggle before it actually can be. We won't let anyone else know that we plan to get married ever because it will make it easier for both of us if either one ever changes. Do you get what I mean? You might meet some Casanova who will sweep you off your feet and you might marry him. Or something might happen to me, especially if I go across, that will harden me or change me in such a way that you and I maybe wouldn't click as we do now. So if we keep our love and plans to ourselves and something like this turns up, it won't be so bad. But you know honey, I believe that our love is so strong it will weather the worst test.

September 21, 1943

It's funny, but it seems I must have my chat with you each day. I think of you so much, it always leads to a letter. This will probably be short but I just had to let you know that I am thinking of you and loving you more than ever. We have declared ourselves to each other and it's total love on both sides. At least on my side.

September 22, 1943

I love you, my sweet. And after reading your letters of today, I think you realize that I do. If I only knew what the outcome of the war would bring for me, I wouldn't wait a minute to marry you. Believe me, I don't want to hurt you. If I was ever wounded in such a way that the injury would be permanent, I wouldn't allow you to marry me. That's why I am sorry that we even fell in love. But honey, it's done now and we can't help it, can we? God will find a way for us. We'll be together someday. Try to dismiss me partially from your mind. It will be easier that way.

September 23, 1943

The record I had in mind is not one of Frankie's at all. It's "It Can't Be Wrong" by Dick Haymes and his Song Spinners. Most any love song reminds me of you, my sweet, particularly "It Can't Be Wrong."

September 26, 1943

Mama wrote me that no one leads a normal life until married and she is correct. My mama is always right. She never misses. (I know you will like her.) You say get married and it will be easier for both of us, but I can't see it. I say wait until the world settles down and then we can go ahead.

September 28, 1943

Your father should have chastised you severely for teaching your kid sister such vile things as "jitting" [the newly popular jitterbug] in preference to arithmetic. All kidding aside, you should teach her both, but don't tell her that dancing is the most important.

September 29, 1943

This will be very short, my sweet. It is to warn you that probably from Saturday on you might not be hearing so much from me. I am being assigned to an outfit in Ft. Fisher, North Carolina. The outfit has been training for about a year now. I imagine they are giving me a chance to get some experience. I am afraid my duties there are going to be very tough. I'll keep you posted. Until later be sweet and believe in me.

Chapter 5

Self-Doubt Creeps In

Ft. Fisher, North Carolina

Ft. Fisher was a Camp Davis satellite camp and firing range for artillery training. Davis and Fisher were both dismantled late in 1944.

October 2, 1943

Hello Dearest,

This is a short note to let you know where I now live and to let you know (I repeat) that you are the one. You know, if this war was over and I was out of the Army, I would never let you out of my sight for one minute.

Ah, but I must stop dreaming about the war ending and, as far as that goes, ever getting back to you. It must be faced, as you said several times before. As for you staying at home, if you do I'll stop writing to you, so there. Believe me, kid, I know how tough it is when you have no way to forget for brief hours. I think of you all the time. I try to get wrapped up in my work but I can't. I am falling down on my duties. If I was no longer a lieutenant, would you still love me? You know they can take my commission for

61

inefficiency and then I would be a buck private. They expect so much from a new 2nd lieutenant that sometimes I wonder if I can hold my position. Time will tell. Well honey, forgive me for writing such a dreary letter but for now that's all I can write.

Love me! Doyle

Here begins a breakdown of confidence that leads to self-doubt and eventually depression—clinically undiagnosed, of course. At the time the army did not treat or even medically recognize the deterioration of mental health; a soldier was on his own to figure things out and get better.

October 7, 1943

Your letter of the 29th came today and I really felt like a heel. You started talking about saving for our future. When I say feel like a heel, I mean I should have married you while I was home. It was after I returned that you and I declared ourselves. But I know and knew while I was home that you wanted to marry and I wanted to marry too, but I still think it is best the way it is. Believe me dear. It is best. *["Declared ourselves" means that Doyle and Juby openly expressed that they loved each other and became more committed to the relationship through telephone conversations and the letters following Doyle's ten-day leave after OCS in late August 1943.]*

Don't worry about the cooking deal, kid, because I can cook, and since you are going to make the living for us, I think that it's nothing but right for me to cook your meals. Oh it would be so nice if only you were here on the bunk with me now. You talk with a great amount of intelligence about owning a home, a car and then having a baby (and in that order). That's the only way to enjoy children. That is, to have security before children. But I bet you and I have children before we have either of the other two. *[Correct bet!]*

But honey, let's try not to have it happen this way. We want our children to have more than we had. Not that we didn't have enough, but we want our kids to have some college. At least two years. It will help them along, you know. If we can first get our feet on the ground, it will make it easier on us (and them) at a later date. I don't know why I dream of things that are far in the future, but I guess it's good that I do. It helps us go through the ordeal we are going through. *[Many of the dreams came to pass. When I read this letter and realize that herein the seeds were sown for my life, my education and my future, I am overcome with emotion. Rarely does one have such a close encounter with one's parents' deepest contemplations at the beginning of their relationship. I am privileged and grateful.]*

You ask if I had mentioned our situation to my mother. Yes, but I wrote her as if it was a secret, so don't ever let on as if you know that she knows. You asked about her response to the information. Well, my mother doesn't believe in war marriages. She saw so many in the last war go on the rocks, and she would hate to see her son Doyle have matrimonial difficulties, so she advises me to wait until the war is over. My mother is a swell person and a straight thinker. She loves anyone that her children love. So my dear, she loves you. She knew while I was home that I was sweet on you. So she suggested that I date some more girls. You see, she was afraid I would marry you without thinking of the lonely nights you would be forced to spend at home. She thinks the same as I do about the girl's side of the question. You think that just a few days of matrimonial bliss will be enough to last you until I return but no, my sweet, after those days of heaven it would be a great number of days of hell. So it is best we wait. And may heaven help us.

October 11, 1943

I am afraid for the first time since I have been in the Army. I'm not afraid to go overseas, but I am afraid of the duties I have now. Presumably they expect me to be a superman. I am so afraid I almost go crazy. Maybe I shouldn't feel the way I do, but I can't help it. I will tell you that you are everything I have now. I love you sweet, as if you didn't already know. If God may grant it, we will be together someday.

October 19, 1943

You asked if there was anything you might send me to make me more comfortable. No honey, there isn't, but it makes me feel so good to know that someone is interested in my welfare. I am afraid to write much because I am afraid that I might alarm you. My spirits aren't too high. I am trying to snap out of it, but it is so hard to do. That's enough of that, however. Just remember I love you regardless of the outcome. You must realize that things are different now that I am an officer, so very different. I sometimes am sorry I let them talk me into going to OCS. It is hard to say, but true.

October 25, 1943

I feel like a heel writing such letters as I do to you. You're such a dear, and for that reason you should throw me along the wayside. I am no good for you. You are head and shoulders above me. I try not to express my feelings in my letters, but it is so hard not to open up to someone that I love. Fear has me in its clutches. Now that I am a lieutenant, I know I should have remained an enlisted man. You told me that once, remember? They expect so much out of me now. I would give anything if I hadn't gone to OCS. Understand me dear, when I say that I just can't seem to adjust myself. Why didn't you talk me into staying in the ranks? I was so much happier there than I am now.

I am afraid my nerves are about shot. If I go into combat, I will be responsible for the lives of about 60 men; before my only responsibility was myself. It's not for myself I worry, it's others.

Don't ever let anyone know what I have written you, will you dear? In fact it might be better if you burn this letter. I'll admit I am a coward and I have tried to overcome it but I can't, so that's that. Well dear, I have said some things here that I didn't think I would ever say even to you. I can't help some of the things I write.

October 31, 1943

Again, I will attempt to write you a good letter. Before I get started, let me impress on your mind that I do love you and always will. I am going through the toughest struggle of my life now. I wish instead of loving you so much while I was home last, I had made you hate me. But there I go, off on the wrong foot. I was going to make this a good letter, but in just a few words I have made it bad.

Don't misunderstand me, sweet, I'm not trying to crawl out. I want you to feel free to do so if you ever want to. I am sticking my neck out, I know, when I write you the way I do, but I can't help it. That one letter I asked you to burn would court-martial me if it was read by some people. Even this one would. So you see what I mean when I ask you to burn them? But no, you are going to keep them. OK, you win, go right ahead and keep them. I wish you wouldn't though.

I spent the night with a couple of lieutenants and their wives the other night. It was so nice to be in a house again. I really wish you had been there. Things would have been perfect. We had a nice dinner and played cards. After a while they brought out candy (homemade) and popcorn. They live at Wrightsville Beach, about twenty miles from here. They are scared to death that they are going to have to move. They have had their wives here about three weeks now and if they move, their wives will have to pack up everything and go home. To be a war or army wife is no good. We will be happier if we wait until the turmoil is over. Then our life will begin. Well so long until next time and please pray for me, my sweet. I certainly need something.

November 8, 1943

Dearest Juby,

Yes honey, you're correct when you say we had better quit writing. It will be better if we just go on our way until a later date. Let people think that we have lost interest in each other. Hell, I don't know what is right. I can't even think. Forgive me for being such a fatalist. I'm licked. It's not that I am a coward—it's that I lack enough military knowledge to carry out my duties. Believe me honey, it's tough to be so depressed.

I am positively ashamed to mail this letter but I must since I have nothing else to write. Well honey, remember my love regardless of what happens or not. So long.   Love, Doyle

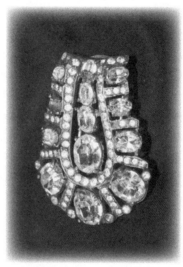

Juby's Christmas present from Doyle, December 1943

The next letter is January 18, 1944. Doyle did stop writing for about eight weeks. Juby says they had a few phone conversations and she kept writing. Doyle had Will buy her a pretty Eisenberg pin as a Christmas present. He did not have a Christmas leave. Juby says that during that time he talked to Will about his conflict regarding marriage and Will told him that if he loved Juby to marry her "by gad." In later letters from Europe, Doyle refers to this time and chastises himself for being so foolish. By the time they resume correspondence, he has been sent to Camp Forrest, Tennessee, for maneuvers.

Tennessee maneuvers: apt preparation for conditions during "The Bulge"

Trying to keep warm

Tenting in the snow at Camp Forrest, Tennessee

Chapter 6

Bare Soul, Open Heart

Camp Forrest, Tennessee

Similar in climate and terrain to Western Europe, Camp Forrest in central Tennessee was a site for large-scale war games and intense training prior to deployment. It was an active army post from 1941 to 1946, named for Civil War General Nathan Bedford Forrest.

January 18, 1944 Just after I heard you say, "I love you." (Ah)

Dearest Juby,

Well my dear, even after I have given fair warning that you should forget me, you insist on my writing to you. My God, I want to write you and hear from you. But if you knew the circumstances under which I am, might I say, masquerading as an officer, you might understand why I haven't written. If only had I listened to you, I would still be an enlisted man and would be doing a good job for your country and mine. When I became an officer, I stepped out of my class.

You know yourself I haven't got a line of bull, and that seems to be what an officer must have. When I say a line of bull, I mean that I haven't the good fortune of being one who talks very freely. Also I have been sent hither and yon so often since I went through OCS that I have forgotten all I learned there. My initiative is gone.

69

In other words, I am worthless as an officer. If only they would release me, I would feel better about the whole matter. I do my best to do my duty, but I am grossly inefficient.

Honey believe me, I wouldn't be afraid if I was an enlisted man, but I'll just have to admit that as an officer, I am afraid. Very afraid. On the three-weeks maneuvers we just came off, I didn't do a damn thing but worry myself almost silly. The staff sergeant in my platoon did everything. The next phase of maneuvers to start any time now brings me something new. I am to be an umpire. I don't know the first thing about it. You know, it's funny how for twenty months I enjoyed the Army and felt I was doing something for my country, but now I am disgusted with it and know that I am just dead weight. What the outcome will be, I don't know. If I disgrace the family name I am sorry, very sorry. No one has said that I am not doing my duty, but I myself can't be fooled. It is slowly driving me nuts. My memory isn't five minutes long now.

Forgive me dear, for writing such a letter, but it's all I can think of. I have gone through hell worrying about it and it seems to be getting worse. If only I had gone to Australia with the outfit I took basic training with, I would at least know my job. But as it is, I don't know what I am about, and the outfit I am with is losing its discipline because of me. My dear, I am a shiftless no-good. About the family name being disgraced—the family won't be disgraced. It will only be me because the family name is high and will remain so. One disgrace can't tear it down. Of course I am not planning anything to disgrace the family, but sooner or later higher officials will hear of my inefficiency and something will happen. I want to thank you for being so patient with me. As I said to you when you called, I might not write again for a long time because I certainly don't relish writing such a letter to one that I love. I would make a good fighting man for some good officer, but I wouldn't be worth a damn as an officer in combat. I can't even look after myself, much less look out after other men. Please don't let anyone see this letter. It is incriminating. You wanted to know what was wrong, and I have tried to write what I feel.

It is so hard to explain. The privates know more than I do about things. They also know that they know more than I do. I only wish that I could bluff, but I can't. It's a great weakness. In other words I guess I have a great inferiority complex.

I told you I may get a ten-day leave in about ten more weeks. Please honey, don't count on it because too many things can happen in ten weeks, and believe me they probably will. I tried to get a leave during these two weeks we're in Forrest, but leaves will not be granted until after the next phase of maneuvers. So that means about eight more weeks, then we will have to move to another camp. I don't know where nor does anyone else. So don't count on seeing me, sweet, for a long, long time. Regardless of what happens, remember that I love you and I want you to always have a loop-hole to free yourself because I don't want you to be hurt—ever. I bet that you think that I am a dope, don't you? Well I am! I don't even know my own mind. The Army is getting me slowly. I hope you understand. Believe me honey, what I have written is true.   All my love, Doyle

February 5, 1944

Dearest Juby,

I am going to try to make this letter a wee bit more cheerful than most of my letters. I have opened my heart out to you in so many of my letters. In fact, if you desired, you could make a traitor of me. I have lost all of my self-confidence to the point of not being able to think of a thing but just how helpless I am.

Enough of that. A lieutenant friend and I have rented a room in Murfreesboro. So far we have been here two weekends, but next weekend we might be stuck out some 20 or 30 miles in the country. If I only had some way to let you know that I am to be here, I would be delighted to have you come up.

I love you honey, and for that reason I can't marry you now. How do you think the Tolbert girl feels now that her husband is missing in action? I wish it were me instead. You would get over it, but she has the child to remind her of the short stay with her husband. Maybe I am a fool, but I still feel the way I do. I have worried so much that I have got myself in a mess. I have gotten to the point where I can't concentrate at all.

I keep saying "can't." Maybe if I started saying "I can," things would be much better. Maybe if I had married you while I was home, I would have a brighter outlook on life. Maybe if I had you here to look after me, I would do better. I am afraid to try it. After the war we will see. Well my honey, I have tinted the letter as usual with melancholia, but please forgive me. I would like oh so very much to talk to you personally tonight, but it is impossible, isn't it? It makes me so sad when I talk to you over the phone, explaining why I didn't call you on Sunday. We will have a chance to thrash this out someday, so be patient. Here's all my love and until later, so long.

Love, Doyle

February 7, 1944

Dearest Juby,

I just returned from the home of the three lieutenants and two captains I wrote you about. They are in my battery and have their wives here in Murfreesboro. The wives tried their best to get me to call you and have you come up some weekend. They would like for you to stay with them. But honey, that is too great a risk to take. Those wives tried their best to find out your name. I told them it was Sally Smith and one of the girls placed a call to Rome for Sally Smith. Of course, I told her that wasn't your real name and she cancelled the call. If they do find out your name and call you, please just thank them for the invitation and politely refuse.

L-R: Rae and Captain Hooper, Ruth and Paul Doorly,
Peg and Captain [unnamed], Eileen Hess

I am a defeatist and have gotten to the point where I am almost defeated. I have prayed and still am praying for strength to buck up and do my job. The position I'm in now will have to have some divine force behind me. It is really funny how when one gets in a tight spot he turns to the very help he thinks he will never need. Go to church for us, will you? Pray for me while you are there. Pray for my prayers to be answered. Also pray that the war will be over soon and your sister can have her husband back and everyone can go home to the ones they love. It will be a normal world again. I have reached the point where I need help from some stronger force. I have let myself say "I can't" until I have come to just that. God will give me strength. He must.   All my love, Doyle

February 23, 1944 [after a leave]

Dearest Juby,

I hadn't planned to write you this week because I am expecting to see you again over the weekend. Can I? But after spending two nights in the field (very, very wet nights), I am back in my room with Lt. Schwartz. We come here every Tuesday night to make our weekly reports. I have thought so much about us since I left you. We are so in love it's a shame. I am sorry that I have set my head on waiting, but you understand. Or at least you say you do. It gave me a thrill when you said that Saturday was the happiest day of your life. I was a fool to write my troubles to you. But you know honey, it did me good to open my heart to you.

Honey, when I saw you and was with you for such a short time even, all my worries were chased away. I did not consider that you might want to do something or go someplace, but I will this next weekend if you want to. I have hopes of beating this letter home. Well dearest, I hope to see you before you read this, but if I don't, just dream of me and let me know about it.

My love is yours, Doyle

Now that they are closer in proximity, they begin to see each other more often. His spirits lift and the marriage dilemma resolves. His new roommate Bruce Schwartz becomes his war companion for the duration.

Lt. Bruce Schwartz, Doyle's roommate at Murfreesboro, Tennessee. They served together until December 1945.

Battery mascot Mickey

Beer party west of Lebanon, Tennessee

Chapter 7

Reversal of Fortune

February 28, 1944

Dearest Juby,

Already my sweet, I am missing you like everything. I arrived here about eleven o'clock today. I was very miserable in Chattanooga. There are so many people there, and the station is so small for the crowd. I was so sleepy, but I couldn't find a place to put my head. Finally the bus left and I got to sleep for a while. Since I only left you last night, there really isn't much to say but to repeat that I miss you and love you very much. Take care of yourself, honey, and write me some news of the hometown. The weekend seems like a dream. I only hope I have another dream like it next weekend. Honey, I am about ready to go out in the field, so until next weekend, bye-bye.

Love, Doyle

March 6, 1944

"A Lovely Way to Spend an Evening" is on the radio. When I heard it, I just had to write you. I am afraid that my love for you shows now because when I visited the home of the lieutenants this morning all the wives started kidding me by saying that I was in love. And I am. I don't care who knows it. Well honey, I started out to say hello and declare my love for you. Hope to see you this weekend.

March 13, 1944

Honey, I just arrived. Took enough time out to shave my whiskers off and here I am, writing to you. I find it harder to leave you each time I have to come back. I slept most of the way to Chattanooga. But from Chattanooga to here, I had to sit on a toolbox. I love you and want to see you now, and it hasn't been but eight hours since I had you in my arms. *[The weekend evidently was more special than most! The only details available are in the following poem written by Juby in reflection many years later. Here also is her account of the courtship.]*

THE ENGAGEMENT
(A Walk through the Woods, Spring 1944)

We walked into the wooded glen
Beside the flowing creek,
Budding trees on either side,
Winter's leaves beneath our feet.

Warm in the sun, cool in the shade,
First robins on the wing
Leaving their nests to taste
New berries of the Spring.

As we sat upon the mossy log
Watching the lazy humming bees
Puffy clouds filled the sky
And we could feel the gentle breeze.

We laughed about our muddy feet,
We talked about the war.
He held my hand and promised me
That he would not be far.

Walking back the way we came
It just seemed to me
That the birds above sang louder.
Were they singing just for me?

My steps felt lighter on the ground.
Skies were bluer, the grass greener
For in my heart I was so proud
To have his ring upon my finger.

—Juby Whittenburg (March 27, 2009)

At Doyle's mother's house on engagement day

From Juby's memoir:

After graduating from Rome High School in June 1939, I took a job typing and sending out flyers for Calder Willingham who was running for tax commissioner. *[This is author Calder Willingham's father.]* I was 16 years old, and this was my first job. He did not win the election so my job ended. I was offered a job as secretary in the office of Alec Marsh and Will Whittenburg who were insurance claims adjusters. Eventually I became Mr. Whittenburg's full-time secretary. He was great to work for, and the additional money was great for me as a teenager of eighteen. One day Will introduced me to his brother Doyle, who had just received his uniform in the army and came by to see his brother on the way to an orientation center. *[This would have been on or about Aug. 12, 1941, according to one of Doyle's letters.]*

Juby at 16

At Will's request, I set Doyle up for dates with several of my friends, but when he never dated any of them twice, he and I finally started dating instead. We had no car so we couldn't go anywhere but to the movies and such, but we spent a lot of time getting to know each other and finding out our feelings for each other. When apart we wrote constantly. One nice time was when he asked me to meet him at the hotel in Lafayette where a couple of his friends were meeting their girlfriends for the day. Several times we borrowed Jack's Model T Ford (when he would let us) to get about. We spent a lot of time with Jack [Doyle's younger brother] and his wife, Betty.

Doyle's mother and sister were afraid we'd get married. Will was all for it and urged us on. Although Will and I were friends and shared news from Doyle's letters to each of us, I felt I needed to change jobs. By this time Tubize, a textile plant, was in full production making rayon and other fabrics (parachute material) for army contracts, and they were hiring throughout the plant. *[Juby's father worked there as a machinist, and the family lived in the mill village.]* I went to work in the Research Department as a secretary. Doyle and I made commitments to each other. Although we were emotionally torn, we knew that we were "made for each other," as he kept telling me. During this period, I was 20 and 21 years old. When the official engagement happened and I had his ring on my finger, I thought it was the highlight of my life.

March 23, 1944

When I left you, it was about the hardest thing I have ever done. Maybe you didn't realize we might not see each other for a long, long time. I hope and pray it won't be very long. Last weekend was the best I have ever spent. I am now about three miles from Kentucky sitting on the ground in front of my tent, so this letter will be short. I just wanted to tell you that I love you and let you know how I felt about the weekend. I just finished letters to Mama

81

and Anne per your request. I should have told Mama before, but now she knows.

Well honey, keep loving me as I love you, and soon we will be married. Keep your chin up—it won't be long.

March 28, 1944

I want to call you now, but if I did I wouldn't be acting sensibly because only last night I was with you. I must tell you what I have heard. The present plans are this: I will be home for ten days the 8th of April. Now remember honey, the Army is always changing. Please don't tell anyone I will be home this date. If I do get the leave, we will live it (the furlough) as man and wife. I love you.

Waiting for a ride to Murfreesboro one week before the wedding

April 1, 1944

Just a short note to bid you good night. I love you more and more. I can't wait until next week. Sometime next week we are to move to Ft. Jackson, near Columbia, South Carolina. I think we are going to move by motor convoy. If we do we probably will go through Calhoun, Georgia, where I can jump convoy if my leave is approved.

I was a little too bold in my talk to you about money. But honey, I will always feel insecure until we have a nice nest egg laid away for some emergency. You see, I am like that because I haven't had too much in my short life and still haven't, as far as that goes. I want to be able to give our children all that they might want.

April 3, 1944 (1 mile west of Lebanon, Tennessee)

Dearest Juby,

This is the first weekend in six weeks that I haven't been with you. I find myself very lonesome for you now. But knowing that I will be with you next week makes me feel very happy. To make sure we get the wedding ring you want, you had better go see Bobby and fish out one to match your other ring. You mentioned that you knew I wouldn't be sorry I married you before the war is over. Honey, I know I won't be sorry. It's you that might be sorry if I am hurt or killed. But if I come back, baby, I will love you to death as long as I am able. The chances are greater that I will come back just as I was when I left. And another thing, I haven't gone yet. I might never go overseas. I want you to teach me to live in the present and not so much in the future, will ya? I might not write again before I see you, so until next weekend remember I love you.   Doyle

P.S. If my leave doesn't come through I'll die. D

Doyle's family during the courtship

Above, L–R: Doyle, Juby, Anne, Betty and Jack

Below, L–R: Mama Whit and Eleanor

Chapter 8

Together, Yet Still Apart

Ft. Jackson, Columbia, South Carolina

April 8, 1944, Wedding day at the church in Rome

When Doyle came home on furlough, he and Juby had to find a minister to marry them on short notice. They met at the church with Juby's sister Frances and Doyle's brother Jack as the only witnesses. Through the years, Doyle often expressed regret about not having their mothers present.

There was no time or money for an elaborate ceremony, and the couple went straight to the bus station after the pronouncement that they were man and wife. They spent a week in Lake City, Florida, where Doyle had worked before being drafted. As predicted, Doyle's unit moved from Camp Forrest to Ft. Jackson in Columbia, South Carolina, while he was on honeymoon leave. The next job was to find lodgings for his bride convenient to his assignment. Juby says that the simplicity of her wedding day was typical for the turbulent time.

April 18, 1944

My dearest wife,

Let me tell you that I love you dearly and I am already missing you. I missed being with you before we were married, but I never realized that being your husband would cause such a change. This is the first letter to my wife, and sweet, it is so natural. To me it seems we have always been married. And then again, our honeymoon was the shortest ten days of my life. When I say that I feel I have been married to you always, I mean things are so perfect and natural that it seems it's always been that way. I wish you were here tonight. I wish we had married long before now. You would have made me take care of my money. I have spent it foolishly, and I dared to worry about you spending our money foolishly. We are going to spend money, but we are going to have something to show for it, aren't we sweetheart?

Now, to get down to business. I want you to come up if we can get a room or apartment. I am going to try to call you tonight and get the name and address of the people you know here. If you want to work, I think that a nice room is all we will need, don't you? Pray for our success in being together my love.

All the love that's in me sweet, Doyle

April 20, 1944

I haven't heard from you since I left but for the phone call. Maybe I expected to hear from you just a little too soon. I only left three days ago. I can see you now: your beautiful hair, your cute face, your sparkling eyes. But really my sweet, I must get down to business now.

I have made an allotment of $200 to our account at the bank. This allotment will continue to go to the bank after I am overseas (if I ever go) even if I am lost in action, captured or what. I want you to go to the bank and sign a card as joint depositor. I have also made a change of beneficiary for $5000.00 worth of insurance from Mama to you. I left a little of it in Mama's name. Is it OK with you?

Honey, rooms and apartments are sky high up here. Forty and fifty bucks per month for rooms; apartments are much more. I have a chance to take half a house with a lieutenant here in the battery for $50 per month. I am still waiting for the address you have. We probably can take that room, and when you get here you can scout around and see if you can find something better. It's left up to you, whatever you want. I am Duty Officer tonight and very lonesome. Give my love to your mother and your sisters. My regards go to your swell father. I'll write your mother soon. "Let's make San Fernando Valley our home." (Bing Crosby just sang it.)

This and the next few letters express the typical anxiety of newlyweds: What next? Choices must be made about financial issues, transportation, living quarters, household management and privacy. Mobilization readiness and the unpredictability of a military at war demand flexibility of this young couple as well as others nationwide.

April 21, 1944

Today I met Vivian. She is swell and you will be crazy about her. She and Bruce came in tonight. They were disappointed you

87

didn't come back with me. It's wonderful to know that soon I'll be able to be with you practically every night and look at you and talk to you. I can't wait.

April 24, 1944

Vivian, Bruce and I spent all Saturday afternoon and night and all day yesterday trying to find something (wish you had been with us), but we never did. Bruce asked off today in order to find a place. I am taking his Duty Office for him while he looks for our rooms. He is going to look for a place with at least two bedrooms and a bath and kitchen so that we might live together. I hope he finds it. If we have to furnish dishes, linens and cooking utensils, should we buy them here? Or do you want to know what we will need and have it sent from home?

Oh yes, about the dresses. I don't know when you will ever get to wear so many dresses. Maybe yes, maybe no. You won't need evening clothes right away, but it would be nice for you to have one dress when you come. There is an officers' party in the offing, however, and you will have plenty of time to send for dress clothes for it. So dear, when you come just bring your street clothes and your nightgowns and things. You had better bring the iron your mother gave you because they are hard to get. Oh yes, call Mama and tell her to send me my raincoat and also those pajamas (both pair).

April 26, 1944

I was in town tonight and saw Vivian. She and Bruce got the two-bedroom, kitchen and bath apartment. It will cost you and me $42.50 per month, but it is lovely. The house is in a beautiful section of town. It is brick and so nice. It is five minutes from camp and only about two miles from town, 30 minutes by bus. Fare to town is only five cents. We are so lucky, sweet, don't you think?

Vivian and Bruce

May 1, 1944

Vivian and Bruce have moved into our cozy apartment. I found out that the dishes are furnished. Oh yes, don't forget your ration stamps. I am going to write Jack tonight and ask him to keep his eye peeled for some pretty 51-gage hose for you. They are hard to get here. Are you going to need money to get here on?

Vivian, Bruce and I went shopping yesterday afternoon and bought all of the staples that we will need for housekeeping. Flour, sugar, coffee, spices, pickles, mustard, dressings, etc.—things that we will have to have. We had so much fun, but we could have had more fun if you had been here. My love to your family. You realize they are going to miss you like the devil. But they want you to be happy. I'll make you happy; I must.   Your husband, Doyle

[See image of ration stamps in the color gallery.]

May 3, 1944

I just got back from dinner and saw a movie with Vivian and Bruce. We had fun, but not half as much as we will have when you get here. When you come, bring an electric coffee pot, a bread toaster, sheets and pillow cases. Call Jack and ask him if there is any way he can give us any extra points for food. Oh yes honey, I bought a membership to the Officers' Club today. They have an orchestra every Wednesday and Saturday night. They also have a swimming pool and a picnic ground. We are going to have a lovely time, I know.

You and Vivian have a good chance to get jobs on the post making from $30 to $40 per week. Vivian had a most wonderful experience today. She rode to town with the mayor of Columbia. He gave her the name of a woman who he assured her would give her a job. He said if she didn't, call him and he would see to it that she got a job. So you see things are going our way. Oh yes, in closing (I'm sleepy honey) we got a lovely gift today from the Hess's. It's a hand-hammered candy plate.

From Juby's memoir:

Our first home following our marriage was on Devonshire Drive in Columbia. It was a nice two-bedroom, two-bath apartment. We shared the kitchen and living room with Lt. Bruce Schwartz and his wife, Vivian. We enjoyed a private backyard where Vivian and I sunbathed while the guys were at work.

Vivian and I took turns with the cooking, and I have to say that she was a much better cook than I was. My mother's wonderful skill as a cook never rubbed off on me. Our grocery purchases were limited due to rationing policies, and often we would be forced to improvise because we'd run out of stamps. I'll never forget one day in particular. It was my time to cook, and I decided to try pork chops and gravy for the first time. As I was preparing the meal, Doyle came home with his captain, having invited him for dinner. I could have gone through the floor. The dinner was a disaster—overcooked chops and lumpy gravy. At least the potatoes and biscuits were edible, in my opinion. He never surprised me with a guest for dinner again.

Entertainment was limited to movies in town, bowling or just walking the streets window-shopping and people watching. Other military people were doing the same thing, and we would run into buddies of Bruce and Doyle and spend time with them. I well remember an officers' dinner and dance where I met more military couples. Doyle and I were teased for being newlyweds, and being five years younger than he, I was referred to as his "child bride." During the evening, I learned that Doyle had two left feet. I had always loved to dance, even taught a little. I would need more than one night to teach him! We had a good time anyway.

This party was my first experience in a social drinking environment. For months to come, even when he would write about parties overseas, I would continually be amazed at how much alcohol the army provided the men. This particular evening was eye-opening to a new bride. Six of us had ridden to the party in one car. When we headed home in the crowded car, with me in Doyle's lap, he became nauseated and asked the driver to pull over. You can imagine my embarrassment, watching my husband be sick on the side of the road in full view of our friends. Needless to say, he got no TLC from me the next day as he suffered the residual hangover. Later on, we were able to laugh about the incident with the same friends.

We were together in South Carolina for a month and then the army sent us to Camp Davis in North Carolina. We knew this would be the last training place before deployment to a war zone, but we didn't know which one. By then the D-Day invasion had occurred.

With very little notice, Vivian and I hurriedly packed and loaded the Schwartz's car, the convoy having left ahead of us. After we were on the road, I noticed that Vivian was weaving and jerking the car on stops and starts. I asked her how long she had been driving and learned it was practically her first time. I was terrified for the rest of the trip. But we made it!

When we arrived late in the day, we followed directions our husbands had given us to an office where we picked up keys to designated military housing near the shipyard. The furnished duplexes were built for shipyard workers, but some were now reserved for military families. We arrived there during a shift change and were welcomed by whistles and yells from men as we passed by. Unlocking the doors to our accommodations, we were met by a hoard of roaches. Quickly surveying the condition of the interior furnishings, we made a hasty retreat back to the office and turned in our keys. We were given a pamphlet listing rooms to rent. Many good citizens of Wilmington offered temporary housing for families of soldiers. We rented a delightful old house owned by an elderly widow and sent word to our husbands of the change in location. We could only see them on weekends, so our landlady felt it her duty to "mother" us, not affording us much privacy.

A short time later, Doyle, Bruce and two more officers found a four-bedroom house and a room in a small inn converted from a single family home, both located on Wrightsville Beach. Since Doyle and I were newlyweds we opted for the inn, the Lucinda. Our room opened to a deck, which we enjoyed greatly. Yes, this was the first "home" we shared together alone. We took our meals and enjoyed entertainment with our friends in the big house, and we spent much time on the adjacent beach. The wives and I became the best of friends, although I was the youngest one in the group. I learned a lot about military life from them, especially how to be nice to the proper commanding officers' wives. Our stay at Wrightsville Beach was the best of times.

"The best of times"

Chapter 9

Separated Again

Camp Davis, North Carolina

For a few short weeks in June of 1944, there was no need for written correspondence since the couple was together enjoying "the best of times." After the D-Day invasion on June 6, US troops began movement across France, pushing the line of battle westward. Doyle's upcoming role in the war was not yet defined. He and his men could only guess what their futures might be or when and where they would be deployed. They didn't know when they would be saying good-bye to loved ones, but it seemed to be imminent.

In early July, Juby suffered appendicitis and rode the train to Rome to have a necessary operation. Doyle stayed with her for a week, but then reported back to duty. They were separated again for six weeks of all-too-valuable time while Juby recuperated at her family home.

FROM FT FISHER NCAR JUL 17 734.P

LT DOYLE K WHITTENBURG ROME GA

TWO DAY EXTENSION GRANTED DUE BACK 19 JULY 1944

CAPT A V HOOPER

July 21, 1944

Dearest Juby,

I realize more and more each time I leave you that I love you dearly. I am so lonesome and lost now. And only yesterday morning I was kissing you. If you were only here now everything would be so peaceful. It always is when you are near me. I love you for just yourself. I just like to know that you are near me. It frightens me to think that we won't be together for some five or six weeks.

I want to apologize, honey, for being such a baby the other afternoon. My eyes were filled with tears, partly because I was going to leave you the next morning and partly because you were mad and fussing at me because I had been out so much that day. But I had been doing things for you. I was very nervous the day after your operation and I guess the leaving, your pouting, and my nerves were too much for me. Forgive me. I was hurt. I love you and want you now! Your husband, Doyle

July 23, 1944

Nothing at all to do but think of you. We could really enjoy each other's company tonight. It is raining and cool. We are awaiting a 60 mph "blow" here. We just got word that it is headed this way. The rain is preceding it. All the men are out on an overnight bivouac. The officers didn't have to go because the post commander declared non-commissioned officers' day today. So they took over as officers and had to take the men on the hike and bivouac.

Here's something that I think expresses my feelings perfectly now and always:

> Let me lie on your breast, like snow
> Cool and apart, for a moment—so;
> Before the flames start...
> Beautiful, beautiful, beautiful
>
> [Source unknown]

July 26, 1944

If you were here now I would be able to see you practically every night because training stopped today. All the 639th will be doing is packing from now on. Today the boys passed their last test before going overseas. They will be leaving soon, I'm sure. I would like to go with them if I am ever going overseas.

July 27, 1944

All the boys in the outfit are very sorry to hear that you had to go home. They want you to come to another one of their dances.

July 31, 1944

I told you when I called you that they are to clear all units out of Camp Davis by October 1. So hurry and come on up. Check on the account after the allotment gets there, and then you can pay the bills. I don't know whether we can live in Wilmington for the remainder of the month or not. Also it will cost about $15 to come up here. We will find it much cheaper living in Wilmington. You can start saving some of our money for future emergencies.

The Unit History, 639th BN *reports a move from Camp Fisher to Camp Davis on July 31, 1944, for the purpose of packing equipment for overseas movement.* "Our packing crews worked night and day making waterproof bags, packing the boxes, stenciling, nailing and banding them and finally loading them on the train. Final proof that this was IT came when we were all restricted to the area" *[Unit History, 639th BN]*.

August 1, 1944

You know what I did last night honey? I read a sex book. It was the one I told you about before. It was very good. *[Details omitted!]*

Well honey, this has been a different type of letter hasn't it? But all of them boil down to the point that I want our love to be the greatest on this earth. I want it to grow in enjoyment of each other, and it has thus far and will continue to do so.

August 7, 1944

I am using red ink because it depicts the love and passion I hold for you. Honey, your letters are like short furloughs to me. Keep writing them often, will you? I need you now. I'll be with you soon, I know. I must.

You are right when you say that fate was with us. If you had been at Wrightsville the other night when the storm hit, I would have gone crazy. The waves from the ocean came up over the sand dunes and flooded the entire beach. The roof of the Lucinda was blown away and the piers at Carolina and Ft. Fisher were destroyed. The bridge across the inland waterway at Wrightsville was damaged and the water was up over it. Everyone at Wrightsville was cleared out by bus or GI transportation. They were taken to the Camp Davis hospital and USO at Wilmington and other places. Ruth and Vivian went to stay with Eileen. Our battalion wasn't used for evacuation, but we were on the alert just in case we were needed.

I wasn't very scared for myself, but if you had been on the beach I'm sure I would have been frantic. Some of the EM [Enlisted Men] in the battalion were three days finding their wives. Carolina Beach is still restricted to military personnel until repairs are made.

Juby on the balcony of the Lucinda

From Juby's memoir:

While at home mending after surgery, I heard on the news that a hurricane had swept away a lot of the beach at Wrightsville and had damaged the Lucinda. I hated that our little inn was destroyed. I no longer had a place to return to. When I came to Wilmington after my recuperation, Doyle took me to see the devastation. We mourned our lost paradise, temporary as it was.

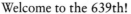

Welcome to the 639th!   Caricature of 2nd Lt. Whittenburg
                             by a fellow soldier

August 8, 1944

Honey I hate to say this, but from now on don't be surprised a bit to hear I have been assigned to the 639th. There is a big fight going on amongst the officers as usual. I don't like to say it, but I think that some of the officers are a wee bit yellow-bellied. I am I'll admit, but at least I am willing to do my job. That's more than some of them can truthfully say. I wouldn't be surprised a bit to learn I am to go overseas with them. Heaven only knows I haven't tried to get assigned. I have done nothing but gold brick for a month now. Another thing (this is secret info), the 639th is to be restricted the 18th of August.

I want to see you tonight more than usual. I need you honey, but please don't try to come up until you are well, because if you came and it caused health complications, I would never forgive myself. The tentative date for moving out could be delayed for a few weeks. One never knows when or where the Army will strike next. Regardless of what happens, our love will hold our spirits up and our spirits will be together through thick and thin. This is enough gloom so I will speak of brighter things.

August 18, 1944 [after a leave]

I have your picture here before me now. It isn't like the real thing but I'm sure glad that I brought it. I can imagine that you are here with me. This letter will be short because I'm sleepy and tired from my trip. I was so happy while I was there with you. When you cried a little I felt like crying myself, but somehow I didn't. I'm back now and I must buckle down to work. I'll be thinking of you every minute of the day.

Sweetheart, I love you more than anything on earth and always will. I'll miss you while I'm gone honey, but just the thought of being able someday to be with you is going to give me strength and power to carry on. You have made a new man of me since we married, dear. In return, all I ask is for you to accept my thanks and love. We'll be together in our letters, won't we sweet? I get so much comfort from just hearing from you.

August 19, 1944

We are about ready to move now but there is no date set. Our advance party left yesterday. We still could be around for two or three weeks.

Your smiling face is beaming down on me now. Every time I look at your picture, I get a funny feeling in the pit of my stomach. Honey, you are about the best loved gal in Battery D. Every day several of the boys ask me how you are. I like to know that I am married to someone other guys like. It gives me a certain amount of ego to think I am married to such a swell gal and am loved so completely by her. I love you and want to see you so much tonight.

I am going to send another footlocker home with some things in it. Save them for us, will you? Oh yes, thank your mother for treating me like one of her sons. Honey, it's a pleasure to be a son of your father and mother. I love your sisters too. Give them my regards. I wish I had a couple of Mary's biscuits tonight. Ym. Ym.

Juby's family, summer 1944
L–R, Little sisters: Frances, Kathryn and Elizabeth;
parents: Mary and Grady

I am about to spend another lonely afternoon in camp. I took Paul's OD [Officer Duty] today so he might spend the entire weekend with Ruth. We have to remove all our AA patches, and I am trying to get a few hundred for you. Don't you think if you crochet them together they would make cute placemats? I think they would be great in a breakfast nook.

I just finished a bull session with a couple of the guys. I had your picture before me and they commented on your beauty; of course they looked mostly at the legs (the wolves). I just went around and collected about 50 AA patches.

Captain Hooper said we might be around for two more weeks. I just sit and dream of the time when we can have our own house and live as husband and wife should. I went to the movies last night. It was a double feature, *Seven Doors to Death* and *Madame Fifi*. I stopped at the club for a beer, and there was an all-girl orchestra playing. They were all hags.

August 26, 1944

I wish I had arranged for you to come up this weekend because I think maybe we will be leaving before the next. I think we are going north.

We were at the USO show which included Borrah Minevitch with his Harmonica Rascals and acrobatic dancers that I have seen in the movies; also a tap dancing team and a songstress that sang with Larry C__ton [name unclear in the original]. It was the best show I have seen since I have been in the Army. Lester sawed a girl in half while he had five GIs on the stage with him to see things well and close. When the act was over he told the guys to shake hands with the very, very beautiful young lady, and as the girl put out her hand, the first guy grabbed her and kissed her for about one minute. Of course the other guys followed suit. The poor girl was really embarrassed. The wolves.

Tomorrow I am to go on camp stockade OD. I might have some time to write. But if I don't, please try to bear it until you hear from me.

From Juby's memoir:

In preparation for overseas assignment, the guys were instructed to remove all insignia and AA patches from their uniforms. Doyle collected AA patches from the guys in his unit who had met me and wanted me to have them (for some reason unknown to me). Not particularly inspired by his idea of making placemats, I had no clue what to do with them. One day when I didn't have anything to do, I reread some of Doyle's letters (as I often did). I was reminded of the practice among enlisted men of hanging pinup pictures of sexy starlets such as Betty Grable and Rita Hayworth near their bunks. An idea came to me—cover my two-piece bathing suit with the AA patches and send him a photo of me wearing it. A very personal pinup for the 639th! It took time to do the sewing and even more time for the mailed photograph to reach him. He got a kick out of it and proudly showed others in his unit. He kept the picture throughout the war, and it came home with him to become part of our scrapbook.

"Always loyal to the 639th"

No doubt the battalion "wolves" howled when they saw this one!

[See duplicate image in the color gallery.]

104

Chapter 10

Moving Out

August 29, 1944

Hello Dearest,

The 639th will be leaving for some other camp pretty quick now. If we were sure that we would be here this next weekend, I would have you come up to Wilmington, but honey I'm afraid we won't be here.

I sent you a footlocker today and the suitcase I brought before. In the suitcase is clothing your father could wear, including a pair of galoshes, boots, a wool gabardine shirt, a green shirt and a field jacket. I also sent a wool blanket, sheets and a pillowcase. All the khaki clothes I would like to have washed and ready for shipment in case I need them. I sent 15 records and the ten-record turntable out of the big radio that was in the day room at Jackson. Ask Will if he will take it to one of his radio repair men and see if it can be fixed. I am going to enclose a key in this letter to unlock the locker. I mailed my Bulova watch today. Let me know if it gets there because I'll be worried until it arrives. I didn't insure it. Let Will have it until I return or need it. The government has issued me a 17-jewel Hamilton so I see no reason to have two watches.

Honey, forgive me for not making love to you so much in this letter. It's been more or less a business letter. We might not see each other for a little while, but when we do we have a lot of tangible loving to catch up on, and it won't be long if we continue to dream of each other.   I love you dear, Doyle

P.S. If you have trouble, push in on the lock, turn the key and she will open. D

August 30, 1944

I shouldn't write what I am going to write but I will. We are going to Staten Island very soon now. Don't tell anyone about it. ... Honey, you have given me all the courage a man could have. I now have something to go over and fight for and come back to. I love you dear. If I wasn't married to you, I wouldn't care whether I came back or not. Now I will come back and to you. I guarantee it.

September 1, 1944

Honey, the present status of the war might change all the plans of the 639th. Our boys over there are raising hell, so if things keep moving maybe the 639th won't have to go. I'm afraid, though, that we might have to go to the SP [South Pacific]. I'm afraid of disease down there; malaria and the like. But I'm not coming back as an invalid, I'm coming back with more zip and wolfishness and devilment in me than I go over with.

I wish you had been at the party the other night. We had a five-piece band, a really good master of ceremonies, a couple of good singers (men), a comedian and a magician. We also had 45 cases of beer. Over a 1000 bottles, and it was all drunk by the men. Of course I had some of the beer. I ate three chicken breasts, six legs, three thighs and two pulley bones. Plus potatoes, beans, corn, pretzels, cheese, potato chips, etc. It was a grand party. One of our kids named Scannella (you danced with him) got drunk and got up and sang "Sam You Made the Pants Too Long." He was really good.

Then he and Brezinski put on a swing-a-roo show. Marollo, our professional Broadway dancer, gave us a lesson and demonstration of elite ballroom dancing. He's really smooth.

Enclosed is a letter from Mama; you will find yourself mentioned in it. It made me feel good when I read what she wrote about you. She speaks of you as a Whittenburg as if you had always been in the family. To me honey, it seems that you have been in the family forever. You seem to have always been a part of me. I just finished playing casino with Captain Hooper. He was my partner. We won. Write soon.

September 2, 1944

I played a game of softball today. We are playing games quite a bit now. We are getting in condition physically to face the job we have trained to do.

I got a nice letter from Mama yesterday. She's a little peeved because she gets her letters from me secondhand. I don't blame her, I guess. I'll write her over the weekend. She really loves that grandson of hers, doesn't she? I bet he runs Mary crazy before it's over. I can tell by the way Mama writes that he's quite a pistol. I'd like to have something to do with giving your mother a grandson. Your mother would make him rotten. She'd do anything the kid wanted to do. I love your mother, she's so good. She's always working to make a home.

I'm really looking forward to the time when you and I settle down to normal living. For now we must be patient, and then we will be together again loving each other bodily. Then we'll have our baby and soon our second and third and maybe even a fourth. So be patient my love and think of me as I think of you—all the time. You're my guiding light now, sweet. Please honey, buy the record "We'll Meet Again" and play it when you're lonely. We'll be together in thought.

September 4, 1944

As usual, all of us are sitting in our private club drinking beer and eating sandwiches a couple of our boys made for us. Six or eight officers who haven't got their wives here are together every weekend. We have set up our own little club in one of the rooms. We play rummy and casino and drink beer. I hope we are still here next weekend, and if you are willing to make the trip, you will be in my arms.

Doyle and Juby were able to spend a short time together in Wilmington in a rented room at the home of the Byrd family. They last saw each other on September 8, 1944. The next several letters were written just before and during his transit. He now had to write on V-mail (Victory Mail) pages, which were then photographed to microfilm for transport, thus reducing bulk and weight. The pages were printed on arrival to the States, reduced to 60 percent.

September 10, 1944

Yes, I know you once said that you did not like V-mail, but I have packed all my paper and this is all I could find. So here 'tis. Dearest I miss you so very much and hope that God will soon have us together again. The next letter you get from me will be from another station so please don't worry if you don't hear from me for two or three weeks. Promise? I'll be thinking of you and all of the swell things you have done for me.

Tonight I had the good fortune to see Ella Fitzgerald. She is really good. Ugly as a mud fence, but good personality and a good sport. I saw Rudolf Frimi's *Firefly* last night. They really have some wonderful talent here. Give my regards to your mother and dad and your sisters and please honey, keep your chin up and don't change from the sweet little girl that I left in Wilmington that morning.

Chapter 11
Deployed

September 17, 1944

Dearest Juby,

Honey, I feel so very close to you. You're all I have to keep me going. We have big things to do together. The world is ours to use as we like and we will use it to our advantage.

We have moved since I last saw you and may move again. I have to weigh my words closely—I don't want to say some things that are on my mind because I might disclose some information that might aid the enemy.

How are your sister Frances and her husband? Please, for my sake, don't let things get you down like they did her. You can take it. And honey, visit with Mama and keep her posted, will you? I will do my darnedest to write you every day so I won't have time to write much to anyone else. It is very difficult to write now and stay within censorship regulations. Up to now I have been writing what comes in my mind, but now there are things on my mind that can't be put on paper. I'm worried about you. You did make a promise to write every day and you have, but the mail hasn't caught up to me, has it?

All my love, Doyle

September 20, 1944

I will try to catch up on my work this afternoon and write you a long sweet letter. We were restricted at 2400 Monday. I know when we're leaving, but I won't tell you just yet. Some saboteur might wreck our train.

September 21, 1944

Honey, this is a note to tell you that I love you very much. Before I go any further, I have a confession to make. I played cards last night and lost $15. OK, give me hell. I deserve it. I was so lonesome for you and the guys were playing, so I decided I would try to pass some time. You made me promise I wouldn't gamble. Write me a nasty letter about it. Sweet, it taught me a lesson. If I had won, I would do it again and probably lose more than I did. Please forgive me this time.

The Unit History, 639th BN *details the itinerary of the overseas movement. Leaving Camp Davis on September 22, 1944, the battalion headed to Camp Gilmer in New Jersey. After final processing was completed on September 28, the 639th rode the train to Jersey City, then ferried across the North River to port. Details and destinations were not revealed to the troops:* "We boarded the SS *Chitral*, a British vessel making its maiden run as a troop transport having formerly been a passenger liner on the Oriental run, and at 0510 on 29 September 1944, embarked for an unknown destination. ...Life aboard consisted of a little training, boat drill daily, eating, sleeping, reading, playing cards, etc. The food was not up to American standards" *[Unit History, 639th BN].*

These next letters were written while aboard the SS Chitral, *11 days at sea.*

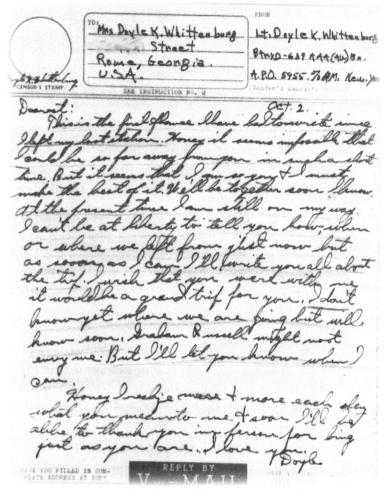

V-mail, actual size, difficult for Juby (and us) to read

October 2, 1944

This is the first chance I have had to write since I left my last station. Honey, it seems impossible that I could be so far away from you in such a short time. I can't be at liberty to tell you how, when or where we left from, but as soon as I can I'll write you all about the trip. I don't know yet where we are going. I realize more and more each day what you mean to me, and soon I'll be able to thank you in person for being just as you are.

October 3, 1944

I find it very difficult writing at the present time. I am limited as to what I can say. I haven't stopped moving for five days and nights now. We have no idea where we will go. As soon as the censor gives us permission to let out the news, I will write you about it. I have thought about you all day and dreamed that maybe someday you and I can make a trip like this together. Well honey, I can't say much on this V-mail, but I can say that I love you with all my heart and would give anything to be with you now. You are all that I have left so please be sweet, my darling, until my return. Here's my heart.

October 4, 1944

I'm writing you letters now expecting to mail them as soon as we land. I can tell you one thing: don't ever make a trip by boat. It's a lot of fun at first, but now I would give almost anything to be on dry land. I do a good bit of dreaming about you during the day and night. Honey, I'll ask you now what you want for Christmas. Of course you might have to buy it yourself because of the circumstances, but please let me know. I am going to send you some souvenirs from the places I go. It seems like ages since I have heard from you. Of course there will be letters waiting when we dock, but for now I will be satisfied with writing to and dreaming of you.

October 5, 1944

Since I last wrote you I have been thinking of the swell time we had together. It was oh so short. Our weekends together, our most wonderful time in Florida and then our stay at Wrightsville. Wasn't it wonderful? Then your stay at the hospital. You didn't enjoy it much, but I enjoyed waiting on you. You were such a sweet patient. Yes, you were. Then the six days at home, just you and me in the Hotel Forrest. Then I left you, and we were apart for a long, long time until you came to me again at Wilmington. You looked so sweet when I saw you standing there in the station in your white coat.

Honey, in three days we will have been married for six months and it's been the shortest six months of my life. I'll be back to you real soon, and we can pick up where we left off. So be sweet and love me because I love you.

Juby in her white coat

This is a well-worn photograph that Doyle carried in his wallet for many years after the war was over.

The unit debarked at Greenock, Scotland, south of Glasgow at the mouth of the River Clyde, and immediately boarded a train for Aldermaston, their destination in England. Doyle's desire to share his experiences with Juby is a recurrent theme in his letters to her from here forward. His detailed descriptions of each adventure and new place he discovered allowed her to learn with him that there was an immense world beyond their hometown. She was able to travel with him via his "word pictures."

I spent six months of 2009 transcribing all 411 of Doyle's letters of love and war. The more I read, the more I felt a growing imperative to embark upon the journey he'd always wanted to take with Juby who was present with him in spirit during his deployment. Many times in his letters he would express his wish to someday return with her actually by his side to the many beautiful places he'd seen. Unfortunately, Doyle was never able to realize his dream of a return trip with his wife, but his letters provided a reliable map for the next generation to follow. My brother Ken and I "bit the bullet" financially and scheduled the trip. During six months of planning, many things fell into place. We were able to learn through the Internet that the main places our father stayed in England were functioning as hotels now. As the plans began to crystalize, our anticipation grew.

A few days before our trip was to begin, a volcano erupted in Iceland and stopped all air traffic across Europe for five days due to volcanic ash. Our carefully planned mission seemed in jeopardy. On departure day, April 20, 2010, Ken and I sat in the Delta lounge at Hartsfield-Jackson International Airport in Atlanta, our flight delayed but not yet cancelled. We knew that no flights had landed in London for five days. We were actually surprised when the boarding call came. The plane lifted off at 8:00 PM for the overnight flight, just two hours later than scheduled. There are no flight horror stories to tell; it was smooth as silk all the way. Since we were on one of the first planes to land in London after the recent air traffic disruption, retrieving our luggage, clearing Gatwick customs and hiring a cab to Aldermaston was exceptionally easy. We arrived at Aldermaston Manor shortly before lunch, April 21, 2010. Dad's journey had taken as many days as ours had taken in hours. Our quest to follow in his footsteps had begun.

Part II

The Overseas Story
England – Belgium – Germany

Of Deployment, Combat and Victory

October 5, 1944, through June 11, 1945

REMEMBERING FALL 1944

The words flow smoothly from your pen
As you write to me each day
From somewhere in the world—
Just where you cannot say.

You write of battles lost and won
Of fear and death and winter's chill
And when the bombs light up the sky
That you're alive just by God's will.

I remember last days on the beach
When we knew you had to go
And the promises we made
To keep our love aglow.

I remember how you smiled that day
With that twinkle in your eye
Assuring me that you'd be fine
While kissing me goodbye.

Now I hold your letters to my heart
And pray that Peace will be
The ending to this warring game
And that you'll come home to me.

—Juby Whittenburg (October 17, 2007)

Chapter 12

On Foreign Soil

The Battery D History, 639th BN *indicates arrival of the battery at the English country estate Aldermaston Court on October 11, 1944, at 0630. The troops were billeted in Nissen hut barracks on the grounds; officers stayed in the manor house, which they called a castle. For six weeks, athletics and vigorous training programs filled the time while the battalion waited for combat equipment to arrive. All personnel were able to visit London and explore England. A recent local publication about the history of Aldermaston parish,* Memories of Life in an English Country Village, *describes the time when the "Yanks" were there. They were awed by the "castle" and particularly captivated by its pet cemetery. The site is now a hotel and wedding venue with a fascinating history going back to the fourteenth century. [See image of Aldermaston Court in the color gallery.]*

October 10, 1944

Dearest Juby, [first of two V-mail pages]

If you received my last letter, you know we landed safely. I am in the most beautiful place I have ever seen. I can't tell you much about the trip yet, but I can tell you that Bruce, Paul, Larson and I are quartered in one of 75 rooms of a most luxurious castle. The furnishings have been removed but for a few large pieces such as hand-carved desks and a harpsichord. First built in 1636 and renewed in 1857, it has a large garden court and all the things that go with a castle. It isn't the type of gloomy medieval castle with a moat that I saw on the way here. I wish you could be here. I love you. To be continued.

Dearest Juby, continued: [V-mail, second page]

Mama could spend months at this place. There is so much to see. I am going to send you a couple of milk glass globe shades that I think you can use on a pair of table lamps. They are very old. I am going to look around for more souvenirs while I'm here. Do you get my mail? Did you get the money I sent? I haven't heard from you since I left. Have you been writing? Keep it up. I miss you more and want you more than ever before. I hope and pray that the war will be over soon and I'll be on my way home. D.

October 12, 1944

Honey, this is the first real letter I have written you since I left. All the others were just notes on V-mail. I can tell you that I am somewhere in England and soon I'm going to take a trip to London. I hope we stay here for the duration of the war. It's like living in a dreamland. Of course I go through the agony of yearning for you, but I am trying to enjoy the castle and surrounding countryside. You don't blame me, sweet, do you? You are having it much tougher than I am. Now that I'm overseas, I'm just as safe as I was back in the States, and at present I have better living quarters. We have a regular living room with a cute little fireplace, a large closet and an army cot per man.

We have a beautiful view from our large window overlooking the entrance of the castle. There are oak trees about ten feet thick at the trunk, huge boxwoods, hemlock and some shrubs that I don't know. A large greenhouse is on the estate, as well as a lake for canoeing (if we had canoes). There are stables with running water in them. The men's baths have private compartments with a large bathtub in each. The men are delighted. There are fancy iron fences and fancy brick walls all around the court. The chimneys are in groups of four, and the bricks are laid in all different patterns. The architecture is amazing. I haven't stopped gasping yet.

The main tower has a clock like our city clock, but the hands and numerals are copper. A gargoyle is on each corner of the tower, and one floor below is a life-sized bronze statue of a Roman soldier with a staff. A hammer made of curved sheet bronze is on the staff. When there is a strong wind, the hammer seems to be rippling. The kitchen consists of large rooms with white tile walls up to eight feet; one for baking preparation, one for actual cooking and one for cleaning up. The oven is in the basement. The dining room, which the officers have taken for their mess hall, is an immense thing. I wish you were here. You would love it.

This place has a cemetery for cats and dogs. Some of the inscriptions are Blakie, Smut, Fredy, Tom, A Faithful Pet, Companion, R.I.P. and the like. Some of the stones in the old churchyard date back to 1600 AD. I have written so rapidly about so many things that amaze me that I might not be making things clear.

I have been to Scotland, and honey, it's the prettiest country I have ever seen. The landscape is beautiful—rolling hills, rock formations and farms here and there. The little villages are just like Christmas cards. No kidding. Every house has its own hothouse for raising plants. The people wanted souvenirs from us, especially cigarettes. The little kids would take them to their fathers and their sisters. They also wanted candy, chewing gum and anything else we had to offer. Kids went crazy when we came around. The older women stood in their windows and waved Scottish, English and American flags as we went by. It was quite interesting to watch.

Our food here is very good. We have more rations at present than we had in the States. My only regret is that you aren't here. I miss you, oh I miss you. Please honey, don't get down in the dumps. Your mother expressed hope that I would keep you cheered up by writing often. I will—just keep smiling in return. I'll be back soon and make up for my absence. Just you wait.

October 12, 1944

This is a V-mail to ensure that you get a letter for this day. I'm sending a letter by regular mail too. I want you to let me know the difference in time it takes for the two types of mail to get there. And I need some three-cent stamps. We can send letters airmail for six cents. Something else in the way of business, my sweet. Don't tell anyone how much money you have in the bank because they might want to borrow some. Please honey, don't let any of my family borrow money from you. Just tell them that it's our money and it will stay where it is until you and I can get our heads together and decide about its disposal. OK? We're getting a raw deal having to live apart for a while, and we might as well take advantage of it. We can live well when we do join each other again. I miss you like the very devil, sweet. They say what you can't have is what you want more than anything else. I do want you. Don't forget—don't loan your money. When you get a surplus, start a savings account.

From Doyle's memoir [written October 13, 1998]:

When we were billeted in Aldermaston, we had physical training while special crews were out gathering up combat equipment from supply dumps in Glasgow, Codding, Southampton and other points of England. Each battery was given permission by the colonel to have dinner dances on weekends. Small signs would be placed on the bulletin board at the Aldermaston pub (beer parlor) announcing the coming party. The mess sergeant would serve ham and cheese sandwiches or dried beef and bologna with potato salad. Drinks were provided: iced tea, lemonade and beer.

Girls who worked in nearby munitions plants were invited. Many were from Ireland, having come to do the war work. Some would pedal bikes 20 miles to these parties—not just for dancing, but to get a square meal. When we opened the door to the serving room, they would fight to get to the table. I have seen them put sandwiches in their brassieres—two or even three—to take back to their billets. I saw one small girl about 18 years old standing back. I approached her and asked her why she was waiting. She explained that she had just come from Ireland and she couldn't break the rule set by her parents: always be a lady. I took her back to the workroom and let her make a selection. She took two sandwiches and two oranges and told me she had never seen an orange. She was going to send one of them to her little brother. She said the bologna sandwich had more meat on it than her weekly ration. When the word got out about the food, more girls showed up than we could handle. We had to place restrictions on how many could come.

We had a small band that played dance music and a guitar player who sang sad country music songs. When he finished, he had every girl there crying. They loved it.

There was an airstrip next to the castle where B-24s landed. The crews were hauling gasoline to Patton on the southern front. All Patton wanted was gasoline for his tanks. I heard he said that they could live off the land but they couldn't find gasoline. The B-24 crews would come in from a mission and their CO [Commanding Officer] would assign certain ones to come to the castle for a hot meal and an army cot to get some sleep after a battle. If I remember right, we took about ten crew members every two nights. These men were nervous wrecks.

The stay at Aldermaston was a good time for us. Reading was only 15 miles away, and we could go there if we didn't have night duty. We were allowed to use our jeeps. We went to London two or three times and were able to see other parts of England and Scotland. I remember walking down country lanes and talking to the older English people working in their gardens. They produced most of their food on small garden spots. Not an inch of their land went untended.

There is a romantic love letter to Juby that would be good to splice into this Aldermaston vein of thought. I may dig it out of the files and duplicate it for here. This is really for posterity.

Doyle did indeed dig out his romantic letter, which he placed after his remembrances of Aldermaston in his memoir. Written October 13, 1944, his letter is a detailed and wonderful word picture describing an imaginary tour of Aldermaston castle (manor) with Juby by his side. My brother Ken and I spent three days at this wonderful place at the beginning of our journey in our father's footsteps. We used the letter as a guide and enjoyed walking about and appreciating the same beauty he had seen more than 65 years ahead of us.

I'm placing the second letter written on October 13, 1944, here because Juby received it before the first one. The reason is explained in the letter.

October 13, 1944 [second letter]

Honey, I feel as if you are sitting here beside me now because I have been talking to you for the past hour. I love you dear. Kiss me will you? Ah. That was sweet. Now I'll kiss you—ahhhhh. Have you received any of my letters yet? I haven't heard from you or anyone since I left. Maybe tomorrow.

Now keep your chin up and I'll be home soon. If you don't mind, read Mama parts of the letter I'm sending to you in three envelopes. Of course if you want it only for yourself, I don't blame you a bit. This letter will reach you first; it will fill in until the longer one comes.

October 13, 1944 [first letter]

Dearest Juby,

Come along for a short walk, honey. Want to? OK. You'd better put on your coat and gloves and take a scarf for your head. Are you all set? Here we go. Wait a minute 'till I find my hat. Where in hell is it? Not here—no, it isn't here either. Honey, you moved my hat from where I left it. Oh! I'm sorry, it's on my head! Rattle-brained me.

Well, here we go out in the dark hall. Honey, I had better put my arm around you. That door to the right is the home of Starnachi, Vought, Morrotta and Kenny. The room farther up on the left is for Rorensteel, Murphy and Larkin. The one farther up on the right—here it is—is for Kessler and Watts. Now we are halfway up the hall and we go up six steps. At the top of the steps is a circular staircase to the third and fourth floors, and then to the tower. I'll take you up there some other day. I have a lovely place I'm taking you now. You'll love it.

On our left is a banister. See the beautiful hand-carved wood-work? It covers the entire banister about five feet high. There is a group of cherubs, little angels, and look honey, at the muscles in the stomach of that bearded man; he appears to be holding that post up on his back with his hands behind his neck. Here honey, step up and look at all the detailed carving—there's a long, pointed basket with fruit coming out of it, a horn of plenty. Look down there and see the main entrance on the first floor. Notice how high and wide the doors are. I'll bet they are twelve feet high and ten feet wide. Huge, aren't they? The receiving room is immense, isn't it? It's wonderful.

I haven't yet shown you what I started out to show you. Let's take a few more steps down the hall, and here we turn right. The door to our right is where Tate, Low and O'Donahue live. To go down we must go right on a landing and twelve more steps; now we are on the first floor.

On our right is a large den. The room is about 50 feet square. The next room is the library. See the massive bookcases? They extend to the ceiling about 18 to 20 feet high. There must have been some wonderful books in here when it was used for a house. Oh, you ask about one set of bookshelves that still has books in it. Come over here with me. If you look closely, you'll see that these are dummy books. Now push on the shelves here. Ha! Surprised, aren't you? Yes, the entire set of shelves swings back and beyond is the den where we were. The man that had that secret door installed must have read a murder mystery or two, don't you think?

Come along to the receiving room. I want you to see this lovely fireplace. The opening for the fire is about six feet high and the mantel piece is ten feet high. See the statues on the end of it? They're bearded men four feet high carved from wood. Now we will walk to the castle chapel down the hall from the library. Before we get there is a bathroom. Step inside and look it over. Up on a tile platform is a hand bowl three times as large as ours back home. On either side of it is an enclosed commode. No waiting here if we both have to go at the same time. It probably was put here for someone who came in from a trip and couldn't wait until he got to the rear of the house. Convenient, eh what?

A few steps down the hall are four beautiful stained-glass windows. There's a picture of the Virgin Mary and Saint Christopher and other biblical characters. Aren't they lovely? A double doorway with brass hinges and a long fancy brass doorknob is on the right. A huge thing, isn't it? Wouldn't Mama love this? Wait. I'll open the door. There. Step inside. Aren't the doors heavy? They are a good four inches thick.

Now we are in the chapel. This room is about 60 by 40. You notice the other end widens out into two little vestibules. One vestibule leads to an outside entrance and the other contains the altar of the chapel. On each side of the pulpit is a leather-covered seat about eight feet long. I imagine the choir sat on each side, don't you? Behind the pulpit is a large oak chair, straight and tall. The minister sat there, I guess. Notice the carved woodwork all around the altar and the stained-glass windows on either side of the minister's chair. Above the outer door are seven stained-glass windows that have coats of arms in the glass. Under each one is "Forster and ____ (the name of the person whose coat of arms is displayed)." *[The lord of the manor was Forster in days of old.]*

Come along with me. Wait, this is a dark hallway. If you don't mind dear, come a little closer. I'll pull you close to me and take you in my arms and kiss you. There. I love you dear. But come along now. Let's go back down the hall to the receiving room. Wrap up good because it's cold outside. Now we go out into the stoop. It's about 12 by 12 and has a tile roof. Notice the design of the floor—many colored pieces of tile. They are so grouped that they form baskets and bowls of flowers. The pieces of tile are about half-inch square, aren't they? *[Doyle had evidently never seen mosaic art before.]*

Now we are out in the front yard. Don't you imagine that beautiful horse-drawn carriages came up to this entrance in the past? There is a tiled wall about 100 feet out. Isn't it fancy? Look at the men playing softball on the lawn beyond the wall. Notice the size of those trees. I'll bet that one is 15 feet through, don't you? Just above us is the tower, about 150 to 175 feet high. Gargoyles and bronze statues of knights are on each corner around the clock, see? On our right are quarters for visiting servants. A little farther to our right are the stables. The stalls for the horses have nice bowls with a hydrant for the horse to shave with. No kidding, it's really there. The floors of the stables are made of red brick tiles. Nice. Upstairs are quarters for the coachmen and grooms.

Past the castle to our right we can see the shrubbery garden. The shrubs are huge. There are flower beds and a lawn. You must see more of it tomorrow. At the end of a ten-foot brick wall is a greenhouse. Now we will turn down this little path. Look here to our left. See the large cedar? The seed that sprouted that tree was imported from the forests of Lebanon. Where were the cedar forests of Lebanon? Was it Palestine? I'm sure it wasn't Lebanon, Tennessee, because the seed was brought here by a lieutenant in the Royal Navy.

Honey, you don't know how much I'm enjoying this walk with you. You're much more beautiful than these things we're looking at. But let's go on, it's growing late. Do you see that little square of hedge over there? It has an opening at one end and there isn't any hedge growing in the center. There is a gated iron fence around the inside of the hedge and stone steps down into the earth. I explored it the other day and found it to be a dungeon. There are three large rooms under the ground. There aren't any torture devices and no skulls and bones. I don't know why. Maybe the man here was a good man and maybe he had good vassals, or were slaves called serfs? I forget. *[Ken and I learned on our visit to Aldermaston that this was the cellar to an estate building that had burned. The iron fence and steps are still there, but not the hedges. Doyle would be disappointed to know there was no sinister purpose for the space.]*

Over there past the entrance to the dungeon is the pet cemetery with graves and monuments to dogs, cats and other pets. Quite nice of the other generations to show their love for their pets this much, eh what? Now honey, on down this path is what I started out to show you. Are you getting too cold to go on? Do you want to go back and get warm and clean up and go to bed? No? OK. We'll go on. You can see it now. Yes, it's the village church and churchyard. Doesn't the architecture remind you a little of the entrance to the Alamo? Remember? It's made of cement, I guess. Notice the iron fence around it. Here, let me open the gate. You're cold aren't you? No? Yes, you are. Honey, you can come down tomorrow and read some of the epitaphs on the stones. It's too dark now. Let's go in the church.

Here we are, inside. Gee, isn't it beautiful? I feel much warmer now. The atmosphere here seems to warm you up, doesn't it? It gives you that good feeling. Aren't the stained-glass windows pretty? Now look there. Someone long ago lost his beloved wife and erected that bronze plaque in her honor. Read the inscription on it, "In behalf of my beloved wife." I hope I won't ever have the opportunity to dedicate something like that to you. I'll die when you do dear, so we'll be together. Look, there's one erected by a wife. I'll bet she was lonely. Come along. Look behind you. Up there is a balcony where I imagine servants sat. What's this? Why it's a grave here in the aisle of the church. I didn't see it the other day. Yes, there is an eight by four slab of marble with the man's name, title, birth and death dates and also an inscription cut into it. Look, there's another farther down and look to the right, honey. I have never seen anything like that. It's wonderful isn't it? It's a carved marble tier set back into an alcove with two life-sized knights of old lying on their backs praying. See, they have their helmets on their chests and their prayer books in their hands. Their heads are on prayer pillows and a seat is at their feet. We're looking at the knights from their left sides. They are up about four and a half feet from the floor. Behind this is a small altar. It's amazing.

At the front of the main auditorium is a most beautiful altar. Look at the wooden fence separating the congregation from the choir, organ and altar. Let's go in. Here we are. Let's go closer. We are now at the kneeling mats just between the organ and choir seats. Honey, this atmosphere has the power to make one think of God, doesn't it? Will you kneel down here with me, my sweet, and pray for us? Pray that the turmoil this world is now in will cease and we, you and I, will be together again in body as well as in spirit and love. Pray that all the men and women, fathers and mothers, sisters and brothers will be together soon. Pray that the boys less fortunate than I will have someone to love them as you love me and they will return that love as I do. Ask God to take care of you until I return. Then I'll take care of you. Honey, you look so sweet there on your knees and in the half-light. (Yes, I peeped.) I love you so. Ask God to bless your family and mine. He'll hear your prayers, I know.

Well honey, it's growing quite late. You're tired now from your long journey, so let's go now to our room where you can take a nice warm bath and go to bed. Tomorrow you can go sightseeing yourself while I work with the boys. I wanted you to see the church because I thought of it when you came to me on the wings of an angel. Thank God you were with me today.   All my love, Doyle

From Doyle's memoir:

Ninety-five percent of my prayers now are prayers of thanks. The other five percent are intercessory prayers. I have had a wonderful life; the Almighty has been kind and good to me. I have asked for strength at times. He always gives it. I actually heard his voice once. He said, "Come down here with me." I rolled toward the voice and fell into a six-foot snowdrift. There was no one there. A mortar shell exploded in the very spot I rolled away from. I felt His presence in other situations but never actually heard Him again. I know that He is there, however. He is everywhere. People don't believe this happened to me, but I can't deny that He spoke to me. Saved my life outright. He heard my prayers and returned me safely to my wife in late 1945. We have three great kids and four wonderful grandchildren. We have our health and each other. Who could ask for anything more?

From Juby's memoir:

I loved the letter describing Aldermaston Court in detail. I could imagine being beside Doyle as he toured the beautiful place. I was glad to learn how much he appreciated artwork. In fact, I learned more about my husband from his letters than I did in the short time we were together before he left. I shared the letters from the war zone with my family and his. We all waited with anticipation for the next one. He was writing daily except during troop movements or battles, but the letters did not come daily. I would go many days without getting one, and then get several. He was having the same experience with my letters. It was very frustrating, but unavoidable.

IN HIS FOOTSTEPS

April 21, 2010: *Ken and I check into our suite at Aldermaston Manor. We explore about, using our father's October 13, 1944, descriptions as our guide. It is amazing how accurate his word pictures are and that so much has remained the same over 65 years. Of course the history of the manor spans centuries; its staying power has been proven through the ages. We are delighted by every discovery that matches Dad's, and we are just as awed as he was. Exploring the manor and its immediate grounds holds our attention during this first day. From the giant fireplace in the reception room, to the rich wood of the many hand-carved figures along the ornate stair banisters, to the exquisite stained glass windows—we, like he, can't stop gasping. [See images of the fireplace and carved banisters in the color gallery.]*

Having read this letter many times through the years, we thought we knew what to expect. Here now in person, we take in the vibrant colors of banners bearing coats of arms hung from ornately adorned ceilings high above. We hear echoes of our own footsteps among the lofty spaces. We count the steps from one level to the other on the staircase that Dad had so thoughtfully measured as he tenderly toured Mom in his narrative long ago. In the library, we identify the secret door masked by "dummy books" and pass through to the next room. We enjoy the smells and tastes of fresh cheese and pickle sandwiches in the dining room where he and his fellow officers had taken their meals. [See image of the secret door in the color gallery.]

We remark that time travel must be a true experience after all—we seem to have done it. Our hearts are full.

After lunch, we venture outside. Early spring has awakened buds on the ancient trees. A breeze sets the daffodil blossoms dancing in rows sloping away from the manor toward the lake. The sky reflects deep blue on the surface where ducks gently coast. We try to imagine a softball game on the lawn, a Nissen hut village nearby and bombers coming and going from a local airstrip. We admire the clock tower with its gargoyles and the smokestacks of fascinating brick artwork. We find the greenhouse, the "dungeon" and the pet cemetery. [See images of the clock tower, groups of smokestacks and the pet cemetery in the color gallery.]

Now shadows lengthen near day's end. We take a stroll in what we think is the direction of the village church, but soon realize that we are off track and don't have enough daylight left to explore further. [See image of the churchyard and village church in the color gallery.]

April 22, 2010: *This day is brilliantly sunny and briskly cool. Our mission is to find the village church that we have toured in our minds so many times. The church is very near the gate to the manor. We don't know how we missed it yesterday. Travel exhaustion, I suppose. It is the Church of St. Mary the Virgin, built around 1150 and partially renovated in 1898. Alas, we find it locked tight and protected by security. We observe from outside. The building appears to be stucco, thus Dad's reference to the Alamo. The wide, tall door of dark wood with patina that tells of the ages is our barrier. The old black metal ring serving as a door pull lifts away at the hinge for us, but does not cause the door to give. We know we will have to make contact with the caretaker or another guardian to let us in. [See image of the locked door in the color gallery.]*

In lieu of entering, we admire the exterior and open the gate of a wrought iron fence in order to explore the adjacent cemetery. We find tomb markers from simple stones to elaborate concrete or marble beds—actually looking as if one could use a bedspread and sleep there. We find dates from the early 1700s all the way into the 2000s. The gravesites are variably tended. Many bloom with primrose. Others are barren. Here and there are items from the living placed in honor of the dead. One gravesite has a watering can, gloves and trowel carefully arranged on top of it. Perhaps the deceased was an avid gardener.

We go back to the manor somewhat unfulfilled. We ask at the reception desk how we might get access to the church. We are given a name and phone number. We call and leave a message and check back several times during the day. No response. Further exploring, we find the library with the secret door to the den, the mosaic adorned portico, the "fancy brick walls" and the "giant shrubbery garden." We take many pictures of interior and exterior features in order to bring the experience back home to Mom.

One curious observation we make is that the manor is essentially deserted. We seem to be alone here. Even at meals there have been only a few quiet patrons. We meet a friendly woman in the dining room. She is here to lead a workshop on business writing for employees of AWE (Atomic Weapons Enterprise). That explains the solitary businessmen we have seen. She says the manor is what remains of a large estate. The majority of the property is now used by the government as the only atomic research facility in the United Kingdom (UK). Let me be clear—this is the only place in the UK where atomic weapons are produced.

Aldermaston is now known more for the ongoing protests against AWE than for its rich former history. Though restored as a hotel and event venue, the manor is not a major tourist draw. Most activity occurs on weekends with weddings and other special occasions. Our new friend says AWE employs 6000 and is "harder to get into than the House of Commons." Ken and I remember our coming of age during the Cold War, an uneasy era born from the initial development and use of the devastating weaponry that ended WWII.

Needing to stretch our legs and clear our heads, we take a walk to the nearby village of Aldermaston. We pass a school with children at play and a row of old brick town houses, each with a bright blue door. In the center of the typically quaint English country town, we visit the Hind's Head town pub where the Yanks advertised dances.

We feel at loose ends because we've run out of goals except for the one we can't accomplish. I have a nagging feeling about it, trying to soothe myself in the event we do not get inside the church. It would mean so much to us because it meant so much to Dad.

We decide to follow a footpath around the lake. Some trees are still bare; others are in bloom. Beautiful native primroses bloom at our feet. At a fork, we decide to take a narrow grassy path instead of the mildly graveled road we have been following. In a short while, we notice environmental mayhem across from us past an old barbed wire fence. We obviously are at the border of the manor property and some other property under siege from development. We keep walking near the perimeter fence. We notice a small sign that says "Do Not Enter—Protected by Guard Dogs." What? Here in the middle of a forest? But we heed the sign and turn around. Not a few paces along, we hear ferocious barks that sound closer and closer. Thank goodness we have turned around. We keep moving, increasing our pace, hearts pounding. The dogs, spooked by our scent, keep barking. They sound increasingly nearer. At last we are far enough away and the barks subside. We learn later the boundary we almost breached is that of the AWE site. We imagine a difficult explanation to Mom if we had been arrested for trespassing on secured government property!

After the evening meal, we head back to our suite to pack for departure tomorrow. As we pass the front door, Ken suggests we go outside to see how the manor looks at night. As soon as we open the door, we hear a cacophony of bells—loud! We wonder why we did not hear them last night, thinking they were from the clock tower. It dawns on me...THE CHURCH! We race toward the sound of bells calling us loudly and insistently. It is nearing nine o'clock. A half-moon is directly overhead. The manor itself is awash with the orange glow of tungsten. And the bells keep pealing.

As we approach the church in the near darkness, we see a light shining through one of the side windows. We can see the ropes of the bells moving and hear laughter among the reverberations of the bells. Ken tries the door and it opens. I sob. A gift has been given and received. A surprise, a moment so powerful and memorable that modern digital documentation seems superfluous.

We walk reverently into the dark sanctuary. The bells continue to toll, and the people in the bell tower continue laughing and chattering in a strong local dialect. We do not call out and make our presence known. There is a soft light in one alcove—the one we had seen from outside. In the shadows we can see old murals, their colors vivid even in the dimness; very close to us we see the horizontal life-sized stone figures in the repose of death Dad had described. We approach the altar. There is a spray of white flowers that have wilted; nearby are fresh flowers yet to be mounted and arranged to take its place. Ken says, "If we're going to do it, now is the time." At the closest step to the front, we drop to our knees in the half-light and thank Dad and God for this moment. We pray silently for our safe return home as he had done more than 65 years ago.

The bells stop for a moment, but not the laughter and conversation in the belfry above. We slip out undetected. The bells peal anew, following us all the way back to the door of the manor. Heretofore never demonstrative of our familial affection, I reach for my brother's hand. He holds mine, and we make our way together under the moon's spotlight from the blue-black sky. The mantra, "All things happen for a reason and when they are supposed to," has once again proved itself to me.

Ken and I will always have this pure moment that defies full description, a circumstance that is not circumstantial and a memory that is ours and ours alone, borne to us across 65 years of time in a place that has stood the test of centuries. We are so grateful to the busy parishioners who, unaware, brought a deep sense of spirituality into our hearts this evening. God blesses us, every one.

April 23, 2010: At breakfast we ask about the bells and discover the ringing of last evening was practice for a wedding. The thought occurs to Ken that the parishioners might be decorating this morning. We go to the church. Success! Three women welcome us and allow us to take pictures.

To his great satisfaction, Ken is able to see the ancient artwork in better lighting. We learn from the current church brochure that the sculpted tomb is one of the finest alabaster carvings in the country. The two figures are not two knights with helmets as interpreted by Dad in error, but represent Sir George Forster and his Lady Elizabeth, Lord and Lady of Aldermaston Manor until death, she in 1526 and he in 1533. Our Aldermaston experience is now complete. We can follow Dad to London. [See image of Lord and Lady Forster in the color gallery.]

October 14, 1944

I hope by now you have started receiving some of my letters. Today was a beautiful day. It rained just enough to make everything fresh. After the rain this afternoon, I walked down to the lake on the estate. One would never think that such turmoil is going on just a few hundred miles away. At the lake, a little bird that seemed almost tame was sitting on a post, and I walked within arm's reach of him. As I reached out to see if he would jump on my finger, he fluttered away. I sampled a couple of chestnuts, but they aren't dry yet. I was surprised to see blackberries still around. I will go back and pick a cup full for my morning breakfast cereal. I plan to fish in the lake soon. Honey, don't be angry with me for enjoying myself. Since I must be here, I may as well see a few interesting things to tell you about.

The British papers are very queer. They don't play up the news as ours do. Maybe they don't care for the spectacular as our editors do. The paper I read today had only one sheet. There are no funny papers. I wonder what the kids read. Maybe they're smarter than our kids and are interested in war news and stock reports.

There is something going on over here that I don't like. The girls are, for some strange reason, going with Negro soldiers. I've been told that the girls think it a novelty. There is some racial trouble over it. Some white soldier sees a British girl with a Negro, and then he politely beats the hell out of the Negro. I don't like it myself.

I struggled with whether or not to include these thoughts, but they illustrate the deeply ingrained prejudice that existed in the United States during segregation and have forced me to face the reality of its influence on my father's thinking. While touring Aldermaston Manor I scanned through a book on display entitled Aldermaston, the Airfield. *It was a collection of articles from local newspapers relating to the use of estate property for the Royal Air Force (RAF) and US Army Air Force (USAAF) during the war years. An article, "Shooting Affray," from the* Basingstoke Gazette *dated October 13, 1944, reveals the following:*

"A scene reminiscent of gangster methods of American films disturbed the peace of Kingsclere on Thursday night, when coloured American Troops opened fire with automatic carbines on the Crown Inn. As a result two American negro soldiers, one a Military

Policeman, were killed and Mrs. Rose Napper, wife of the licensee, died a few hours later. The affray started because coloured Military Police had trouble with some of the troops. A number of the men apparently went to camp and secured firearms. They returned and stationed themselves behind the low wall of the churchyard on the opposite side of the road to the Inn. At 10:00 pm when the Military Police were leaving the Inn, the soldiers opened fire and the bullets spattered against the hotel and windows. Mrs. Napper, standing behind the Public Bar, was wounded; one of the coloured soldiers died immediately, and the Military Policeman, on rushing to the door, was hit and collapsed some yards down the road. Jeeps were used to scour the area and we understand that several coloured Americans are now being held in military custody. ... Widespread sympathy is felt for the husband and sons of Mrs. Napper in the tragedy which has befallen them."

This violent incident occurred the same week Doyle arrived at peaceful Aldermaston. I wonder if he knew of it, and I wonder if "trouble with some of the troops" relates to the interracial dating that he describes. I also wonder if the incident is correctly reported or tainted with racism.

October 14, 1944 [second letter]

Most of the officers left for a weekend in London. I haven't got enough money to make the trip. Don't send any money here because from now on American money is no good. We're going to be paid in English money, and we have already had all our surplus cash exchanged. Since they have opened the officers' club here, I won't have too much money to spare. It's compulsory, we must join.

October 15, 1944

This has been a very long day. I read *The Case of the Lame Canary* [one of the Perry Mason series by Erle Stanley Gardner].

One of your favorites, remember? It was good though. I have also slept quite a bit today so that I would get my mind off of you. But alas, I dreamed of you. During the week I make out OK, but on weekends I start reminiscing and find it very hard to remain happy. There's still no word from you. As for me, since I'm away from the States, I couldn't have a better setup. Plenty to eat, not much to do, and a world of historic places to see. I wish you were here to make my enjoyment complete. Some of the officers back from town tell me there is quite a bit of silver on sale in the stores. Maybe I can send you some of it.

Rumor has it that girls around here are very promiscuous. One story goes like this: There was a garrison of soldiers quartered in pup tents, and every night girls would gather nearby in the hay stacks. The boys, of course, met them there. One of the boys went through the chow line twice for about two weeks. They found out he had a girl in his pup tent, and he was feeding her from the chow line. Cute, eh?

Today I didn't go out of the castle but once and that was to the Battery office to get mail the men had written. Each day I read and censor about a hundred letters. The boys are pretty good. There are only a few things I have to take out. It's funny—at first the letters they wrote to their wives and sweethearts were so stiff and business-like, but now they are used to censorship and cut loose with some lovely letters. All of them wish the war was over and they could get back to normal living. Some of the boys have written to several girls and asked them to wait for them. Bunch of wolves they are.

I'm going to church in the morning, and then I'll wash some clothes. I haven't heard a word from you or anyone since I left the States. Well honey, here's all my love for you and my best regards to your family.

Before the war, Doyle's experience had been limited to work in north Florida and west Alabama after growing up in north

Georgia during the Great Depression. His coming of age occurred in a family with a very strong widowed mother who struggled to raise three boys and two girls. In his memoir, he attributes his own sense of character and morality to his mother's tutelage.

Now his awe at this historic and beautiful foreign setting is mingled with culture shock, a term not yet current in 1944. He describes the English news outlets, the village customs and especially the wartime mores and morals or lack thereof. His provincial American sensibilities are greatly offended in England, and he continues to refer to "loose women" in various settings throughout his European experience.

Chapter 13

In England
Waiting for Mail

The letters at this time are mostly on V-mail and often repetitious, expressing a longing for mail and having nothing to do or write about. I have omitted some and excerpted most. Entertainment such as pop music, movies, shopping, sightseeing and hosting dances fill the long restless days until equipment becomes available.

October 15, 1944

I hope I hear from you tomorrow or the next day. It will raise my morale 100%. The men sure are anxious to get mail. We aren't where we were supposed to be. Our mail at present is going to another place. Don't forget honey, send me some snapshots of you. I enjoy these I have so much. They are here in front of me now.

October 16, 1944

We still don't know how long we'll be here. Maybe for the duration. Maybe not. I hope it is for the duration, however, because it is really nice. Next weekend I'm going to London. I want to see Westminster Abbey.

There are more tall tales coming in about how hard up the women are here. If it's true, a married man would find it very embarrassing, don't you think? One of the sayings of the women when wolfed at is, "I don't feel romantic tonight, but if you buy me a couple of beers I'll be very romantic." One of the pilots nearby said it was surprising to see how easy the women are snowed under after two years of Yank snow. The venereal rate in London has grown to a terrific amount. You see things on the streets that you would be shocked to see in a park at home. But such is life in wartime. The girls miss cigarettes more than anything else. I probably will be missing them soon. They are rationed over here, and we are only allowed three bars of candy per week.

It's too bad we can't be together now. But if it hadn't been for the war, we probably wouldn't have had the chance to fall in love. It's good that we can give the war credit for something, isn't it?

I noticed a pair of stone steps today between the kitchen and the dining room. They have been there so long that the servants' feet have worn down the steps about five inches on one side. The steps up to the second floor are worn about three inches. For now honey, that's all.

October 17, 1944

Honey, I've missed you so very much today. I am having trouble keeping myself busy. So I think a great deal. It isn't good. If I don't hear from you in a day or two, I'll scream. ... I found a leather-bound, pocket-sized celluloid sheet picture purse today. I have all of your snapshots so I can easily look at them. I want some more, OK?

October 18, 1944

Honey, just to keep you informed about the place here, there are beautiful Persian cats running around. All of them are solid black. They really are nice cats. I still haven't been any place, but I will go to town tonight. From reports I have heard, the women around here have no compunctions at all. Girls 14, 15, and 16 are on the loose. A stick of chewing gum or a cigarette seems to be their price. I can't authenticate this now, but maybe after tonight I can. They come up to you on the street and try to make you, and when you say you aren't interested they say, "I blow candles, too." You can use your imagination on what the expression means. Another story is about a 16-year-old girl receiving six boys in one night.

How are the sisters, the mother and the father? Are they keeping my little "ruen bruin" cheered up? You're keeping yourself busy planning our future life together, aren't you? You're going to be the sweet one to adjust me to civilian life. When I get restless, all you'll have to do is put your arms around me and kiss me—then everything will be all right. I certainly am glad you pounded some sense in my head. I would just die if I didn't have you to come home to. Thanks for being my wife, sweet.

We have sent 20 percent of the men on 48-hour passes so they can see England. I might go on a pass after payday. I'm financially embarrassed at the present.

I have been censoring mail, and it's pathetic in some cases. Some of the men's wives are expecting in the near future, and the guys are brokenhearted because they can't be there. Others have had anniversaries since we have been here; others write to several girlfriends, make love to them and ask them to wait until the war is over, but all the time they are married. (Wolves.) Honey, I would like very much to be with you tonight. Maybe I can. I have been with you several nights already since I left.

October 18, 1944 [second letter]

Some of the men got mail today; for some reason I didn't. Maybe tomorrow. It's now 2215. Paul, Bruce and I just got back from a nearby town. Everything was dark when we got there, so we didn't see much. We went to a dance hall in one of the theatres. It cost us 35 cents or a shilling and six pence, written one and six. The girls there were very cheap. We stayed 30 or 40 minutes and then went to the Officers' Red Cross Lounge. It was nice. We had coffee and a sandwich. Cost us 50 cents in all, including transport. I met up with a guy I finished school with. Wish you had been along. Here's all my love darling, and I'm counting the days till I can see you.

October 20, 1944

We went into town again tonight for a dance at the Officers' Red Cross Lounge. Would have enjoyed it if you had been there. Good GI music. Nurses were sitting everywhere, but I just couldn't get my mind off of you. Maybe I could have broken the monotony of being here if I had talked and danced with some of them, but somehow or other I couldn't. I guess that I just simply love you. That's all.

October 21, 1944

Darling, I know now how you felt during the time I wasn't writing to you. Remember? It was last November, December and January. Here it is now 23 days and I haven't heard a word.

October 21, 1944 [second letter]

Tonight we had a movie here in the castle. I had seen it before. Remember *Lady in the Dark*? I used my imagination and you were with me. I enjoyed sitting by you.

October 21, 1944 [third letter]

Here I am again, starting another letter after stopping just long enough to light a cigarette. I would like for you to get a box of gum from Jack and send it over. Gum keeps me from smoking too much. Will you, kid? By the way the kids here say, "Any gum, chum?" We say, "None handy, sandy." Cute, eh? I'm going into town tomorrow. I have been in twice, but both times at night and I didn't see anything because of blackout. I saw GIs and British girls backed up in doorways of stores loving each other up. Five years of war has really brought havoc to the British homeland. I hope the girls back there never get half as loose as these here.

October 22, 1944

I have been thinking all day about just why, as soon as you and I got married and started really living as we were born to live, we were taken apart. Maybe it was to test our love. But you know and I know that our love needs no testing. I have been sent to a place where there is all the temptation in the world to make me untrue. Honey, I know now that you are the only one. I was out last night and two Wrens (equivalent to our Waves) came over to where we were playing a bar room game called Push-ha-penny. Of course we were nice to them (Paul was with me). They did everything to interest us in tagging along with them and were surprised when we didn't. I enjoyed listening to them talk. One was a Scot named Sadie; the other was a registered nurse called Christi. They really loved their Scotch whiskey. No, I didn't buy them any drinks. They bought their own. Well honey, I love you with all my heart and still want you. Oh, I want you. I haven't received any mail yet. *[The Women's Royal Naval Service (WRNS or Wrens) was created in 1942; Women Accepted for Volunteer Emergency Service (WAVES or Waves) was an official part of the US Navy.]*

October 23, 1944 [two letters on V-mail]

Honey, mail came today but none for me. I'm going crazy if I don't hear from you. Bruce got a letter from his mother. It took only twelve days to get here. I know you are writing, but I don't understand why I can't get any of the mail. Maybe tomorrow.

Hello again, my sweet. We have just finished a game of bridge. We have a radio on in our room and the best of programs. The AEF [Allied Expeditionary Forces] stations in the vicinity really put on "jive" programs for us. We have decided that our castle here provides the best entertainment to be found anywhere near.

October 24, 1944

Christmas isn't so far away now, and I am at a loss as to what to send you. Most everything here is rationed, and what isn't is so expensive I can't afford it. I have resolved to refrain from writing checks. You will have to buy gifts for our families. Remember honey, my family doesn't go for expensive gifts. A shirt, a tie, a slip, a pair of hose and the like. But my dear, you are my present. Buy yourself something nice for your gift from me. When I do find something here, I will supplement what you have bought with my small offering.

October 25, 1944

"Georgia on My Mind" opened the "Jumping Duffle Bag" program this morning, and that is what I have on my mind all the time now—something in Georgia and that something is you. I love you baby!!! That's all.

October 25, 1944 [second letter]

I just got back from a movie. We have our own free movies here about three times a week. The one tonight was *The Nelson Touch* (British name). It was *Corbitt K 324* in the States. Maybe you saw it.

October 26, 1944

I have been playing bridge and listening to the radio tonight. The songs make me so very homesick for you. Wish I had something new to tell you but there isn't anything new. One thing, this place was the quarters of WAAFs [Women's Auxiliary Air Force, support for the Royal Air Force] back in 1940–1941. Mary Churchill was stationed here. At that time all the original furniture was in the place. Battery C has their first party tomorrow night. They have a hundred girls coming here for it. The guys will be hard to control. In fact they aren't going to try to control them.

October 30, 1944

I found something today for your Christmas present. I hope you like them. You won't have any use for them yet, but when you start our home they will be lovely. I went through five antique shops, and honey, they don't realize the value of the items they have for sale.

October 30, 1944 [second letter]

Hello sweet, here I am again after hours of bridge. I'm getting quite good at the game. Bruce and I couldn't get the cards at all. We lost in games but won in points. So if we had been playing for money, we would have won.

October 31, 1944

As of night before last, I am entitled to wear the European Theatre Ribbon. Yes'm, the 29th makes 30 days away from the States. Honey, they have been lonely ones without you and without any word from you. It is now 1055. I must get a letter this morning. I just must and I will, I know. Hope you have heard from me. Have you?

I'll court you just like I did when you were my girlfriend, forever and ever. I have so far, haven't I? I want it to be like that. We must always be sweethearts, and we will. I look at these girls over here and offer up special thanks for my one favorite American girl. That's you, kid.

November 1, 1944

Honey, today I got letters from Will and Mama. I was glad to get them, but disappointed because I didn't get one from you. It's funny. I have written you more and Will less than anyone else. It doesn't make sense. ... I went to a nurses' dance last night and it was a brawl. Really rough. I had to pull Kenny out of a fight with a lieutenant colonel. I drank a lot of beer and some grain (hospital)

145

alcohol mixed with orange juice. Shortage of whiskey. I was disgusted before I left.

November 2, 1944

I went into town today and bought some things for our house. If you don't like them, you can sell them to someone and make a nice profit. I'll tell you what I paid for the items. Brass fireplace set, $2.50. Round earthenware set, $4.50. Small china vases, $7.00. Two sets of old earrings, $1.85. A cameo brooch, 70 cents. The cameo I want when I return. I want a ring made of it. The set of earrings were so old I thought you would like to have them. I'll pack them well. There will be more.

November 3, 1944

Well honey, the Battery dance that I have been planning has just ended. It was a great success. Plenty of food. That's what the girls were interested in. I didn't dance any because the colonel made an order that officers would not dance at enlisted men's parties.

November 4, 1944

Hurrah!! Today I got your letter written on the 23rd. Honey, I feel so much better now. I love that letter. I'm a lucky guy, you know. Yes, I'm proud of you. Not because you are thrifty as you intimated, but because you are just you. That's all. You asked me to be true to you. Don't bother with mentioning it again, sweet. Every English girl I've seen makes me appreciate you more and more. I mean it, sweet. *[At last, the end of the mail drought—37 days without a letter from Juby.]*

November 5, 1944

I was in town last night with the convoy as company commander. I sat in the Officers' Lounge all evening and thought of you. Honey, I just can't see how a single man can stand it here.

He has no dreams to ponder over. I'm sure glad that we decided to marry before I got over here. I used to worry you would marry someone else like the Air Corps boy you went with. I would have regretted it to my dying day if you had.

November 8, 1944

Just got in from London. It was quite nice, but I don't care to go again. I saw all the places I have heard about. Wish you could have been there. It would have been more fun. I'll write more later.

November 9, 1944

As you know from my short note of yesterday, I'm just back from a short leave in London. I caught a train at a nearby station, rode to the closest town and then changed trains to go into London. I got onto a "tube" (called subway in America) to Piccadilly Station and then went upstairs to Piccadilly Circus. From there I went to the billeting office where I was given a room in Lincoln House. I stayed there two nights and it didn't cost anything.

I saw all the places that I have heard and read about. It wasn't foggy as it was pictured, thank goodness, but really black at night. I saw Houses of Parliament, British Museum, Westminster Abbey and Cathedral, Trafalgar Square, Buckingham Palace (Changing of the Guards), No. 10 Downing St., St. Paul's Cathedral, Hyde Park, St. James Park, London Bridge, Tower of London and all the rest.

Something happened while I was in Piccadilly Circus. After being propositioned about 50 times by hustlers, I was jostled to a dark alley by three civilians who I'm sure were after my money. Luckily I used my head. I caught a glimpse of one of the guys in the half-light. I clipped him with a hard right to the chin and turned and ran like a deer. I looked back and saw the other two thugs picking him up. I really hit him with all I had. I was lucky. They couldn't have taken me for much, but I didn't want them to take any.

All in all, I had a good time. I ate my meals at an officers' mess in the ballroom of the Grosvenor House. The ballroom is as big as half a football field, surrounded by a balcony with lounges and a bar. When you enter you have to walk all around the balcony to get to the dining room downstairs. They feed 500 officers per meal. In one hotel I busted in on a private party where lords and ladies were dining. Really stiff shirts, I tell you. I left London Wednesday. I used the "tube" to get to the Paddington Station and boarded the train to a town nearby [Reading] where I went to see *Going My Way*. I met Bruce and Roinestad at the Officers' Club where they were having a dance. While there, I wrote you a short note and sent postcards to your sisters. I got back to camp about 2330 last night. Wish you could have been on the trip with me.

SHAFTESBURY AVENUE FROM PICCADILLY CIRCUS, LONDON.

Postcard from London

IN HIS FOOTSTEPS
April 23–24, 2010: The Lincoln House is still operating as a hotel. Ken and I stay two nights there and are able to walk to the Grosvenor

House, now a five-star Marriott Hotel. We find the ballroom and have a drink in the lounge. We make a toast to Dad, of course. We also manage a bus tour from Hyde Park, which allows us to see each of the sites mentioned by Dad, even the changing of the guards at Buckingham Palace. We are not able to drive by 10 Downing Street due to post 9-11 security precautions. We try to imagine London during the Blitz, intense bombing by the German Luftwaffe for 57 consecutive nights, but cannot. Our only problem is trying to determine when it is safe to cross a street. More than once we are nearly run over by taxis appearing from nowhere. Like Dad, we find London "quite nice but don't care to go again."

November 11, 1944

I have just come upstairs from the officers' party. This is the first we've had since we've been here. We had some champagne and beer. Wish you could have had a glass or two of the champagne. It's pretty good. Only five years old. Some of the officers wanted to have women there but those who did were outnumbered. We had fried chicken, ham, cheese sandwiches, pickles and several other things.

November 13, 1944

Today I found a box for the things I bought you. They will be in the mail tomorrow. I have packed the vases and pots in one box and the fireside set in another. Also a coral rosebud and another trinket. Soon I'll send you a lovely bracelet made of three-pence pieces. I hope the things I'm sending don't break. I have packed them well in a wooden box and have put excelsior and egg crate packing all around each piece. Let me know how they are when you get them.

Tonight I went the rounds of the battalion. I saw two basketball games in the gym and a bingo game in the service club. About 300 of the guys were there. It cost three pence per card to play. It's the first time we've had bingo. The guys really enjoyed it. Cash prizes were from the gate receipts. Thursday I'm going to Salisbury for boxing; we have a four-man team that is really good. Want to go? You'd get to see a lot of bloody noses, cut eyes and stuff.

Just before I started writing, I had a few letters to censor. All the guys are writing home for silk hose, lipstick, silk panties and slips to give to the girls in exchange for you know what.

It's now 2345 and outside I hear the trucks from town. Every night we send in a convoy for the men who go on pass. Some of them go to a girls' hostelry nearby and others go to the nearest town. Lights went on in London last night. London has been blacked out since three days before England went to war. Over five years now.

November 14, 1944

I'm planning on buying you something each month with the money I get here. I just have to watch my expenses. We want to save for our baby and house, don't we? You ask me how much I get now for myself. Here's how it stacks up [each month].

Assets		Liabilities	
Base pay	$150.00	Allotment	$200.00
Rental Allowance	60.00	Insurance	6.75
Subsistence (food, etc.)	42.00	Meals (average)	18.00
Overseas pay	15.00	Dry cleaning	5.00
Longevity pay (time in)	7.50	—	—
Total Assets	**$294.50**	**Total Liabilities**	**$229.75**

$294.50 minus $229.75 = $64.75 for purchasing things for you and for my own entertainment. Plenty. We can't do much purchasing at the PX because everything is rationed. My weekly ration usually costs about 70 cents. Don't worry about what money I have, kid. It's better off in the bank back in the States. OK, it's settled.

I first considered the previous accounting too mundane to include. By virtue of second thought, I found the information about a soldier's financial status crucial to the truth of this entire narrative. Money issues in the post-Depression, wartime era drove the life choices yet to come for this young couple and for others like them. I am intrigued by how little they had and how much they eventually accomplished with it. We of the baby boom generation and our children reaped the benefit of our parents' prudence and should have learned from it. Did we?

November 15, 1944

These guys here in the room won't let me take time each night to do a little laundry. They always insist on playing bridge, going to movies, basketball games or to town. When they are here, I can't do a damn thing. I must join in with them. They won't take no for an answer. Tonight, however, I'm Duty Officer and I couldn't go into town with them. They are due back now. They probably will burst in any time.

I have a nice fire going here in the fireplace. I'm sitting in front of the fire in my underwear with my feet propped up on the ledge just below the mantel piece. Just behind me is my bunk and beside it is a radio. They just played "We'll Meet Again." Now the song is "My Secret Heart." All the old timers make me think of you. In fact sweet, everything reminds me of you. While I was washing my things tonight, I thought of how you used to do my socks and underwear. You were so willing to help keep down expenses. You're just swell, that's all. I enjoyed your description of your new dresses. Wish I had a ticket for you so you could get new shoes. Wish I could see you in your new clothes. I have read your letters of yesterday over twice tonight. Last night I went to sleep with one of your letters in my hand. I love them darling.

November 16, 1944

All the guys are in Salisbury tonight to see our battalion boxing team fight. It's too cold to make the trip so I didn't go. I am leaving in the morning for Liverpool for a couple of days' business for the battalion. We were to fly up, but some of the men wouldn't fly so I've got to go along by train with them. It made me so damn mad. By plane it is only an hour, by train about twelve. I haven't heard from you since I got seven letters the day before yesterday. I was going to bed early tonight, but I started making some V-mail Christmas cards and now it is 2330. I must stop staying up so late.

Christmas card on V-mail

November 19, 1944

I left here Friday morning for Liverpool. Got there about 2030 on Friday night. Stopped in London for two hours on the way up and went through Birmingham, Coventry and several other towns. On the way back, we drove through in a jeep. It was a miserable trip—cold, wet and dark—and we had to drive with very little light. I led the convoy and had to be very careful not to overrun turns because I had quite a few trucks behind me. We made it in eleven hours. We were in Liverpool overnight. Didn't get into town, but I did find something for you.

November 21, 1944

Honey, I'm very tired tonight. It is now 0115 of November 22. We have been working late. I'm afraid it will be a very long time before I'll get the packages. If you don't hear from me for a while dear, just remember that I love you, miss you and think of you always. I've written at least one letter per day so far and will continue to do so as long as I can, but we can never tell where we will be tomorrow.

November 24, 1944 [first of two V-mail pages]

I have thought of you continuously since I last wrote. We are now on our way to France. You have asked me to let you know where I am. Maybe I shouldn't, but you know dear I try to give you your every wish. You won't have any reason to worry because I know where we are going and it will be far from any fighting. Now I will tell you in inexpressible words how much I love you and miss you. I'll send you some things from France.

[V-mail, second page] Honey, I want to talk a little while longer. I have sent you a pamphlet from the place where we were. I can't say in writing what and where it was, but we were allowed to write about the place without mentioning names and to send the booklet.

From that, you can find out just where we were. Wish you could have been there. It was wonderful. There were rooms we could have lived in too. There's no justice.

I wrote you about my trip to Liverpool and now I have been to Southampton. I have so many things to tell you about when we get together. For a while I want to be silent and love you. Then we will talk.

Chapter 14

Crossing the Channel

The Battery D History, 639th BN, *recounts that battery drivers arrived in Aldermaston via trucks from Liverpool on November 18, 1944, having been sent by train to obtain them. By November 21, guns arrived and underwent thorough maintenance overnight before departure the next day. The battery officers, men and equipment were dispatched in series; first to Hursley for overnight, and then to the port of Southampton, England, to board Liberty vessels for embarkation to an unknown destination. The ships SS* George R. Dewey *and SS* Leopoldville *are mentioned in the battery history, and Doyle names Liberty vessel* James Nelson *in a letter written on May 17, 1945.*

November 25, 1944

Dearest Juby,

Undoubtedly the US Army has published that all personnel had plenty of turkey for Thanksgiving. Well, that's a lot of malarkey. We have been eating "C" rations for four days now. But it's part of the game, I guess. I hardly know what to write because I have already written four V-mails and I have covered everything that can be said. There's a lot going on, but at present I can't say anything about it. *["C" rations are individual canned precooked meals intended for temporary use; "A" rations are fresh food; "B" rations are packaged unprepared food and "K" rations are survival rations.]*

I am glad that you and Boots and Frances are having good times together now. I'm sorry that Boots didn't get to be alone with her husband. It wasn't his fault and I'm sure she understood, but dammit, his mother should have known. You and I will never have that trouble. Mama knows that we want to be alone and we will, kid, always.

Keep your eyes open for an electric icebox and an electric stove. If you see one at a bargain, buy it because we will need it later on. Anything you see that we will need, go ahead and buy it. Of course there is the problem of storage. Maybe you can arrange that. By the way, I got twelve of your back airmail letters day before yesterday. It was nice to hear from you.   I love and miss you, Doyle

November 26, 1944

This morning I was awakened with a start. There was a spewing or hissing noise and when I opened my eyes, steam and fog had filled the room. I first thought the ship had sprung a leak. I quickly started to put on my clothes. Some of the guys ran up the hatch stairs in long underwear. It was really funny. We soon learned that someone had opened the wrong valve on the main deck. After about two minutes, everything was quiet again. Someone said that the 639th had been awakened at reveille in every conceivable manner now, and it's true.

November 26, 1944 [second letter]

I have been out on deck looking over the shoreline of France through a pair of field glasses. I can't tell much about it because it's too far away. We have been in harbor for about 18 hours now, waiting for a pilot ship to come after us. The men are getting a little restless. But as long as we are here, we're safe. We don't know where we'll be next, so I'm in no hurry to get there. It might be rough. They tell me that there's some fighting going on in parts of France and I'm not mad at anyone.

November 27, 1944

My sweet, up to now I have written at least once a day. I don't know how long I can keep it up, but as long as I have time and a decent place to write, I will do so. Wish you could be with me. Up until now it could have been possible because there has been little hardship. We haven't had anything to eat but canned beans and meat for the last four days, but it could be worse. I have a lot to tell you when I get back. Give my love to your family and Merry Christmas to all. I love you darling and would like to be with you tonight.

November 28, 1944

Hello again, kid. It's now 2230. Still haven't landed yet. Still eating "C" rations. I have been dreaming of a meat loaf or hamburger steak cooked by you. We hope to move in tomorrow morning. It has been nice on board. We've kept warm and dry. Much better than what we probably will have when we dock. I'm out of cigarettes, but luckily I have two pipes and tobacco so it isn't too bad. We aren't doing a thing but waiting. We don't even have a regular time to get up. Just a lazy life. But we have too much time to think of how much happiness we're missing by not being with our wives. If we think too much, we get down in the dumps. We can't get that way at this stage of the game.

Pasted inside Doyle's helmet

Chapter 15

In France
Awaiting Combat Assignment

November 30, 1944

Dearest Juby,

Honey, tonight my thoughts are of you and you only. I never think of Mama or my brothers or sisters—it's always you. I am in France. I am on the ground tonight in a pup tent. The weather isn't too cold but there is heavy dew. My nice bedroll makes me very comfortable. If I had a letter from you I would be happy, but I haven't. So I must wait. Honey, my piece of candle is about gone, so I must stop now by saying I love you dearly and hope you are praying for my return soon. Until later I am your own.

Love, Doyle

December 1, 1944

Having a little chat with you has become a part of my day. I think of you and what you are doing and what you and I will do when the war is over. I'm in my bedroll now; my pup tent is over me and a candle is supplying light and heat. I haven't told you what I have in my bedroll, have I? Well I have three blankets, a mattress, a comforter sewn on three sides to make a sack and inside is a sheet tacked on all four corners. If you were only in it with me. Oh, boy! I love you darling.

We have been blessed with nice weather since we landed. Hope it keeps up. Bruce has his tent just beside mine. Kessler and Frank Kenny are behind us. We are the four horsemen now. The captain and Murphy are on our list. We don't get along so well. They are sleeping up the line. *[This is a reference to Captain Hooper. There was some grumbling about him during the training days in the States. Time and war experience to come eventually lead to greater respect.]* Hope to tell you something about France soon. I've only seen the countryside so far.

December 2, 1944

Only 23 more days until Christmas. Wish I was in the States so I could buy you something nice for a gift and hand it to you on Christmas morning. I have two of your pictures pasted inside my helmet. One is the cute one of you made in Florida. You know, the one with you sitting near the palm tree. You have on white wedges and the checked skirt and the white top. The other one is of you standing by the palm tree. You are so sweet-looking in those pictures. I have them pasted on with adhesive tape. Sweet, I love you with all my heart and want to be with you. If I wasn't married to you, I couldn't do what I'll probably soon be doing.

December 3, 1944

It's raining now honey, but it isn't very romantic. Mud is everywhere. It's cold too. But our morale is high. All we are doing now is cleaning our equipment. Since it started raining, we haven't even done much of that. We haven't had a chance to see much of France yet because we haven't gotten any leaves to travel around as we did in England. Maybe later. I'll tell you about France when I can.

I had a shower yesterday in a US Army movable shower unit. Hot water and all. We were allowed to stay under the water six minutes. I really needed a shower too. Remember kid, I have a special shower in mind for our house. The rest you can have as you want it. But the shower is for me. Remember now darling, I miss you and want you something awful. I love you sweet. Your letters here got censored.

December 4, 1944

I'm still writing from my bedroll—under my pup tent by candle-light. Don't know what I'll do when the candles burn up. I'll still write though. Don't you worry. This letter tonight might be the last you'll get for a while, but I'm writing every day if possible. Let me know if you get the packages and what condition they are in. Hope you get them by Christmas. If you hear Will or Jack, or anybody as far as that goes, say anything about how tough things are over there, let me know and I will personally punch them in the nose when I get back. If I didn't have dreams of you, I couldn't go on. You are my inspiration. I love you darling and am only waiting until I can prove it to you. I just burned the top of the letter with the candle. So sorry.

December 6, 1944

Today I took a bath in a 30-gallon gasoline can. It made me feel so much better. Tomorrow I am going to wash some clothes if we are still here. I had my hair cut today. It is now about a half-inch long. It feels so good. Of course I'm not much to look at now, but when I get up in the morning all I have to do is brush my hair and I'm ready to go. It's much cleaner to have it short. I still can't tell you anything about France. All I have seen yet is just like the hills of Tennessee. Of course, some of the towns we came through were really torn up. Here's millions of kisses, kid.

December 7, 1944

The last letters I got from you were received just before I got on the boat to cross the Channel. Most of them were written before you had heard from me. They were your first letters after I left you in Wilmington. I am so confused with your letters. I got some nine days after you sent them, and then I got the older ones, and none since. No packages yet either. They say we will get mail at our next stop. We are to move anytime now.

The battery history identifies the location of the pup tent bivouac area as Betrimont, France. They were there for eleven days, departing on December 9 by motor convoy headed toward Belgium. They stayed overnight in Mons, Belgium, and the next night near Theux, before moving on to their destination of Honsfeld, a few miles from the German border and very close to the front line. Overall, they covered 300 miles in two and one-half days. The first combat assignment began December 12: "We were given the task of making Hitler's last known and best type of weapon ineffective by destroying all rocket bombs possible which were launched in the sector we were defending. We experienced no unusual occurrences during the next four days except that of executing our assigned mission. We had considerable difficulty firing accurately on these targets due to poor visibility" *[Battery D History, 639th BN].*

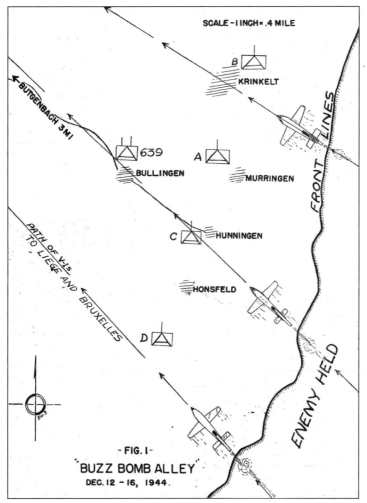

Belgium: V-1 trajectories in Buzz Bomb Alley, December 12–16, 1944
(Map from *Unit History, 639th AAA AW Battalion*)

While considering a visit to frontline areas where Dad had served, I learned of a Belgian guide, Michael Baert, who specializes in personal tours for families of WWII veterans of the European theater. He is especially expert in the Battle of the Bulge. We corresponded for about six months, working from details in Dad's letters. Michael booked lodgings and organized day trips to specific portions of the Ardennes Forest where Dad's experiences occurred. As our itinerary took shape, Ken and I greatly anticipated following this path through combat zones and beyond.

Chapter 16

In Belgium during "The Bulge"

December 11, 1944

Dearest Juby,

I have missed two or three days writing, my sweet. I'm sorry, it couldn't be helped. But I have been thinking of you every minute. When you learn that I'm somewhere in Belgium, you'll understand. I haven't received mail since I left England.

Yes, I'm in Belgium. If I told you I was sitting in the kitchen of a house, you wouldn't believe me. No kidding honey, there's nothing to worry about. It's cold here, but the cold doesn't hurt like at home. There's about twenty inches of snow outside. Darling I must stop now and go check my gun positions. I love you more and more each day. Be sweet.   Love, Doyle

December 13, 1944

Hello kid. It's still Belgium and still more snow. It ain't fair. Me a Rebel and way up here in Yankee snow land. I have never seen snow like this before. I walked to one of the gun positions today, and it was up to my waist in the drifts. I'm looking for a chance to kill a deer. We are allowed to shoot them. I killed a rabbit today. ...

I don't seem to want to think of anything but you. You're my guiding light forever. I have a star in my ribbon now.

Postcard of the cathedral in Rouen, France
Doyle later writes, "Honey, that cathedral is no longer like that.
It has been bombed and shelled almost beyond recognition..."

December 13, 1944

I'll tell you of the towns that I saw in France. I was in Rouen, Le Havre and many smaller places. Rouen has really been smashed. Le Havre is practically leveled. I sent you some cards from Rouen. Most towns in France have been ripped up rather bad. In Belgium I was in Mons, Namur, Huy, Spa, Liège, Theux and many other places. The towns in Belgium aren't in such bad condition. I'm living much better here than in France. As you already know, I lived in a pup tent there and it rained every day. Here it snows instead. The air is very clean.

This was Doyle's first combat position, deceptively comfortable. His platoon in Battery D was shooting at buzz bombs in "Buzz Bomb Alley" from positions on the southwest outskirts of Honsfeld, a town less than three miles from enemy territory. This area, nestled in the Ardennes Forest, was considered secure. It was a place for battle-weary troops to recuperate and "green troops" to get their bearings before assignment to hotter areas. Antiaircraft units were attached to various army divisions to provide protection as needed. By now, more than five months after the D-Day invasion, most of France had been liberated. The Allied Forces were aligned through eastern Belgium and France and poised to fully engage the Germans in their own homeland. The war in the Euorpean Theatre of Operations (ETO) was considered nearly over.

On December 16, the Germans launched Operation Watch on the Rhine. Infantry, artillery and the well-equipped 1st SS Regiment, 1st SS Panzer Division, led by SS Officer Joachim Peiper, attacked in full force at Honsfeld. Overcast skies precluded Allied intervention by air. The 639th Antiaircraft Artillery Automatic Weapons Battalion, attached to the 99th Infantry Division at the time, switched to antitank (AT) mode. The resistance slowed the Germans as they moved through Honsfeld and other towns on their way toward US fuel dumps in the area. Thus began the most costly battle of WWII, leaving 19,000 American dead. It took until January 25, 1945, to reestablish the front line of December 15. This German counteroffensive was referred to as the Ardennes Offensive or the Von Rundstedt Offensive, after the German field marshal whom the Allies assumed to be in control. The American press used the phrase "Battle of the Bulge" referring to maps showing the German intrusion into Allied-held territory. Doyle could not describe the situation in full until February. When he couldn't write to Juby, he'd later apologize and say simply, "We've been busy." Information from the 639th Battalion and Battery D histories inserted below explain just what "busy" meant.

*Still in Belgium
22 Dec. 1944*

Dearest July:

December 22, 1944 (Still in Belgium)

It has been five or six days since I wrote you. I'm sorry, but it couldn't be helped. Circumstances have changed my plan to write every day. You probably know what I mean if you have read the papers or listened to the news. I'm safe and sound now, but for a while I wasn't. My sweet, I could only think of you during those days. Ask me about it someday. I'll tell you, but I don't want to talk of it to anyone else. You understand, don't you? I sent you a set of knives from a town we were in [Honsfeld]. I love you darling, and I apologize for getting you into all of this. I don't deserve such a sweet, lovely girl as a wife. You're all I have now, and someday I'll repay you for this anguish you suffer. Please keep your chin up and smile. Know that I'll come back to you soon and we will start our home together. I love you. Sorry to hear that the Lytle girl's husband was killed. "Se le Gar" as the French say. [*C'est la guerre*, that's war.]

Eyewitness accounts written a few months after the event best convey the intensity of the initial attack. December 16, 1944, was the true baptism by fire for Doyle and other members of his unit. After victory in Europe, the battery history was compiled based on accounts by the troops involved:

"On 16 December 1944, we received our first artillery bombardment which began at 0615 and continued all day. ... About 2000 our Battery Commander issued orders to load all equipment and wait for further movement orders. We received orders from Battalion Headquarters at 1930 to prepare to evacuate with all possible equipment. The shelling became so intense [and close to our gun positions] that we were [forced to leave organizational equipment behind]. This continued action, along with information received from various Infantry reconnaissance patrols, verified the report that the Germans were launching a full scale attack in this sector. ... Our first gun section departed at 2030 by infiltration and the evacuation was not completed until all personnel were accounted for by Battery Headquarters.

"By midnight we were all a ragged, dirty and swearing bunch from trying to find space to load CP [Command Post] and communications equipment in absolute darkness. It was strewn on every vehicle that any space at all was or could be made. We all had to hit the dirt every few seconds and sometimes we'd land on one of the other fellows. Tailgates were sagging and trailer tongues were packed. The clear voice of First Sergeant Max A. Shepp could be heard giving instructions in a quite orderly manner and they were carried out as fast as possible under the conditions. ...

"Buzz bombs were coming over at the rate of one a minute, but the gun crews ceased firing at them as our tracers were giving the enemy, only 1500 to 2000 yards away, perfect coordinates to lay 88s on. We soon realized how close Jerry [the enemy] was and personal equipment started rolling downstairs [to be] piled in the driveway of the house that we occupied. The equipment was soon loaded on every available vehicle and the men piled on wherever they could. The 88s were now really beginning to rain in and flares were being dropped in and around our entire position. Everyone breathed a sigh of relief when Captain Hooper gave 'march order' and our Headquarters section completed the evacuation by leaving the CP at 0300, 17 December 1944, just ahead of the enemy advance" *[Battery D History, 639th BN]*.

The battery and battalion histories further detail the regrouping and reassignments made during the days following evacuation. Reorganization of headquarters occurred at Malmedy, Belgium, where Battery D, about four miles east of Malmedy, covered the approach to that town from Butgenbach. According to the Unit History, 639th BN, *after contact with the 99th Division:* "it was decided to hold at all cost and to consider no further withdrawal." *Surprised to discover that 40mm guns were the only defense, the elements of the First Division that arrived in relief of the 99th called the battalion* "the Ack-Ack who wouldn't run." *D Battery gun sections and M51s of B and C Batteries were then attached to the 110th AAA Gun Battalion to assist with antitank defense two miles southeast of Spa, Belgium, headquarters of First Army.*

On December 21, D Battery was assigned to support the 30th Infantry Division and moved to AT roadblocks along the Stavelot-Malmedy sector to defend against tank advance by the Germans: "Our organization continued to contact the enemy and received constant strafing and artillery bombardment. ... In spite of our losses, our gun positions stood fast and the morale in the Battery was excellent. We were still taking all the enemy had to offer and our combat discipline was unexcelled" *[Battery D History, 639th BN]. According to the* Unit History, 639th BN: "We had little contact with D Battery during the first two weeks of the Ardennes, and it was not until they rejoined us in January that we got the full story of the heavy fighting they went through around Spa and Stavelot."

On December 23, Batteries A, B and C were assigned to anti-aircraft protection of the Butgenbach Dam, taking them out of frontline contact, but not before damage was done to A Battery, tragically hit by bombs from friendly planes. "Only D Battery remained in the Battle of the Bulge. They continued to fight an active war around Stavelot and later La Gleize. ... It was in this sector that the spearheads of Rundstedt's armor struck north with [their] greatest vehemence" *[Unit History, 639th BN]. On December 23, gun section No. 4 of D Battery was reportedly attacked by an ME 109, but knocked it out of the sky with an M51.*

D Battery operated with the 30th Division until rejoining the 639th Battalion on January 24. The German attempt to flank Liège was halted by the 82nd Airborne and 30th Infantry Division on the northern shoulder of battle. "High tribute was paid to D Battery by the CG [commanding general] of the 30th Division for its support in throttling the last death throes of the Wehrmacht's advance into the Ardennes" *[Unit History, 639th BN]. The official report from Historical Officer Capt. Franklin Ferriss, submitted January 24, 1945, and declassified May 24, 2001, details the combined effort to defeat the 1st SS Panzer Division, known to be Hitler's elite unit. Of this division, Joachim Peiper commanded the 1st SS Regiment, an armored unit with the most advanced tanks. The enemy also deployed the 3rd Parachute Division, dropped behind the lines to create confusion.* (Franklin Ferriss, "30th Infantry Division, Ardennes, 16–25 Dec 44." Web. 27 Nov. 2014.) *A report submitted in January 1945 by the AA Section, Headquarters Twelfth Army Group details assignments and methods used during late December 1944, when antiaircraft gun crews, including Battery D, 639th AAA*

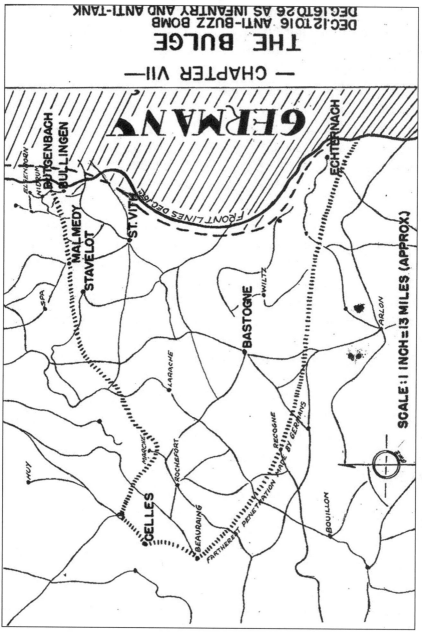

GERMANY

FRONT LINES DEC.16

RED LINE DEC.26

EISENBORN
WIRTZEN
BUTGENBACH
BULLINGEN
ST.VITH
MALMEDY
STAVELOT
SPA
ECHTERNACH
WILTZ
BASTOGNE
LAROCHE
ARLON
MARCHE
ROCHEFORT
RECOGNE
MADE BY GERMANS
HUY
CELLES
BEAURAING
FARTHEREST PENETRATION
BOUILLON

SCALE: 1 INCH = 13 MILES (APPROX.)

The bulge produced by German penetration into Belgium in December, 1944
(Map from *Unit History, 639th AAA AW Battalion*)

AW Battalion, were employed in an antitank role in support of the 30th Infantry Division. The report also makes recommendations for future employment of AAA in an antitank role. ("Employment of AAA in Antitank Role" reproduced from "Antiaircraft Artillery Notes," HQ ETO, No. 15, January 1945. Web. 27 Nov. 2014.)

Due to censorship of combat locations and details, Doyle was not able to describe these events until weeks later when conditions and locations had changed. Details are found in letters written on January 29, 1945, and May 17, 1945, and in his memoir, written during the 1990s, forty-plus years after certain poignant events.

From Doyle's memoir:

An enemy encounter one morning during the Bulge was a perfect example of how unforgettable pathos can emerge from a single incident. One of the gun crews was dug in halfway up the slope of a ridge about 500 to 600 feet high. A crew member spotted an ME 109 working its way up the valley at treetop level. A warning was signaled and the gun crew moved the azimuth angle toward the plane. When it came into close range, they opened fire.

The tracer bullets were in front of the plane so the pilot turned his plane up the hill directly toward the gun position. I was visiting the gun crew at the time, and as the plane pulled up over us, we could see the bullets from the 50-caliber machine gun crash through the plastic glass and actually see the pilot slump forward. The plane rose quickly and crashed about 200 to 300 feet on up toward the top of the hill, immediately bursting into flames. We could not get very close for a long time. When the melted metal cooled, we examined the remains. All that was left of the pilot were his leg bones at the pelvic area, and the body juices had apparently preserved his billfold which we found in his hip pocket. We were able to identify him and learned he was 14 years old. His picture showed a very handsome blond boy. His papers included a leave when he returned from the mission. I cried for him. We turned the papers over to grave registration for proper attention.

Downed Focke-Wulfe FW 190A, originally misidentified as an ME 109

The battery and battalion histories as well as Doyle's memoir mention the downing of an ME 109 by D Battery guns. This photograph from Doyle's collection is a small contact print. When enlarged and clarified, the plane was identified to be an FW 190A, the last mass-produced aircraft to see action in WWII.

December 24, 1944

Hello, my sweet. Tomorrow is Christmas. Wish I could be there with you. But I can't. I hope that Santa Claus will be good to you. I am afraid that Santa won't find me this year. Remember this time last year? I was acting like a damn fool by not writing you. I love you for showing me what a fool I was. I'm so glad you are my wife. I dream of our past and our future together all the time. I'd go crazy if I didn't have you to dream of.

There isn't anything I can tell you about myself at present. It is extremely cold here. Only my feet get cold, really cold. ... I have only seen Paul once since I left France. I see Bruce every day. Frank Kenny and I work together. I see Captain Hooper once a day. He doesn't ever think of his men. Frank and I have to go out and beg, borrow or steal stuff for them. But I guess that's war.

HEADQUARTERS
MAYFAIR 169
24 December 1944
CHRISTMAS MESSAGE

Nine days ago at dawn, you Officers and Men of the Battalion were suddenly thrust into an already critical situation as antimechanized front-line defense. Events since then clearly prove that the action that morning was the opening round of Hitler's last-ditch stand to save his army and the German nation from complete and final defeat. The seriousness and magnitude of that thrust has been acknowledged by our own High Command.

During these nine days, you have successfully accomplished four important missions, including a front-line defense totally unsupported by other friendly forces. You have withstood repeated efforts to remove you from battle by concentrated artillery fire and aerial bombing. You have met the Luftwaffe and drawn first blood. You have fought the enemy on the ground under conditions of his own choosing.

Through it all, you have stood firmly and shown skill, courage and bravery under the most adverse circumstances, reflecting high credit upon yourselves and the Battalion. Praise of your performance has come from every quarter and my pride in you is unbounded.

To us, this cannot be a very Merry Christmas. We can, however, take occasion to be grateful that we stood our battle-baptism with comparatively small personnel losses. As we prepare for future operations, resolve to avenge those who gave their lives that another year may bring Merry Christmas to us and our families at home. For each one of you, my Best Wishes.

W.A. Cauthen. Lt. Col.

December 25, 1944

We are static again and I have a few minutes each day to write you. This is Christmas day. I am thankful to be able to spend this Christmas even here. Things are quiet now, but for a while they weren't.

You are always in my mind, my sweet. I love you more each day. My only regret is that you have to spend Christmas alone. I could cry at times because I know you are there alone. You won't be when I return, my dear. I'll stay with you forever and ever. I love you. I got your V-mail letter of December 4th. First in about four weeks.   All my love, Doyle

Juby alone, Christmas 1944

Chapter 16: In Belgium during "The Bulge"

From Doyle's memoir [written December 17, 1992, "1944,
A Christmas to Remember"]:

I have a story that must be told to ease my flashback mechanism. For nearly forty-eight years, at Christmastime a feeling of desperation or depression suddenly hits me. It can be triggered by hearing beautiful music or seeing a person less fortunate than I, but mostly by being around children in any condition: smiling, joyful or excited, crippled or sickly, sad or mistreated. I am transported back to events that took place in Belgium, December of 1944, during the Battle of the Bulge.

After we were relieved, that is, joined by other troops, we began to lick our wounds. It was almost Christmas. We had not bathed in about 18 days. It was too cold to even shave regularly. Snow was everywhere. We had been promised turkey and dressing for Christmas. Early on Christmas Day I was called to come to Battery Headquarters in a fancy hotel in Spa, Belgium, that had been all but abandoned. This town was known for its world-famous mineral baths. Just across the street from the hotel was a bathhouse. It was built next to a mountain from which came a stream of hot water just right for bathing. When I went into the hotel, I was already angry with the battery personnel who had it so easy compared to what my men had been through.

When I went through the door, I saw the battery officers sitting with four or five women. They were having a glass of wine. I became even angrier and started shaking my finger in Captain Hooper's face. He responded by opening a door to reveal a large room with a staircase. Seventy-five to a hundred children, ages four to eight, filled the room. They had been found in a safe haven with the women. Headquarters had planned a Christmas party for the kids in one and a half days. The Captain had arranged for each platoon to have a skeleton crew on the guns while others came in to bathe, eat turkey and play with the children. He had not told us until it was our time to come. It was my platoon's turn next. My jeep driver and I sped back to the platoon to get the men on the way to the hotel.

The battery carpenter had covered the staircase with boards and covered the boards with a canvas truck tarpaulin. He found two sets of wheels and made two soap box derby cars for the kids to ride down the staircase. The women had made rag dolls and stuffed them with strips of German army blankets. When we left the States, we used our sporting goods as dunnage. Baseball gloves, bats, volley balls, footballs, the works. Each boy got one sports item. We had to show them how to use a glove. They had never seen one. They knew about soccer, however. It was a glorious Christmas after so much horror. Nineteen forty-four was my worst and my best Christmas, and I hope to never have another one like it. All Decembers since have brought me back to Belgium in my heart.

Christmas Day was a dreary low-ceiling day just as the last twenty days had been, but the 26th day of December was a day to be remembered. The sky broke during the night and the next morning the sun came up bright, bright, bright. The Americans, the British and, I believe, every other country that had aircraft to offer must have flown over that day. I have never seen so many airplanes in the sky at one time. As far as you could see in every direction there were aircraft, flying low, flying high, going and coming. It was great. The war was about over.

Many other incidents of note during these violent days are recorded in the battery and battalion histories. For instance, Allied-held Malmedy was bombed severely for three days by Allied planes, killing and injuring American soldiers and local civilians. On December 26, the house in Francorchamps that the 2nd Platoon of D Battery used as a command post was bombed and strafed, injuring many. The details are given by Doyle in letters to come, written weeks after the events occurred.

December 29, 1944

I have just gotten up from a night's sleep in a bed for a change. I didn't rest much. The absolute quiet was too much for me. It's funny how restless one gets when accustomed to a lot of noise and then it is very, very quiet. I have heard that the papers in the States really went berserk on the news of the fighting. It was tough, yes, but not as alarming as the headlines back in the States seem to make it. I'm sure you and Mama are worried about how I came out. Well I can now say that I had a few narrow escapes, but at present the situation looks rather good. We have a good army here and we can take care of ourselves. *[Juby remembers hearing about battles from radio reports, newspaper articles and the short news reels shown in movie theaters before the featured show. She could only guess whether Doyle was involved, and worried silently until she received letters written after the event, even though they contained few, if any, details.]*

I am assuming that you received the stuff from England. You said you and Mama were going to try to put the broken pieces back together. I'm sorry it is broken, my sweet. It is such a problem to try to pack anything well over here. I'm enclosing the receipt for the set of knives I sent from Honsfeld. Hope that you get them. They might have been captured. I don't know. *[I remember the set of pearl-handled knives. Mom used them on special occasions for many years before they were ruined in her first dishwasher.]*

This is most beautiful resort country. Want to come here with me someday?

Chapter 17

Coping in the Ardennes

January 2, 1945

Dearest Juby,

Just today I received the box of stationery I asked you to send me. You didn't include stamps. It really doesn't matter though. We don't have as much trouble getting stamps here as I thought we would. I'm glad you sent the blotters. I need them. The airmail envelopes are nice too.

I can now say that I have really seen frontline action. My only hope is that I can get myself and my men safely through this thing and back home. With God's help, so far we haven't had a single casualty in our platoon (Lt. Kenny's and mine). Honey, it was really hot for a while. Nothing to worry about now though. Please don't ever think I'm trying to keep things from you. You must realize there are some things that can't be told. We can tell about action we have been in two weeks afterward, and even then we can't paint a word picture of it.

I bought some trinkets today. They cost me the whole amount of 155 francs or about four dollars. There is a cameo setting for Mama and a pair of earrings for Eleanor. Maybe I'm crazy honey, but they intrigue me. It's two o'clock in the morning. I must sleep.

I love you with all my heart, Doyle

January 3, 1945

It is good to be able to write you each night again. I'm so very sorry I had to miss, but I had a few things to do as a soldier. So far honey, I've been a good one. You've made me a good soldier. I love you, my sweet. I got a letter from Mama today. She said you were full of surprises. She was amazed at your thinking so much of our home. I have just stopped for a cup of coffee. Had a bull session with Cpl. Dean and Sgt. Hardee. The topic of conversation was home, of course.

January 4, 1945

I have been censoring letters and studying up on my court-martial procedure. I have a couple of guys I must attempt to defend tomorrow. They have been charged with a misdemeanor. They are guilty. All I can do is try to get them off light.

The guys and I have been "bulling" again about our experiences. When I start writing you, they always start telling of amusing things that have happened and I just have to stop and laugh with them. Honey, I've got the best bunch of men I could ask for. I wish you could have met all of them. Remember T-5 Jelle? He's the kid that grabbed you from me that night in Columbia. He's my jeep driver. He and I have had some narrow ones together. He's a little jumpier than I am, and at times he gets on my nerves. But all in all, he's pretty good. He's from Wisconsin. We may go see him someday. He asks about you quite often.

All the snow has melted here but for a few of the deeper drifts, and there's quite a bit of mud. The fields look so green and fresh, just like spring in Georgia. But it will turn cold again and there will be more snow, I know. Honey, things are so humdrum here that it is hard to think of things of interest to write. Nothing happening except inspections, inspections. They get on my nerves. I have a German rifle that I picked up, so if I'm permitted to send it home,

I might. I don't want the damn thing, but I know how I was when I was a kid—a piece of German army equipment was something special to have. By the time our kid is eight or ten years old, he'd like to have something from the war. There was something I meant to send you while I was at the front: a skull and crossbones and an emblem from a German SS trooper uniform. The two S's look like streaks of lightning. I could have gotten dozens of them then, but I never did. Now it's too late. I thought you would like them for your scrapbook. (I mean *our* scrapbook.) *[Doyle never was able to get a German rifle home. He did send a helmet, sword and other uniform patches, which we still have in the family.]*

January 5, 1945

I missed writing to you last night. I might as well tell you what I was doing. I have been under terrific pressure lately, and yesterday we got our monthly ration of whiskey. It consists of one bottle of Scotch and one-half bottle of gin. Bruce, Sgt. Cobb, Sgt. Jensen and I locked ourselves in a room and started playing bridge and drinking Scotch. We played until two o'clock in the morning, and Bruce got so drunk I had to put him to bed. I was rather tired and went to bed myself.

I got three of your old letters and two from Mama today. She gave me advice. She told me not to gamble. You know what I was doing when I read the letter? I was playing poker. Funny, eh? I won six dollars. Don't worry, sweet, I only get $52 per month and I buy something for you, then use what's left to entertain myself by playing poker or buying beer.

In one of your letters, you asked me to send some tweed. I'm not in England now, but I did try to get tweed and plaids when I was there. In England you must have points for such things, and I couldn't get any. If I go into a large town here that has some, I'll send it to you. I mailed a bracelet which you'll have to have repaired because it is missing one link.

Every time Mama writes, she tells me how much she enjoys your visits. She told of you and Boots calling on her. She said she had more fun that afternoon. Now I must say so long until tomorrow.

The battery history reports a move on January 5, 1945, from AT positions near Malmedy and Francorchamps to AA defense positions near La Gleize: "At this time we gave up our fine hotel and all its comforts and returned to live as combat men" *[Battery D History, 639th BN].*

January 6, 1945

I wish you were here with me now. The place I'm in is just like the movies. It's hard to describe and explain. Things are nice now. Of course, one never knows just how it will be the next minute over here. But we can't worry about it. We go on laughing and joking. If we didn't we'd go nuts. It's almost nine o'clock at night now, and we should be getting our mail soon. It has been coming in rather regularly lately.

January 8, 1945

I didn't write you last night. I had something to do. Forgive me don't you? I found something for you today. I say found it—what I mean is that Saul brought it to me to send you. He's the one that gave me the set of knives I sent you from Honsfeld. Yes, I have been there. What I got today will probably have to be my personal gift for your birthday and our anniversary. It is a most beautiful cuckoo clock. It has a hand-carved front. The hands and Roman numerals are carved from ivory. The weights at the bottom that wind up the cuckoo alarm weigh about five pounds apiece. I think it is so very cute and nice, and honey, it didn't cost us a cent. I'll continue to send you things from different places, my sweet. This antique clock came from La Gleize.

January 9, 1945

It continues to snow. There's about two feet of snow out now. I walked to the gun crews today, and in spots it was up to my waist. Never saw so much snow in all my life.

January 10, 1945

I got a letter from Will today. The second one since I left the States. Guess that he doesn't have much time to write, but I don't care as long as you are writing. Will's letter amused me. He told me I had better stop writing to you of the women of England and France. I laughed and laughed because he doesn't know that you and I tell each other everything. I have no secrets to keep from you, so if I happen to go to a dance and dance a number or two, I'll let you know about it.

January 12, 1945

Things are quiet here. We need it, however. Maybe we can rest a little now. Got another letter today from Will. He told me about his problem: his dog. If Will vomits when he steps in canine fecal matter, he should be over here for a while. He would turn inside out. Nothing will ever bother me again. He didn't beef too much about things, and I'm glad because anyone in the States should thank his or her lucky stars that they are there. I'm not beefing myself. I'm glad to be able to help out here, but I don't like for people to write me about how tough things are at home. Such as rations and the like. I know that everything might be humdrum back home, but I'll swap with anyone there. Darling, you have led me through all of the very trying days. If it wasn't for you, I would have given up several times. I have drawn a comic letterhead that you might like. Are you shocked my sweet? (Ha.)

185

WHEN THE LIGHTS GO ON AGAIN!

January 13, 1945

I didn't write last night because it was very late when I finished censoring the guys' letters. I'm kept very busy now because I have the 2nd Platoon by myself. Lt. Kenny was evacuated. He was hit when he and I were bombed and strafed in our CP not so very long ago. He wasn't hurt seriously but was sent to a hospital for about a month. He hasn't returned yet, so it keeps me rather busy. ... I got a box of Hershey bars from you yesterday. I was delighted.

The battery history reports that on December 26, 1944, the 2nd Platoon command post near Francorchamps was destroyed by enemy aircraft. Second Lt. Frank B. Kenny, platoon leader, was injured and evacuated. Tec. 5 Richard A. Vuoncino, Aid Man from the Medical Detachment, was injured by bomb fragments yet treated several wounded men before submitting to treatment himself. Second Lt. Whittenburg became platoon leader for several weeks and submitted paperwork which resulted in Vuoncino receiving a Bronze Star in addition to the Purple Heart.

From Doyle's memoir: A bomb hit directly in an old antitank gun position on the road in front of our CP. I was eating a breakfast unit of "K" rations. I still remember what it was: egg and ham (canned of course) with a raisin bar and powdered coffee—now called "instant." I had just put my feet on the table, leaned my chair back, and had one bite of egg and ham on a hard tack (cracker). I heard the plane and the tell-tale whine of the bomb, then very quickly the blast. There were two walls between me and the bomb. I was blasted about eight feet and hit against the wall. When I stood up, I realized I was soaked with kerosene spilled from a can next to me. A piece of bomb fragment or machine gun bullet had pierced the can. I suffered with chemically burned skin for days afterward. If my feet had been on the floor, I probably would have done the same thing Frank Kenny did. When he heard the sound he jumped up and opened the door, leaving himself wide open for a hit from fragments. Yes, he was given first aid on the spot and later evacuated to have a piece of metal removed from under his scapula. Being unable to move quickly taught me not to be in such a hurry to do things, just stop and think it over. I took over leadership of the platoon for several weeks and later had the pleasure of returning Frank Kenny to our unit after his recovery.

January 13, 1945, continued

I'll tell you how I look now. I have just finished shaving, so my face is clean. I have grown a mustache I think you will like. It is long and goes from my nose down and beyond the corners of my mouth. My hair is about one and a half inches long and, for some strange reason, it stands up now. I don't part it; I comb it straight back. The barber didn't cut it even, so it has a wave in it. I'm almost seasick now from looking at it! I have on a high-necked sweater underneath my OD [Olive Drab] shirt. The shirt is open at the neck, giving me the appearance of a sporting man. You know—ascot and sport shirt. In fact honey, I look almost handsome. "Stop it Doyle," you're saying now. But I do look a little bit handsome. I must brag on myself. No one else will.

I found something that you can give Will. It's a small beer stein. You may be a little angry when I tell you where I got it, but here goes. I turned on my charm for a barmaid. Of course I had spotted the mug, so I had an ulterior motive. She said, "*Souvenir de* ___." I'm still within 25 miles of the town and can't tell you which one it is [Spa, Belgium]. I have some cards I'll send to you and the kid sisters just as soon as we move farther from here.

January 14, 1945

"I dream of you when day is done" [lyrics from "When Day Is Done"] is on the radio now. There were never any truer words, my sweet. I love you and it hurts me that I can't be with you. "San Fernando Valley" is now being played—"I'm packing my grip..." Hell, wish I could. You know what trail I would hit. Yes. The Georgia trail. It will be a wonderful day when I can start home.

I made something today for Elizabeth and Kathryn. When I was in the States, all the girls were wearing charm bracelets. I made a couple for them. I used a broken dog tag chain as the bracelet part and then used a link from the chain to fasten the charms on. I have picked up the charms here and there. Found all of them in wrecked homes and the like. They all are very interesting. Most of them are religious medals worn by Catholics. There are a couple of coins on them too. Hope they like them.

The news sounds good today. Hope we keep it up. We have rigged up our radio so the boys out on the guns can have music. We have learned to live well while we can because at times we have to live in tents. You see, we have power plants as part of our equipment so we string wires and have lights and music. It isn't bad since we have to be here. We try to make it as enjoyable as possible.

I have just censored about 150 letters. It's a pain in the neck. I have to sign all of them after reading them. But I got myself into all of this. It's my own fault that I went to OCS. It isn't bad, though. I read a Jewish boy's letter tonight, and he was telling his parents of visiting the only Jewish family in the nearby town. He was telling why only one family was left. Most of them left when the Germans, or "Bosch" as the French and Belgians call them, first came. The ones that were left were treated so terrible that it makes me shudder. I had rather not tell you of it. The father of the family he visited was taken away by the Germans. It isn't nice, what's been going on. We are putting a stop to it and soon. *[This was Doyle's first bit of knowledge about Jewish persecution and the Holocaust.]*

Some of the things the guys write are interesting, but most of them are dull and monotonous. One kid has been writing a week now trying to convince his wife that what just happened was for the best and that they can try again. His wife had twin boys but they died a couple of hours later. She had written him the weights of each. He wrote back his recommendations for names for the babies. It's pathetic, but "se la gayr" [*C'est la guerre*], as the French say. There are so many things in the letters I read that make me more thankful each day for our good fortune. My first sergeant's baby was born dead at term since he came over here. He told me that it was so very hard to do any comforting at such a great distance. He said his wife had bought about $300.00 worth of baby clothes. Sometimes we feel sorry for ourselves, my sweet, but we are mighty well off in comparison to some others. You agree? We have a beautiful life to live together ahead of us. It will be so wonderful.

The battery history of Battery D, 639th AAA AW Battalion, reports that the battery returned to Stavelot, Belgium, on January 16, 1945, with the new mission of AA support to the 551st FA Bn. While there, Doyle's good friend Bruce Schwartz was promoted to 1st Lieutenant.

January 17, 1945

My sweet, we have moved on as I told you we would. It is much easier mentally now than it was about one month ago. It's hard work, but not so nerve-racking. I guess I'm getting used to it. We are comfortably set up now. Have already made myself two cups of coffee and two cups of cocoa. Some life, eh? War is so very different from maneuvers. Honey, I'm being a good soldier and a good officer. You have done your part for the Army and the country, sweet. You made me a new man. If every man had a woman like you, we would have a better army. I want to do a lot to end this thing.

Honey, I really have a good platoon sergeant. He's tops. He deserves to be made an officer. Also, the boys are good. They work well together and they believe in me. All of us respect each other. They mind me, and I try to carry out all of their good suggestions.

Honey, didn't you say you went to a war show? Well, I'm seeing the show of shows every day. At first it was horrible to me and then it grew to be pathetic. It still is, but it doesn't bother me anymore. Nothing bothers me anymore. But I still have that soft spot in my heart that makes me a peace-loving, comfort-loving person. Yes honey, I still have the touch. I'll never lose it. My love that's mounting each day is proof that wars and their dark sides will never make me a hard man. It does make some men hard and cruel. I'll admit that I am now, but when the war is over I'll forget it all. Just like that. And I'll be the most wonderful husband in the world.

January 18, 1945

It has been nine days since I heard from you. I know some days you are very, very busy. Will tickles me when he says he hardly has time to write. I have found that if one will utilize his time, there are always 15 or 20 minutes each day available for writing. That is enough time if you write what you think. You know by now by the peculiarity of my letters, I just start and write what I think.

It has warmed up enough to rain instead of snow now. It's miserable outside. I'd much rather it would snow. You don't get wet when it snows, but you do when it rains.

Oh yes honey, don't be surprised to learn that I'm a first lieutenant sometime in the next six months. You see, the War Department has out a new ruling that a second "loui" who is in good standing for 18 months or longer will be promoted. Tomorrow, January 19, I will have been in grade 18 months, and I have been told my promotion has been requested. It will take some six months for it to go through. It will mean a little more money for us, my sweet. I'm already doing the work of a first and a second. I'm the only officer in the platoon. As I have said, I have a swell platoon sergeant and also all of my men are aces. They really work for me. They are a bunch of daredevils. I have to watch them sometimes because if I don't, they will be out looking for trouble. All I'm looking for is a trip back home to you.

I'm having it fairly easy now. Only when we move do we have to work. The poor kids out on the gun crews are the ones to get the credit. They stand continuous guard for 14 hours—two hours on and four off. It's really rough in this cold weather. Just made my second cup of cocoa since I started this letter. Have my shoes off and my feet on a hot brick. Comfy, eh? I'm writing on my operations board. It's a large board, something like a biscuit board, and it has a draftsman's T-square fastened underneath. I'm really an operator now. I enjoy it, even if it is hard work. I have to like it or I'd go nuts. You ask for pictures, my sweet. It's a tough proposition. Cameras and film are hard to get, and the censor is hard to get pictures by. So I can't promise any just yet. When the war is over,

Bruce is going to send us some of the ones he is making. Bruce and I have been getting along swell for the last two months. We are really working together.

Honey, I just got through looking at the snapshots I have of you. You know you're so cute and beautiful. I just love you, that's all. Wish I could tell you in person. I'm enclosing a poem that might express your feelings. I like it. *[Doyle enclosed a typed copy with his own underlining. I found various versions of this poem online, credited to different sources. The earliest I located was dated February 24, 1945; others were posted on military blogs very recently. I found it touching to read comments about these classic verses posted by spouses of soldiers now deployed to the Middle East. The words strike the same emotional chords now as they did for my parents more than sixty years ago.]*

LOVING A SOLDIER

Loving a soldier's not all play
In fact, there's very little of it gay;
It's mostly having, but not to hold,
It's being young, and feeling old.
Loving a soldier's all milk and no cream
It's being in love with a misty dream.
It's getting a Valentine from an Army Camp
And sending a letter with an upside down stamp.
It's hoping for a furlough you know won't come
It's wondering if he'll ever get home.
And when he does come, it's laughter together
Unconscious of people, of time, and the weather.

It's hearing him whisper his love for you
And your murmuring whisper that you love him too
And then comes the wonderful promise of love
And knowing that you're watched by the Father above.
And loving a soldier's a good bye at the train
And wondering if you'll ever see him again.
And reluctantly, painfully letting him go
When inside you're crying for wanting him so.
Then you watch for the word that he is well
And wait thru a long, dragged out, no-letter spell
And your feet are planted on sand, not sod
And your course of strength comes solely from God.
Loving a soldier is undefined fear,
And crying until there are no more tears
And hating the world, yourself and the war
And stomping and kicking until you can't fight anymore
And then giving up, and kneeling and praying
And really meaning the prayers that you're saying.
And when the mail comes, you bubble with joy and
Act like a baby with a shining new toy
And now you know he's far away
And you just keep loving him more every day.
You are so proud of the job he's helping get done.
You don't care anymore if living's not fun—
Then you grit your teeth, and muster a grin
You've got a fight and someone who's in

You've got a war, and you'd better help win.

And then comes your birthday, you're a year older today

But you feel just the same as you did yesterday.

You're not. You've changed; you're wise, more strong

You can weather this war if it's twenty years long.

You'll work and you'll sweat every hour of the day

Your job will be hard, but you'll sure earn your pay

You're tired and weary but you're doing your share

You're helping the soldier to win over there

So, loving a soldier is bitterness, tears,

It's loneliness, sadness, unidentified fears

It's fretting, and sweating and loving,

It's nothing to take for a darned lot of giving,

No, loving a soldier is really not fun

But it's worth the price, when the battle is won!

[Original source unknown]

January 19, 1945

I sent you a *Yank* last night in several envelopes. I want you to save it for me. I'd like for you to read the article about Malmedy and Stavelot in particular. Let your father read it too. It'll make your blood boil, sweetheart. You'll see then why I'm now a fighting man. I happen to know it's true. Not propaganda this time.

Yank *was a weekly magazine published by the US military, 1942–1945. The correspondents were soldiers of enlisted ranks. The magazine was edited in New York and distributed for publication in other locations for military personnel worldwide.*

MASSACRE

American soldiers who escaped from German slaughter pen tell how guns were turned on medics and unarmed prisoners of war.

By Sgt. ED CUNNINGHAM
YANK Staff Correspondent

ALMEDY, BELGIUM—Early in the afternoon on the first day of the counteroffensive along the Western Front a convoy of Battery B, a field artillery observation battalion, was moving along three miles south of Malmedy on a road leading to St. Vith. About 300 yards beyond the crossroad of the cutoff to St. Vith, the convoy was ambushed by riflemen, machine gunners, and mortarmen hidden in the surrounding woods. All the American vehicles halted immediately. The men jumped off and took cover in the ditches lining both sides of the road. Several minutes later they were flushed out of their hiding place by Tiger tanks from an armored column which lumbered along the ditches spraying machine gun fire. Other tanks quickly knocked out some 24 American trucks and other vehicles. Armed only with small caliber weapons the Americans had no alternative but to surrender.

The Germans had other U.S. prisoners taken earlier, including five military policemen, two ambulance drivers, a mess sergeant, several medical corps men, engineers, infantrymen and members of an armored reconnaissance outfit. All these prisoners, totalling approximately 150, were herded up on the road where they were searched for pocketbooks, watches, gloves, rings, cigarettes and weapons, all of which were taken from them. They were ordered by their captors to line up in a snow-covered field south of the crossroads.

While the Americans were lining up, an enemy halftrack mounting an 88 gun made an effort to swing around and cover them but was unable to do so. In lieu of that, the Germans parked tanks at either end of the field where their machine guns had a full sweep over the prisoners. Just then a German command car drew up. The German officer in the car stood up, took deliberate aim at an American medical officer in the front rank of prisoners and fired. As the medical officer fell, the German fired again and another front-rank American dropped to the ground. Immediately the two tanks at the end of the field opened up with their machine guns on the defenseless prisoners who were standing with their hands over their heads. No effort had been made to segregate the non-combatant medical corps men, all of whom were wearing medic brassards and had red crosses painted on their helmets.

When the massacre started, those who were not wounded dropped to the ground, those who had been shot. Flat on their stomachs with their faces pushed into the snow and mud, the Americans were raked by withering machine gun and small arms fire from the column of tanks which began to move along the road 25 yards away. Each of the estimated 25 to 50 Tiger tanks and halftracks took its turn firing on the prostrate group. One tank and several German soldiers were left to finish off those who had not been killed. The guards walked among the American soldiers and shot the wounded. They kicked others in the face to see if they were really dead or just faking. Those who moved were shot in the head. One American medic got up to bandage the wounds of a seriously injured man from his own company aid unit. The Germans permitted him to finish his work. Then they shot both him and his patient.

Fortunately the guards were not too thorough in their search for Americans who were pretending death. Several of the prisoners had escaped injury and others were only slightly wounded. About an hour after the armored column left, several of the survivors—including some of the wounded—decided to make a break. Fifteen men made the first attempt. While their guards were some distance away, they jumped up and ran north up the road toward Malmedy amid a hail of machine gun fire from their surprised captors. At the

US Army medic and another soldier lie where they were
dug out of the snow in Malmedy, Belgium. The corpses are
numbered to keep track of them during the investigation.
(Corbis Images)

IN HIS FOOTSTEPS

April 25–27, 2010: Traveling from London under the Channel via Eurostar fast train, Ken and I meet our learned guide, Michael Baert, in Brussels. We rent a car and head toward Liège and southward from there. We stay in Malmedy for three days, taking day trips to the specific places where Dad's mission was carried out. We learn that there were many massacres during the Bulge along the deadly path that Peiper's SS troops took through Belgium, beginning in Honsfeld. We travel among the killing fields where plaques and monuments mark each spot where Allied troops had been captured, made prisoner and then systematically murdered. The most famous is the site of the so-called Malmedy Massacre where American prisoners were gunned down by Peiper's SS troops on December 17, 1944. Eighty-four were left dead in the snow. A few escaped to tell the tale. Weeks later, after the Allies drove the Germans back and the snow began to melt, members of the 30th Infantry Division found the field with the frozen bodies. The recovery occurred on January 14–15, 1945. Attached to the 30th at the time, Dad knew of the recovery, but only spoke of the horror occasionally through the years. He said that road signs had been switched, confusing troop movement and leading to death for some and safety for others. Ken and I are humbled to see fresh flowers placed at the monument sites by visitors and locals who continue to honor the American dead these many years later.

January 19, 1945, continued

The boys in my platoon headquarters and I have really fixed ourselves up. We have a stove in each of four rooms of a house that was shelled. The house is a duplex, and the side we're in wasn't hurt too badly. The other side is a total wreck. We have blankets over the windows and have electric lights because we have our power charger with us. We also have a radio connected to our telephone lines. By doing this, the guys on the gun crews pick up the broadcast by telephone out where they are. Out there, the men have dugouts large enough to sleep eight men and have stoves for warmth. We really live while we can here, sweet, because we never know when we must move on.

January 20, 1945

I have just finished censoring the mail for the guys. Today was just the same old routine. I inspected the gun sections and came back to make out my reports. I went out again in the afternoon and had a short bull session with the boys on the guns. I slipped in the snow and fell into the straddle trench latrine late this afternoon. Very embarrassing. I stripped off my clothes where I was and went inside to put on a new suit from skin out. You see honey, we were fortunate (or maybe unfortunate) enough to be left in a town abandoned in a hurry when the Bosch came through. We were left to defend it and we did. Before the troops came back to resume their previous positions, we took advantage of the equipment they left and equipped ourselves well with clothes. It was nothing but right. The civilians were taking everything, so we ran them off and took over ourselves. You can see why I threw away the things I had on when I slipped and fell into the latrine. I was quite a mess. Have you ever straddled a straddle trench? It's quite difficult I tell you.

Tonight I was in Battery Headquarters. While I was there, I recommended my platoon sergeant for a battlefield commission. He certainly deserves it. There were three others in the battery also recommended and only one will be made. I hope my boy gets it. He's good. *[This refers to First Sgt. Max Shepp. He did get the commission.]* Hope I get my first lieutenant soon too. You and I need the money.

January 21, 1945

Honey, today Bruce made first lieutenant. I'll be next. He graduated from OCS about two months before I did. I can't write too much about what I'm doing. Censor restrictions!! If I could only get one letter, just a short one, I could write and write for days and days. The reports have it that that one mail boat had trouble and had to dock in England and the other is having engine trouble somewhere in the Atlantic. But maybe they have a good engineer and will get it into port soon. ... I'm going to get the address of the guys in the battery so if we hit a town that one of them lives in we can call on them.

January 22, 1945

Sometimes I wonder if my family misses me. Eleanor hasn't written me since I've been over here. Neither has Jack. Will has written a very few times. Mama gets a letter off about every week. I haven't heard from Mary, but I'm sure that she's busy. Maybe I have brought it on myself. When I was in Florida, I'll admit I didn't write as much as I should.

Honey, we have been in the same position now for five or six days. We are getting restless now. We want to move on, and we will shortly I guess. We get on each other's nerves when we stay in the same position too long.

I hope that Freas and Mills aren't transferred to infantry. It's no good, sweet. I thank my lucky stars that I didn't go to Columbus. It would have meant a little longer stay with you, but honey, the chances of an infantry officer ever coming back to the States are very slim. The boys on the line really have it rough. *[Infantry training occurred at Ft. Benning in Columbus, Georgia. It remains the "Home of the Infantry." In 2009 the National Infantry Museum opened near the gates of Ft. Benning. It is a stunning interactive museum covering over 200 years of American military history. The high-tech exhibits invoke a reality unattainable in the typical static museum display. I highly recommend a visit there.]*

I'm lucky to be with AA regardless of how much I want to be with you now. We'll be together soon and it will be wonderful. I can come home from work, hang up my hat and coat, pull you up to me and give you a good loving. [*I remember as a child seeing Dad come in after work and go straight to Mom, who would be at the stove cooking our supper. He would grab her in a bear hug and lay a big kiss on her.*]

January 23, 1945

Honey, today I went into town and had the best bath that I have ever had. You probably have read about the famous Spa mineral baths. A huge granite building is built over a mineral spring. The water is piped into the bathing rooms. There are about a hundred of them in the building, each with a copper bathtub that shines like a new penny. The tub is on a platform with steps used for getting to the tub. At one end of the tub is a copper box with steam pipes in it for heating a towel. The water runs in the tub and out again as you sit there, and it's up to your armpits all the time. I hadn't had a bath for four weeks, and that alone made it wonderful. But to have the hot water bubbling between your legs and up your back was really good. Fifteen minutes in the tub was the limit. It seemed so very short to me.

Now here's what you won't like, I know. There were women attendants. They weren't bashful; neither was I. Mine kept drifting in while I was in the process of undressing, I asked her to wash my back and she did. Don't worry honey, she was around 50 years old. I gave the woman ten francs for her services. She drew my bath and cleaned the tub when I was finished. It was really nice to get clean again. Tell Will about it. He'll envy me because I know that he has heard of the Spa bath. I think I sent one of your sisters a postcard picture of the place.

Postcard of bathhouse, Spa, Belgium, 1944

Radisson Hotel, 2010

IN HIS FOOTSTEPS

April 29, 2010: *The site now is occupied by a new Radisson hotel; Ken and I stay here and take mineral baths in shiny copper tubs of the nearby Spa Thermal as Dad had done. The experience is our respite from travel weariness. We, too, appreciate the pampering of attendants. [See images of copper tubs in the color gallery.]*

January 25 is considered the official end of the Battle of the Bulge, the front lines of December 16 now restored near the Siegfried Line, Germany's 390-mile antitank defense system known to Germans as the Westwall. The Allies regroup and prepare for the final push into Germany.

January 26, 1945

I got a letter from Mama today, and I want to quote something that made me feel good. Did it ever make me howl, you know, like a wolf! Here 'tis: "Juby calls me every time she gets a letter from you. She came in the store to see me yesterday afternoon and she looked so beautiful. She had a very becoming new hair-do, wore a white crocheted pillbox hat and had on a black chesterfield with white gloves. She looked like she had just stepped out of *Vogue*." End of quote. Wow!

January 27, 1945

My sweet, I got the sweetest letter from you today. You told me about trying on my clothes. It did me good to know that someone sheds a tear for me now and then.

I got Christmas cards from Freas and Eileen and Ruth and Paul. Freas mailed the card from an infantry camp in Louisiana. Hope he doesn't have to go overseas as an infantry officer. Honey, it's really rugged. They (the ones who come out alive) really deserve the credit. He expressed his wishes for a reunion of the gang of

Wrightsville Beach. Maybe we'll get to see them all someday. *[Juby and Doyle returned to Wrightsville Beach in 1947 with friends they met after the war. Alas, the "reunion of the gang" did not occur.]*

Honey, you must forgive me for being so brief tonight. I've been very busy. We've just completed a move. I'm much safer now than before. There's nothing to worry about. Good night my sweet. *[This move was to Verviers, Belgium, to give the unit a chance to rest and get equipment ready for the advance into Germany.]*

IN HIS FOOTSTEPS

April 25–30, 2010: For three days in Malmedy, we stay in a lodge overlooking the peaceful valley in which the town is nestled. A nearby pasture can be seen from our windows where we watch deer and donkeys grazing side by side. We are reminded of places back home in Georgia where cattle and deer can similarly be seen dining together. We enjoy personal attention and good food, some things familiar and some not. This is my first experience with Belgian endive, white rather than green due to being purposely grown in the dark. Lightly steamed, it fairly melts in one's mouth. Michael is not with us in the evenings, so we struggle with the language barrier. We try to use French words and phrases that pop into our heads from French classes taken decades ago. Comical at best, pathetic at worst!

Resting each evening after lengthy excursions, I try to absorb and process the impact of things I have learned during the day. Being at the sites of so many events I've long heard and read about is overwhelming, and I have not yet reached the full depth of my emotions. It is hard to imagine the reality of the past horror in this absolutely exquisite place. The spring-green rolling hills, the patchwork vistas of distant tree farms at various growth stages, the fresh breezes of clean air—Belgium is beautiful.

Each morning, Michael meets us after breakfast, simple and continental (the breakfast, of course, but maybe Michael too). He is over 70, soft spoken and very knowledgeable. After a lesson with maps of Peiper's path, we head out to the Ardennes Forest. We find the forest floor to be lush, green and mossy under the tallest trees I have ever seen. Michael says they are second and third generation firs that are farmed, logged and replanted. We ask why the space has not been memorialized as a battlefield and learn that only one area has been so designated and protected. He reminds us that the whole country was a battleground in more than one war. The entire countryside cannot be set aside and rendered nonproductive. Point taken.

For the three days in and around Malmedy, then for a subsequent two days as we "invade" Germany, Ken and I climb in and out of foxholes, eight-man dugouts, large L-shaped dug-ins (oriented for maximum protection) and bunkers in the Ardennes-Eifel-Hürtgen forests along the present German-Belgian border. I must not have inherited Dad's ability to estimate footage, as I have no idea how to describe the sizes of these spaces. The only thing I can say with certainty is that they were of variable sizes. Ken and I together would "fill" some of them, yet others would be deeper, wider and longer, approximating the size of a room in a medium-sized house. I have to admit to using a latrine for its intended purpose!

We visit many memorials, including the American cemetery at Henri-Chapelle and a German cemetery in Bastogne. Most German tombstones read simply "Ein Deutscher Soldat" (A German Soldier) because German dog tags were made of cardboard and deteriorated rapidly.

American cemetery at Henri-Chapelle; 7992 stones

Cemetery at Bastogne, where 6807 German
soldiers are buried, six per stone

We see the killing fields of several massacres. In Belgium, it seems the war was over only yesterday. Memorabilia has been collected and effectively displayed in museums across the region. German and Allied equipment left behind has been incorporated into a landscape of remembrance.

Rural castle, 2010

We see an isolated castle nestled among rolling pastureland; cattle peacefully graze on the lawn. Peiper is reported to have stayed in the adjacent farm buildings because he surmised the Allies would expect him to be in the castle. He put POWs in the castle in his stead. We saw a small bridge reportedly blown up by the Allies just before Peiper's tank column got there. He was quoted as saying "The damn engineers!" It meant a re-routing and significant delay for the German advance. Such delaying tactics gave the Americans time to strengthen and to stop the enemy from meeting its goal of dividing the British and American armies and capturing fuel depots of the area.

We take pictures in Stavelot, St. Vith, Honsfeld and other places where Dad had been and often talked about. We hear important stories at each spot and fear we will not be able to remember them well enough to retell. The town of St. Vith is newly built because it was completely destroyed by bombing. There is a German Tiger tank on display in La Gleize. There are monuments of apprecia-tion in many places, well kept and honored with fresh flowers. We take note of mention of the 30th, the 99th and the First Army. We notice that "E" Company of the 101st Airborne (active on the southern shoulder of the Bulge near Bastogne) is honored by recent moviemakers—Band of Brothers.

Memorials to American units

Francorchamps is a disappointment to us because the house where Dad's CP was bombed is nowhere to be found. We know it was there in the mid-1980s because a member of his unit, Frank Kenny, sent Dad photographs of the repaired and functional house. We assume that the missing house was in a section taken when the Circuit de Spa-Francorchamps for motor racing was developed. Formula One car racing is what the town is mostly known for now.

We see the Dragon's Teeth of the Westwall (dubbed the "Siegfried Line" by American troops) crossing pastures and

207

through forests. These concrete "teeth" were linked beneath the ground as one long barrier to the advance of tanks. The angle of the graduated rows caused an advancing tank to rise up, exposing its vulnerable underbelly to fire from pillbox bunkers embedded in the ground. Over the years, nature's debris has built up the earth so the teeth seem shorter. Moss growth softens their outline and masks the erstwhile harshness of war. We learn that the underpinnings are so extensive that removal would not be worth the cost or the damage incurred in the process. Extraction only occurs as needed, such as for road construction. [See image of Dragon's teeth in the color gallery.]

Of all these places, the lonely forests make the most memorable impression. Only birdsong breaks the silence as we wander through remnants of a fierce tug-of-war battle. We learn that the lower branches of the towering trees have been trimmed for better access. At the time of the actual battle, the branches were to the ground, making movement and visualization difficult.

We learn that the Americans lacked winter camouflage, so villagers gave them white linens to slit and put over their heads. An interesting aside: we learn that local brides, lacking availability of fabric, would make their wedding dresses from scavenged parachutes. We smile, thinking of the fabrics for parachutes made in the plant where Mom worked while Dad was overseas.

We learn of the deadly tree-bursts resulting when bombs detonated upon striking the canopy above, causing the trees themselves to splinter into wooden shrapnel. Loggers continue to find remains of soldiers who died in the forest; they are reverently recovered and turned over to authorities for identification and return to their home countries. Many are yet to be found.

Memorial marking the spot where PFC Robert
Cahow died in the Hürtgen Forest.
His remains were found 56 years after his death.

In the protected acres called Hasselpath (Remembrance Place), dedicated in 2000 with the cooperation of Belgium, the USA, the Federal Republic of Germany and the town authorities of nearby Büllingen, we hear artillery fire in the distance. Are we imagining it? Is this an echo from 65 years ago when this timberland was occupied by American and German units in turn? No, the sounds we hear are real. Adjacent to this hallowed battleground where so many fiercely fought and died is Lager Elsenborn Camp, a multinational military training facility available for Belgian, Dutch and German military exercises. The irony does not escape us.

Exploring bunkers and foxholes in the Ardennes and Hürtgen Forests.
It is here I noticed that my brother has the same stance as our father!

Returning to Malmedy, Michael takes us to a church in the center of town to admire the church and abbey and see the memorial associated with the Allied bombing of civilians and American troops on December 23–25, 1944. Dad wrote about the tragic results in a letter dated May 17, 1945, which reviewed his travels and experiences in Europe. On stone tablets are inscribed the names and ages of 200 civilian casualties of the "friendly fire." Victims include the elderly, infants and all in-between. Nearby we examine the entrance to a shelter in the mountain where 300 citizens hid out for weeks under deplorable conditions—no food or water or other supplies—during the Bulge.

While writing in my travel journal late in the evening, I hear a loud, startling thunderclap that reverberates through the nearby hills. The bombing of Malmedy? I can't imagine the terror of the thing.

Chapter 18

Respite in Verviers, Belgium

January 28, 1945

Dearest Juby,

Went over to see the doctor today. I have a couple of frozen toes, but they will be OK. I was told to sleep with my foot high and soon I'll get some feeling back in them. I'm lucky to come out as well as I have. Some of the guys have really had tough luck.

The Russians are going to end this war for us, it seems. They'll send me home to you. We've moved away from the front. At times I am sorry because now we have too many inspections. It seems that inspections are allergic to the front lines, but they bloom forth in the rear areas. To have six weeks of frontline duty so quick is quite an experience. It's all over now, and you and I can breathe a sigh of relief.

I wrote you, I think, of a show featuring Marlene Dietrich that was to take place while we were at Honsfeld. It was to be the very day we ended up withdrawing from Honsfeld when the Germans broke through. Of course it was cancelled! We got a big kick out of saying the reason for the breakthrough was that the Germans wanted to see her legs. Well anyway, today the show went on in a nearby town. I sent 22 men from my platoon. They said it was very good. I'll send 22 more tomorrow. I can't go because I have to take care of a court-martial tomorrow. I'm the Assistant Defense and Paul is Defense. I saw Paul yesterday for the first time in about seven weeks. You see, we are now back with Battalion after weeks of detached service. It was rather nice to operate alone.

Good night, Doyle

"On 16 December 1944, 3:30 am, company 'B' pulled into Honsfeld. The little village was the rest center for the 99th Division's 394th regiment. The captain commanding the center was having

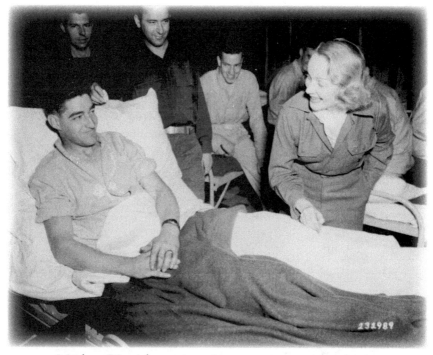

Marlene Dietrich, motion picture actress, autographs the cast of Tec 4 Earl E. McFarland at a US hospital in Belgium, where she was entertaining the GIs. (National Archives)*

---

*Tuttle, November 24, 1944 111-SC-232989 National Archives, Online Public Access [OPA] Electronic Record (ww2_47.jpg).

a frantic day. He had been getting ready for a visit by the actress Marlene Dietrich to entertain the troops. He hurriedly sent her back and started pulling together a scratch defense force of 99th troops and a few guns of the 801st Tank Destroyer BN. ... Jeeps and half-tracks filled with cooks, engineers, and office personnel, in addition to stray artillery pieces and antiaircraft guns lost from their units added to the total confusion." (Don Smart, "Terror at Honsfeld, The Story of Company B, 612th Tank Destroyer Btn," *World War II*, Vol. 16, Issue 4, page 50, November 2001. Web. 21 Oct. 2014.)

January 29, 1945 (Somewhere in Belgium)

I guess you wonder where I got the typewriter. Well, I got it when the Germans broke through. I'll try now to tell you what happened to me during the Germans' drive. On our first mission, we were sent to the exact spot where the Germans had massed their thickest concentration of SS and Panzer troops. We performed our mission for about three days [December 12–15] and were just getting fully set up when lo and behold, the surprise attack began. We held off the Germans for about 14 hours and then learned we had nothing to support us; the high moguls of the Army weren't sending us the help we needed. So we made escape plans.

The first plan was fool proof, we thought, but the Bosch had already surrounded us, and the second plan was the only possible escape route. After fighting some delaying action and causing the Germans a great deal of trouble, we decided we were no match for the Tiger tanks that kept coming at us. I told the men to get their stuff together and be ready to go. After that, a shell hit our line and we had no communications. I had to walk out to the positions to give the men more instructions, and on the way a shell came over. I could tell by the whine of it that it was coming straight for me. Not having a slit trench close, I hit the dirt in a ditch alongside the road. When I got up, I was muddy from top to bottom. I didn't mind because the shell hit about five feet from me at the top of the bank I was behind. If it had been two feet farther, it would have been over the bank and I wouldn't be here to write you tonight. When we started our withdrawal, we had been under artillery fire for almost two days [December 16–17]. We finally pulled out of the positions, and 30 minutes after we left the town [Honsfeld], the Germans took it over. Close shave number one.

As we came down the road, we barely missed running into German paratroopers that had just landed. We maneuvered out of close shave number two. We knew by now that some unseen Power was with us. We moved on to Malmedy [December 17], staying there for about five hours. We were then ordered to Spa to set up roadblocks [December 18]. In that sector we stopped the German drive and started to move gradually forward. We were in Francorchamps near Stavelot when our platoon CP was strafed and bombed [December 26]. This was the third time an unseen Power took me in hand. We moved from Francorchamps to La Gleize where we also did well. From there we moved to Stavelot. All during the battle of Stavelot, I had my CP only about a mile away. I saw a lot there. One day my driver and I slipped into Stavelot where street fighting was going on. We stayed long enough to get a few holes in the jeep top. Quite a thrill! You bet. We had moved within four miles of St. Vith when we were ordered to the rear for another mission. I haven't heard a gun fired now for about five days. I'm as safe now as a newborn babe. I couldn't tell you about all of this earlier because of censorship.

Now I'll tell you how I got the typewriter. When we moved into Spa, we were told to stay there and officially surrender Spa to the Germans. We couldn't see it that way, so we fought the Germans off. We and a 90mm outfit were the only troops that stayed. I took a truck into town and went to a hospital that had been evacuated— most equipment left behind, including the typewriter. Civilians were having a big time in the place getting food, clothing, supplies and whatnot. The boys and I ran them off at the point of our rifles and got needed equipment—blankets, clothes, food and medical supplies. It was left to be captured by the Germans, so we took it instead. What was left wasn't captured, thanks to us. Now you know that I have been busy for the past few weeks.

February 1, 1945

Honey, I didn't write last night because I had to move one of my gun sections. I went over the position by map with Captain Hooper, then I had to take my Chief of Section out on ground reconnaissance. When I returned I had a flock of letters to censor for the boys, and by the time I finished I was very tired. I went to bed and dreamed about you.

The guys here in the CP and I have just been shooting the bull about our narrow escapes. It is all very funny now, but at the time it wasn't funny at all. Now that it is so quiet, everything seems to get on our nerves. We lived at such a high pitch for a while, the quietness doesn't seem natural. You see, we got into frontline action and stayed there so long that we became accustomed to it, so it is actually nerve-racking to stay so far back. Yes, I'm safe now. So don't worry about me. In one of your letters you said that you wondered if I was in the drive. Well honey, you can rest assured that I was. My outfit was the outfit that stopped them in a certain sector of the Bulge.

I just got three letters from you written on the 28th, 30th and 31st of December. I am glad to hear you were just a wee bit worried about me. I'll admit things weren't so good for a while, but it was a great experience for me. I often wondered how I would feel under fire. I certainly know now. I'll tell you all about it someday. ... I got the package of sugar-coated fruits that you sent. The guys here in the CP send their thanks and so do I. Here are a couple of paragraphs for your mother.

Miss Mary, I'm sorry I had to pull your daughter into this war. You once said to me you hoped I wouldn't have to go overseas. In fact I think that it was about the last thing that you said to me when

I left from my six-day leave. I told you I didn't think I would have to go, but deep down inside I felt I would.

I hope Juby is taking it as well as I think she is. It will be only a short time now before I'll be home. I'm really sorry we couldn't have gone on living together as we did in Columbia, Wrightsville Beach and Wilmington. We had so much fun together. Wish you and Mama could have visited us in Wilmington. You would have enjoyed it. I have just completed five weeks of frontline duty. For this reason I am a bit weary. I want to thank you for having such a swell daughter for me. You know I love and miss the kid like the very devil.

February 3, 1945 (It's really the 4th)

I have just finished a day's work. I'm working very hard now, but it helps pass the time. Captain Hooper told me the first of the month that I would be a first lieutenant about the 15th. Are you proud of me about getting a battlefield promotion? Enclosed are photos of a couple of the guys. Keep them. We may visit them someday. Their names are on the back. *[There are so many pictures of "the guys" in the scrapbook I can't tell which these would be. Most are pasted in, so the back is inaccessible.]*

February 5, 1945

It made me laugh when you said Washington and New York might be bombed. Don't worry, kid. It won't happen. You want to know what army I'm with. You should know by now. I think I slipped and told you once. I got a letter from my sister Mary today. It was the sweetest letter I ever got from her. She seemed quite concerned over my predicament.

Honey, I'm getting quite good at understanding these Belgian people. I get a big kick out of talking to them. I'm living with an old fellow and his wife. The old man speaks German, and the old lady speaks French and German. I understand German better than French. I can't speak very well yet, but I'm learning slowly.

It's really funny how we go about putting our point across. You'd laugh your head off. My communications man is a scream when he gets started with them. He's Italian and he speaks with them for a while in English and then in Italian. He really screws them up when he does this. What a laugh.

I was the defense counsel today at a court-martial. I'm the appointed Assistant Defense Counsel and Paul is the Defense, but he went on leave to Paris this morning and left me holding the bag. I lost both cases. But if you know military courts as I do, you know that a man hasn't got a chance after his charges. It was quite an experience to act as a lawyer. I'm getting quite a bit of good experience in this man's army. Good night sweetheart. I'm looking forward to our honeymoon together.

February 7, 1945

Did I tell you I finally got a package from Anne and Will? Yes, I got a fruit cake. It was very good. I have received three packages from you. One manicure set, one box of chocolate and one box of crystallized fruits. One from Mama, one from Eleanor when I was in England and one from Ann.

When I get home, I never want to leave you again. You know I didn't want to leave you this time, but there's a regulation against taking wives to the wars. I wouldn't want you to see what I've seen anyway. I'm so glad this isn't happening to our country. We're losing some fine young men, but not many of our womenfolk are suffering as the people over here are. I realize that you and many other wives and also mothers are eating out their hearts, but the women over here are doing that and doing without things the women in the States could never stand to do without. You said in one of your letters, my sweet, that you could only buy one pair of shoes a year. Well honey, be thankful because I've seen things much worse. I don't feel sorry for the smokers in the States either. My sweet, the cigarettes are coming to the fighting front. That's where they are needed. I've been there. I'm not exactly at the front now, but I'm still close enough to appreciate plenty of cigarettes. I get plenty too, so don't worry about sending any to me.

Honey, where I am now things are humdrum in comparison to the previous few weeks. I was less than a mile from Stavelot when the Germans were there, and when St. Vith was retaken I was only four miles away. Your father will know of these places from the news.

February 8, 1945

I just got a letter from Mama after her return from Pensacola. From what she said, you made quite a hit with Luke II [Doyle's young nephew]. You are sweet and beautiful enough to make a hit with all the men. Mama said that Luke II went all over the house saying,

Doyle's sister Mary (Mrs. Luke Cain), Luke II and Luke I

"Juby, Juby, Juby." Honey, I go around all day thinking "Juby, Juby, Juby." I dream of you at night, and during the day I have you on my mind every minute. Tonight I will get a little bit more sleep. I have already censored the mail and it is only 2215. I'm clean for a change. I took a shower today, the first since the bath in Spa.

I wish Mama wouldn't take Mary away from Luke. It isn't right. Suppose Luke went to sea all at once? Luke would never get over it. Neither would Mama. You can tell her this if you like.

February 10, 1945

Today I got a replacement from Georgia. You should have seen the look on the kid's face when I told him I was from Georgia. He lives somewhere between Augusta and Savannah. He seems to be a good man. He's been over here and in Africa for 22 months. I'd like to see him get home for a while. Maybe I can arrange it for him.

Let me tell you about where I'm living now. My CP is in a farmhouse. My men and I (nine of us) have three rooms in the farmhouse. There is a mom, pop, grandmother, four daughters, a son and an unrelated girl who is here because her home was destroyed. The father is about 60 years old and the mother, 50. One daughter, Lucy, a brunette, reminds me so much of you. She's 21, and her sister Anna, a redhead, is 19. Their sisters Marie and Jeanine are also redheaded. Jeanine is 17, and the visiting girl is 12. The boy is 14. The family name is Jamar. The old man speaks very little French, mostly German. He was four years a prisoner of the Germans in the last war. They are such a nice family. I'm going to try to send you a picture of them for our scrapbook.

Jeanine is very intelligent. In four months she has learned English by herself, and it amazes me how well she does. She has been selected by a famous doctor here as a student. She's remarkable. She seems to be about 12 years old until I start talking to her, and then she seems to have the mind of a much older person. She painted the blue bird picture I sent to you. She said, "Your blue bird of happiness will fly to your Madame." Sweet gesture, wasn't it?

The old man killed his hog the other day. The mama brought us a large piece of the most beautiful pork roast I have ever seen. It was so very good. This month I got one bottle of Scotch, a bottle of cognac and a bottle of champagne for my monthly ration. I gave the Scotch and cognac to the boys here in the CP. Then I went next door where the old man and the old lady were sitting and asked if they would have a drink of champagne with me. The old man said, "Wee" [*Oui*, yes]. I didn't know if the old lady would drink, but she did. And there happened to be an older lady there, about 85. She had three drinks with us. Honey, I sat there and talked with my hands with them for about two hours. You should see me making motions to explain my words. It's really fun, and you'd laugh your head off.

IN HIS FOOTSTEPS

April 27, 2010: *Ken and I meet members of the Jamar household, Lucy, age 87, Marie, age 85, and "the boy" Godefroid, age 80, at the farmhouse in Ensival, Belgium. It is a welcomed occasion, and we are all delighted with each other. I can now relate to trying to communicate with hand gestures across a language barrier! We tour the home, now owned by another family. The "old man" died in 1950, having been kicked by a horse in the chest. His wife died in the mid-1960s. Jeanine had weak lungs and died in 1969. Anna is in ill health in a nursing home. The surviving three are vivacious. Our guide Michael and Godefroid's son Stephan communicated for months, making this meeting possible and memorable. It is indeed.*

From the base of the driveway, the house looks exactly like the picture Dad sent home but for a pole bearing electrical wires and a paved driveway, rather than dust and gravel. Everyone talks at once during our tour, with much picture-taking. We are shown the room where Dad slept and the room where he and his buddies played cards. The kitchen has a huge fireplace in front of which we stage group pictures of the surviving Jamar family members whom Dad knew and loved. This is a lively and energetic group, especially the elderly, whose exuberance grows by the minute. Godefroid remembers that Dad was kind and talked a lot. He says Ken looks like Dad. He tells us in those days they had 30 cows, and the women had to do the work.

It occurs to me that Dad's reference to Godefroid as "the boy" in his letters was because he probably had no idea how to spell his name. They all are thankful we came—it is a very big deal. There are two reporters present who take pictures of Ken and me and interview Michael since he speaks French and knows our mission. We will be sent the published article later. Stephan says that when Michael called him several months previously, he thought it was a joke. None of them ever thought Americans would come to see them. All over the country there is evidence of Belgian appreciation for Americans. Ken and I are deeply touched. [The news article follows this chapter.]

February 10, 1945, continued

The people here wear Dutch wooden shoes for work around the *ferme* or farm, and when they go inside they park their shoes outside, walking around in the house in heavy woolen socks. They treat us swell. The old lady bakes bread each week on Saturday and gives us bread. Here's how she makes it: she puts a great amount of wood (small twigs) into the oven and sets fire to it. The fire heats up stones lining the oven. After all is burned, she pulls the ashes out and puts the bread in the oven. The loaves are round and about five inches thick and twelve inches in diameter. Boy, is it good.

I wish you could be here; it's really very interesting. The girls work very hard on the farm. They shovel cow sh___, I mean manure, and push it away in a wheelbarrow just like a man. One of the girls, Lucy, has hands bigger than mine, and they are calloused just like a man's.

She is a cute girl however. Every one of them is very attractive. I'm going to send a picture of them soon. One of the boys has a roll of film he got from home, and he has already consented to take a picture of the family for me. I've enjoyed my stay with them as much as I possibly could without you. Every time I see this girl Lucy, a lump comes in my throat because she looks so much like you. I showed her the pictures of you, and she was amazed at the likeness herself.

By the way, sweet—speaking of pictures—today I had a chance to stop in town and have some of those six-poses for 10 francs, ten-minute snapshots made. I've tried to get some better photographs made for you but these are the best I could do. They aren't bad. I'm sending you four. One I gave to Vuoncino in exchange for the one he gave me, and I'm sending one to Mama. Put them in your scrapbook if you like. They were taken in Verviers, Belgium.

What Doyle looks like in February 1945

Honey, remember when I was describing my appearance in one of my letters? [letter of January 18, 1945] Well, one of these pictures is just what I intended my description to convey. You can see by the pictures that I'm not losing any weight and that I'm still the same in looks. You said in one of the letters you wondered if I had changed in looks, but you knew I hadn't changed otherwise. No honey, I haven't changed a bit. Yes I have too. I love you more than I did when you last saw me.

Tec. 5 Richard A. Vuoncino

I got two letters from you yesterday. Only took eight days to get here. You said you enjoyed my letter of January 13th because it was interesting. It was Kenny who was hit with me that day, and I don't know how he is doing because I haven't heard from him.

Honey, I wrote you about sending a cuckoo clock. I guess that that will have to do as your first anniversary wedding gift. The first is wood, isn't it? It is a lovely clock. I'll be sending other things from time to time. The clock should be there by April 8th. I hope you like it. Wish I could be there on our first anniversary, but I don't guess I can. It seems only yesterday that we were standing there in front of the preacher. Honey, I'll never, never forget that day. Not ever! I was so very happy and I've been happy ever since. Sad because I can't be with you, but so very happy to know that you are my wife. Well sweetheart, "Bon wee" [*bonne nuit,* good night] for now, and I'll see you again tomorrow. [*I just love Dad's phonetic spelling of the French and German words he picked up on his adventurous path.*]

February 13, 1945

My sweet, I'll explain the picture that is enclosed. It is a photo of the Belgian farmhouse where I now have my CP. The girl I wrote you about gave it to me to send home. I'm now writing in the room with an X on the window. The trees are apple trees. Jeanine wrote the verse on the back. She is quite a poet, it seems. You can tell that it rhymes. She translated it as best she could. She's a sweet kid and very interesting. She has told us so much about the German occupation. Things that she has related aren't very nice. But I can tell that she is a true Belgian and had to put up with the German occupation as best she could.

Dairy farm

Comme le flot sur que le vent chasse,
Et vient, a nos pieds mourir
Tout passé, tout lasse, tout casse
Tout excepte le "souvenir."

Jeanine Jamar, February 11, 1945

Like the windswept wave
That comes to our feet to die
Everything is gone, everything is weary, everything is broken—
Everything except memory.

[Translation, Gayle Wurst]

When we came to this house to live, I saw that I must do something and do it fast. Really cute young girls in the house and me with eight Yankee soldiers who are very susceptible to having things to do with cute girls. I laid down a gentleman's agreement with the guys that it would be perfectly OK with me if they found a girl somewhere nearby to go see, but it would be strictly hands off in the house where we are living. Compre? [*Comprenez*, understand?] Well, things were fine until I realized that the one I least expected to ever go for a girl fell head over heels for Lucy. He was always following her around like a lost puppy. She would come into our CP room to get water, and he would get right up close to her and just look at her. He would mumble such things as, "You talk to the other boys; why don't you talk to me?" She can't speak a word of English. Honey, he was going nuts. He would get up at five in the morning to go out in the cow stalls and shovel and haul cow sh___ so she wouldn't have to do

225

it. He did the same in the afternoon until about seven at night. I transferred him to battery because it was one-sided. After she saw him leave in the jeep, she asked Jeanine to ask me if he *parté* for good and when I said yes, she was so grateful. The guy scared her to death. I don't blame her because he certainly had a gleam in his eye. So you see my sweet, I have troubles other than those caused by the Germans. *[Following in my Dad's footsteps, I was able to meet Lucy and discovered she remembers this incident to this day. It is the anecdote that triggered her memory to pinpoint Dad's identity. The family had hosted various officers over several months.]*

Paul and I had a couple more cases to try today. They seem to keep us busy. If it isn't one thing it's another. Honey, the weather is so very beautiful now, just like springtime back in Georgia. The fields are so green and fresh, and the trees are beginning to bud. It's lovely for walking through the country. *[Ken and I were able to experience the early spring in Belgium and we agree with Dad.]* I'm very lonesome for you. I listen to music on the radio and wish so much that I could dance with you. I'm getting so damn tired of people I can't talk to. That's why I enjoy talking to this kid Jeanine who speaks a little bit of English.

Honey, it doesn't look as if I'll be away from you much longer does it? Unless they decide to send us to the South Pacific to help end it there. God, I sure hope they don't. By the way sweetheart, we made quite a name for ourselves when we were protecting Spa, and only D Battery was in on the praise. I'm rather proud of it myself. We have a good bunch of guys, I'm telling you. *[The following commendation is printed in the* Unit History, 639th BN.*]*

HEADQUARTERS

ELEVENTH ANTIAIRCRAFT ARTILLERY GROUP

APO 230, US ARMY

1 February 1945

SUBJECT: Commendation on Outstanding Performance of Duty

TO: Captain Alan V. Hooper, Commanding Officer,
          Battery "D," 639th AAA AW Battalion

THRU: Commanding Officer, 639th AAA AW Battalion

1. I wish to commend you and the officers and men of your
    battery for your outstanding work while attached to this
    Group during the Ardennes offensive from 21 December
    1944 to 24 January 1945.

2. During this period your battery operated as a separate bat-
    tery with the attendant complications of administration
    thrust upon you at a time when tactical defense was of prime
    consideration. Your defensive positions in the 30th Division
    area which were coordinated with the Division AT and DT
    defenses and with the defenses of the 143rd and 110th AAA
    Gun Battalions, were superior and worthy of the highest
    commendation. Your problem was made more difficult
    because your guns were widely scattered in order to give

effective cover for the principal anti-mechanized defenses of a sector which the Germans never cracked but your battery still was able to maintain communications and carry on.

3. You and your men were called on for dangerous and difficult tasks during this period, which were performed willingly, expeditiously and in a superb manner, and I take this opportunity to commend you on your ability as a leader and to extend to you and your men my heartiest congratulations on a job well done.

> s/Harry P. Newton
> t/HARRY P. NEWTON
> Colonel, C.A.C.
> Commanding

February 15, 1945

Honey, the life we're living now isn't at all like I expected it to be in war. The first eight weeks were worse than I expected, but now we get so tired of doing nothing that we almost go crazy. They say that war is made up of long periods of boredom and short periods of excitement. It's true.

February 16, 1945

Honey, I don't know what I'll be doing next. You know what I did last night after I wrote you? I helped a cow have a calf. I was sitting here in the CP shooting bull with the guys when all of a sudden the boy that lives here dashed in with a long line of French lingo and a lot of excitement. I finally got his point—I should come out and help him and his father. At first I thought the Germans were returning.

I went out and there was the cow with her calf just barely protruding from the vagina. Only the front hoofs and the nose were out. Mr. Jamar put a rope on one of the calf's legs and with a few motions told me and the kid to pull the rope while he held the cow's head. We pulled and pulled, and for a while I thought I would have to get one of our two-and-a-half ton trucks and throw out a winch to bring the calf into this world. But in about a minute we gave a big pull, and the calf's head came sliding through the opening. From there on it wasn't so hard. You see the head is the largest part because of the bone. It can't be compressed. When the calf was halfway into this world, the farmer grabbed a gunny sack and caught the calf as it came on out, preventing it from falling to the floor. The kid and I rushed the calf to the calf stall where the kid grabbed a handful of salt and slapped it into the calf's throat. With a few motions and a few words, he explained to me that the salt made the calf cough and it started him to breathe. It was very interesting.

Honey, during the entire operation I kept thinking of you and a child. Not that the cow reminded me of you, but that there was something being born into this world to be loved. Gosh, I wish we had a baby. I see babies every day. Mothers push them up here from the city nearby. They come to buy milk. When I look down the hill and see them coming, I always go out and play with them. They don't know what I'm saying, but I can almost always get them to smile at me. There was one today about five weeks old, and it smiled so very sweet at me. We're going to start a baby as soon as I can get back, aren't we honey? Sure we are. *[They did!]*

Forgive me for writing you about a cow, but I got a great kick out of bringing that little calf out into this world. It gave me a very strange feeling. The calf is doing very nicely today, thank you. Also the cow. Now I'm a godmother. Ha. A second calf was born last night but the cow didn't need any help, so I got to sleep through it.

So you see honey, when you get out into this world of ours anything may happen. I do have a lot to tell you when I get back. But for now I can tell you I love you and I'd like to have every one of those "jerks" together that have been talking to you and kidding you about untrue husbands (including sister Eleanor) and give them a talking to.

From Doyle's memoir:

While we were near Verviers, my platoon CP was in a farmhouse. I enjoyed my stay there. A 17-year-old girl spoke English fairly well. She and I talked often. We had three rooms in the house. The Army paid for their use. *[I asked the Jamar family about this and they said, "No, the only payment was in the currency of the day—cigarettes and candy." Godefroid ("the boy") said he collected cigarettes from the various soldiers and then sold them. He earned enough money to buy himself a bicycle. It is possible that the younger generation was not aware of a contract between the parents and the US Army.]*

We had just finished our baptism of fire in the Bulge. We distinguished ourselves in the eyes of our superiors and finished the operation with few casualties and little loss of equipment; that is, in comparison with the enemy's casualties and losses. We came out of the action with a proud attitude. We were in this town for regrouping and rebuilding for the next offensive drive. We had time to reflect; we were in a mood of remembering and enjoying certain things of the past and especially enjoying the present. Verviers was a great place and period of time for us. *[Lucy and Marie told Ken and me that many of the troops were still in shock when they first came. They were silent and had faraway looks in their eyes. This much-needed interim provided time for healing of the body and spirit.]*

The Unit History, 639th BN *refers to the Verviers assignment as the interim between two battles. Verviers was a target for the Luftwaffe due to its value as a communications and supply center. Though the last major air attack occurred on January 1, there remained the danger of "hit and run" attacks by individual planes seeking targets of opportunity. Reorganization for the upcoming push into Germany sent many divisions through Verviers:* "We had a fair share of kills during the Verviers mission and no target in the area was successfully bombed while we were there" *[Unit History, 639th BN]. Second lieutenants received overdue promotions.*

February 17, 1945

Today I walked around to all of my gun positions. I enjoyed it so very much. It is about six miles, but the weather is very nice now. I walked in my shirt sleeves. Such a lovely day.

I am enclosing another picture of the farmhouse and a picture of the four girls I wrote you about. Reading from left to right they are Anna, Jeanine, Marie, Lucy. Anna, I have heard, went out with German soldiers. Jeanine is the one studying to be a doctor. Marie has sewn shoulder straps on all of my GI shirts. Five of them. Some of the guys here said I had better do a lot of explaining if I sent the pictures of them, but I know I don't have to explain to you. I have made the vow to you and God to be faithful to you, and honey, I am. So for this reason I don't have to make an explanation. Three of the girls are very cute I'll admit. They have been very nice to me, and when they showed me the picture I wanted it to send to you, so they gave it to me. *[See images of the farmhouse in 1945 and 2010 in the color gallery.]*

L-R: Anna, Jeanine,
Marie, Lucy, 1944

Marie and Lucy,
2010

Notice the size of Lucy's hands.

L–R: Marie, Lucy, Godefroid, Stephan, Leigh and Ken at Ensival

L–R: Godefroid, Lucy and Marie enjoying photos from 1945

February 20, 1945

Honey, last night I was very busy preparing for a ceremony presenting Certificates of Merit for outstanding service to some of the men in the battalion. It was quite impressive. At the end I was made a first lieutenant. Yes, I was made the 16th of this month and I have just now gotten the orders on it. I have increased our allotment to $225.00. Just think honey, we'll get to save $100 more every four months.

February 22, 1945

I'll tell you the only interesting thing I've done lately. The people that I live with asked if I could obtain transportation for moving their cousin from one hospital to another here in town. She had been hit by artillery shrapnel in Stavelot. I took one of my trucks and went over to the hospital. The doctor was busy with an operation and couldn't give her a last-minute checkup, so I stuck around for about two hours. I talked with several of the doctors and some civilian patients that had been hurt by bombs, shells, etc. It's really a shame, honey, that innocent people are hurt and killed the way they are.

The girl was brought downstairs and transferred from the pushcart stretcher to our GI litter. The nurse wouldn't let me help, so I didn't insist. The damn nurse didn't know what she was doing. She reached down and grabbed the girl around the neck and someone else took her feet to lift her. When they did, the girl screamed to high heavens. Damn, I was sorry for her. It was all so unnecessary. Well, Jelle [the driver] and I carried her to the truck, put her in and drove slowly to the other hospital. When they brought out a pushcart stretcher, we didn't give the nurse a chance to hurt her this time. We slid our hands under her back and had a girl raise her legs as we raised her body, lifting her without allowing her body to bend. She was so very grateful for it. The pain had been so intense at the first hospital that she dreaded being transferred from one litter to the other. But we did the trick.

She told me a lieutenant staying in her house at Stavelot was killed by the same burst that injured her. She showed me the wound on her arm. It was almost healed, but it certainly was a nasty look-ing scar. She also was hit on the calf and on the buttocks. She was too bashful to show me those wounds.

Tomorrow morning a Red Cross club-mobile is coming to my CP to bring doughnuts and coffee to the boys in the gun crews. An American girl will bring them. The guys will enjoy having her. She will be the first American girl that they have seen since we left England. No, I take it back. Some of them did get to see Marlene Dietrich on the stage.

L–R: Jeanine Jamar, Leona DuPont

From Doyle's memoir: In 1947 I received a call from my mother. She said, "Doyle, there is a mail here for you from Belgium." I did not know who would be writing me from Belgium. I asked if there was a return address. She said, "Jeanine Jamar." The letter was really from the girl I had helped transfer to another hospital. She and Jeanine had composed the letter to thank me for being so gentle that day. She sent a photograph of her and Jeanine. These are the things that soften the harshness and horror of war.

Dear Mr. Doyle,

Allow me to thank you for all you have done for me. Do you remember the little wounded girl you have carried with so much care during February 1945? I am so happy to be able to write to you at last and thank you most heartily. You have not forgotten either, I hope, little Jeanine Jamar. We both send you our most friendly compliments. I hope you are in good health and very happy to be again together with Mrs. Whittenburg. When I see Lucy Jamar, I try to picture her to myself.

I could never forget the dear big brother who was so good for the little wounded unknown girl from Stavelot. Now I am much better. I remained seven and a half months in hospitals. The doctors thought I would never more be able to walk. It is a real wonder. I am in a convent waiting to be quite recovered, for I have no family anymore.

I enclose a few photos from Stavelot after the Von Rundstedt Offensive. I hope you will enjoy them. You will see again a corner of our dear little country which you have helped liberating.

If Mrs. Whittenburg allows it, I should very happy to hear from you. We send her, Jeanine and I, our kindest regards. To you, Mr. Doyle, we express our deep gratitude and send our most sisterly greetings.

Leona DuPont

Stavelot after the Von Rundstedt Offensive, 1945

A festival in remembrance of US soldiers, August 1945

Dad decided it would be inappropriate to correspond with these girls, fearing jealousy on my mother's part. I read their letter over and over again through my childhood and adolescence. The letter has a place of honor in the wartime scrapbooks, as do the pictures they sent. Evidently the episode was as intently noted and remembered by the girls as it was by Dad. He told and retold all the stories of his interim in the farmhouse at Verviers. Mom never objected.

February 27, 1945

There is nothing new happening. I just visit the boys at the guns and lately I have been walking my rounds just to help pass the time. At night we shoot the bull and maybe play a little poker. I played a couple of rubbers of bridge with Bruce, Jensen and Cobb tonight. I enjoyed it, but was very sleepy. The Battery CP is too hot. Oh yes honey, I think I wrote you about our aid man. I put in for the Bronze Star and the Purple Heart for him. They came through the other day. I got a bigger thrill out of it than he did. It made me feel so good. [See letter of January 13, 1945.] You asked me what the star is for. It's for the campaign of Germany. We might get another for the Battle of the Bulge. It takes the War Department several months to decide whether an engagement warrants a star or not.

The Battery D History, 639th BN *reports that Tec. 5 Vuoncino was awarded the Bronze Star* "for exceptionally meritorious conduct in the performance of outstanding service" *and* "Second Lieutenant Doyle K. Whittenburg was promoted to First Lieutenant and First Sergeant Max A. Shepp was commissioned Second Lieutenant—the first battlefield commission to be awarded to our Battalion."

March 1, 1945

Cute isn't it? I'm writing you this letter on the stationery that Battalion Headquarters is having printed for us. These are sample sheets and I spilled coffee on this sheet. I'm sorry. You might like to cut out the two rabbits and use them in our scrapbooks. The rabbit looks as "cocky" as the men did after their wonderful showing in the Battle of the Bulge.

March 3, 1945

My sweet, this will be a very short letter. ... I am enclosing a negative of a picture of me made in Verviers, Belgium. I didn't get to see the picture, but the negative seems to be OK. It was taken on the edge of Ensival, a suburb of Verviers.

From Doyle's memoir:

When we received the march order to leave Verviers, one gun in my platoon was on a very steep hillside. When it was placed there, the ground was frozen solid. When spring came upon us, the earth thawed, leaving an impossible situation. Impossible to everybody

New 1st Lieutenant

but the Army. My men cut trees, made A-frames, figured out how to use the winch cables on the trucks, a pulley, some rope and a lot of ingenuity. They picked the gun completely out of the mud, swung it all the way up the hill and hooked it to a truck ready to roll. We could have done the same thing during the Bulge but did not have time. We had to fight to save our necks.

Before I left Verviers, I went by the medical clearing station where recovered wounded were held until the unit they left came in and claimed them. I went by to see if anyone was there from our battalion. As I walked in the door, Frank Kenny ran to me. He was glad to see me. He had been there so long they were about to send him to another unit. We had moved many times in the last few weeks, and army paper had not caught up with us. I signed him out and took him with us to our new location.

239

VERVIERS ENSIVAL

Sur les traces de son père

Leigh Callan refait le périple de son papa durant la guerre. ■ GDS

La vie réserve bien des surprises... Ce mardi, Godefroid Jamar, habitant de Pepinster, recevait la visite d'une Américaine, Leigh Callan. Une visite par comme les autres...

"En janvier 1945, nous avions abrité durant trois semaines un lieutenant américain, Ken Whittenburg", se remémore Godefroid Jamar, aujourd'hui âgé de 80 ans. *"Nous rencontrons à présent sa fille! Cela me fait presque pleurer."*

Comment la jeune femme a-t-elle retrouvé la trace des anciens amis de son père? *"A la mort de son père, il y a 4 ans, Leigh Callan a découvert un coffre contenant 430 lettres. Des lettres que son père envoyait à la mère de Leigh durant la guerre afin de lui donner des nouvelles. Après avoir lu ces lettres, la jeune femme a décidé de reproduire exactement le chemin qu'avait parcouru son père. Ce qui l'a amené ici."*

Ici, c'est à la Houckaye rouge à Ensival. En effet, c'est là qu'habitaient Godefroid Jamar et ses quatre sœurs en 1945. Pour retrouver cette maison, Leigh Callan a fait appel à Michel Baert, guide de la Bataille des Ardennes. *"C'est très émouvant ce genre de périple"*, souligne celui-ci, également présent aux retrouvailles. *"J'ai tout de suite accepté de l'aider. Mais je n'avais qu'une photo ancienne et un lieu: Ensival. Cela n'a pas été facile, mais on y est arrivé."*

Ce mardi, c'est avec beaucoup d'émotion que Leigh Callan serrait la main de Godefroid Jamar. L'Américaine, effectuant son périple avec son frère, logeait encore quelques jours à Malmedy avant de reprendre la route et de terminer le parcours de son père. «

A.H.

News story from *La Meuse*, April 27, 2010, Ensival

In Her Father's Footsteps

Leigh Callan retraces her father's World War II journey

Life is full of surprises. This Tuesday Godefroid Jamar, who lives in Pepinster, received a visit from an American woman, Leigh Callan. A visit like none other...

"In January 1945, we welcomed an American lieutenant during three weeks, Ken Whittenburg," reminisces Godefroid Jamar, now aged 80. "Now we meet his daughter! It nearly makes me cry." *[Ken is Leigh's brother who also visited. The American lieutenant was their father, Doyle Whittenburg.]*

How did the daughter find her father's long-ago hosts? "At her father's death, four years ago, Leigh Callan discovered a box containing 430 letters that her father had sent her mother during the war. After reading them, she decided to retrace her father's exact itinerary. This brought her here." *[Leigh's mother gave 411 letters to her.]*

"Here" is the "Houckaye rouge," the house in Ensival where Godefroid Jamar and his four sisters lived in 1945. To find the location, Leigh Callan called upon the services of Michael Baert, a guide to the Battle of the Bulge, who was also present at the meeting. "This type of trip is very emotional," said Mr. Baert. "When she asked me to help her, I accepted immediately. But I only had an old picture and a location: Ensival. It was not easy, but we succeeded."

Last Tuesday, it was with great emotion that Leigh Callan shook Godefroid Jamar's hand. She and her brother, with whom she is traveling, would remain a few more days in Malmedy before taking to the road to finish retracing her father's wartime path.

A. H.

[Translation, Gayle Wurst]

Chapter 19

In Germany
The Roer Pocket

March 4, 1945

Dearest Juby,

Tonight I'm not angry with anyone. I have just today been through Aachen and Duren, Germany, and honey, if that's what war does to cities, I'm more than glad to be away from you a while to prevent it from happening to us in the States. I never dreamed that a town could be beaten so badly. You can imagine, maybe, a town the size of Atlanta leveled to nothing but a pile of bricks and debris. The two towns I saw today were just that. Leveled. There were no civilians whatsoever in the cities. It did me good to see it because I don't like Germany or Germans. I hope all their towns are torn up like these two because if they are, it will take them 50 years to build them back. Now honey, you are probably worrying about me being in Germany. Don't. We are still 12 to 14 miles from danger.

Honey, I guess you already know we were in Verviers, Belgium. I am allowed to tell it now in my letters. You know, it's surprising how efficient the Army works once it moves into battle. Paperwork and red tape are done away with, and everyone gets down to business.

TAKING DUREN

It's true!

Concussion turned this statue of Bismarck around so the man who built an earlier German empire faces away from ruins of Duren, levelled by First Army advance. Now he's a Signal Corps phone pole.

This is about the best Building in Duren. I've told you before that it is about the size of Allant a.

This might be my jeep there I know!

Annotated page from *Yank* (issue and date unknown)

Duren, taken from the Germans only a week ago, has clean streets thanks to our engineers. However, all the buildings are just piles of brick. It's amazing how quick they cleaned up the streets.

Well sweet, I have a hard day tomorrow, so I'll stop. Just know that what I saw today makes me love you more than ever. Frankly, I'm glad I can be here fighting for you and our country. Honey, I wouldn't have it happen over there for anything. Darling I love you and want to be with you.   Yours forever, Doyle

IN HIS FOOTSTEPS

April 30, 2010: Ken and I visit Aachen and tour the cathedral. It is the only building to survive the bombing with relatively minor damage. We are told that a bomb hit it but did not detonate. We are shown the comparison between the old surviving stained glass and the panels in the dome that had to be replaced.

March 8, 1945 Germany

Honey, this will be short and sweet—just a note to tell you how much I love you. I'm sorry I haven't sent you anything since the bracelet and clock. You see, here in Germany we can't buy anything and we aren't allowed to send home things we find. There are lovely things all over too. I haven't received any mail in days now. I hope I get my birthday present soon. We were moving on my birthday [March 5]. Honey, I must go to work now. Please don't worry because I'm in Germany. I'm still way behind the lines.

The Battery D History, 639th BN indicates a mission to protect supply routes and bridges on the Roer River. Lt. Whittenburg's position was Nideggen, Germany, which is described as a ghost town east of the Roer on a high mountain overlooking the river. The place was in ruins following bombing in advance of the First Army movement, with few options for a CP site: "Lt. Whittenburg and Tec. 5 Arthur N. Jelle once again came across with the best spot that could be had. It had three walls and a roof, but Pfc. James

245

F. Decker, our Platoon radio operator, later built a fourth wall and did a very good job indeed" *[Battery D History, 639th BN].*

It took me a while to understand this: When Doyle went on reconnaissance, he was doing advance preparation for a move to another sector. He and his jeep driver Jelle would survey the new area for buildings that could be used for headquarters and billeting. Later and deeper into Germany, he describes forcing people out of their homes, aided by Pfc. William Saul, a Jewish American soldier who gave the commands in Yiddish. To quote Doyle's newfound French phrase, "C'est la guerre."

March 10, 1945

Hi ya, kid. Here I am again after two days of not talking to you. You should know by now that I write when I can. I was busy moving my platoon into Germany. Yes, we are here in [Nideggen] Germany. I wrote you once from Duren and I was in Aachen. We are still west of Duren a good distance. I can't say where but there's no danger. When I was in Duren, Churchill and Eisenhower were there. I didn't get to see them, but I saw the C-47 they flew up in.

The picture from Rouen, France, I did recognize. Honey, that cathedral is no longer like that. It has been bombed and shelled almost beyond recognition, as have many buildings and cities in France. In Germany, all the towns are ruined. I'm glad because it will take Germany years to build back.

I received a letter from your father. Tell him that German-made pistols have been very hard to get. Maybe I can get him one soon. Even if I do though, I can't send it. I will have to bring it home. I can mail a German rifle, but I can't mail a pistol. I am going to enclose some pins that I picked up along the road. I may send you other things too.

Honey, I'm enclosing a letter you sent me. I want you to read it over and I'm sure you will realize just how I felt getting such a letter after moving into Germany. I'm sorry I sent the picture of the Belgian girls, and I am sorry I told you of the Spa bath incident and about the sewing I had done. I should have realized that you, being a woman, would let your imagination run away with you. Honey, if you will forgive me this time, believe me, I won't write of these simple contacts with other females. You said you wanted me to write you everything and up to now I have, but I had better stop because it seems to bother you a great deal. I have told you that you are the only one now and forever, and I mean it sweet. But honey, because I love you so much I want you to know of the things I do. You asked me once never to keep things from you and I haven't. I got two other letters from you yesterday. They were so sweet and when I got the one I'm sending back to you, it being the latest one, I felt rather bad. But honey, I know how you feel.

At this time Juby decided to quit sharing her letters with the family. Eleanor was particularly relentless in pointing out the opportunities for infidelity and was certain that every soldier, including her brother, participated. Juby was young and naïve (her word) and doubt easily germinated; thus, there was frequent need for assurance such as shown in this letter.

Just an explanation of the badge I'm enclosing. Thought you might be interested. If you remember back in 1939, I believe, Hitler asked all healthy women to start having babies for their Führer. Well, this badge was given to the girls when they had their first baby. It is interesting don't you think? Thought maybe you would like to have it. Wish I could give you a badge to wear for having my first baby. *[See image of Nazi pins in the color gallery. The badge described here is in the center of the picture.]*

Bruce's CP personnel on the Roer

Lutz, McLaverty, Marollo [a professional dancer], Shepp, Kelly, Patterson, Arsenault and Scopoletti

Chapter 20

The Rhine at Remagen
The Ludendorff Bridge

March 13, 1945

Dearest Juby,

Forgive me, my sweet, for missing last night and the night before, but when I tell you all about it you'll understand. I have just finished moving my platoon from the Roer up to the Rhine. Yes'm, from where I am now, I can see several of the castles on the Rhine. Never did I expect to see them. They are beautiful, I must say. I am very safe here. At my last position I was in Nideggen, Germany, on the Roer. I'm sending the pictures tonight. While I was on reconnaissance I had a little time, so I went into Bonn, which I heard had been taken. Well it had, but just a few hours before I came into the city. There were a few snipers around, but I didn't run into any danger. That's the closest I've been to Germans lately, other than prisoners. All the houses here have white flags sticking out the windows. There are very few civilians around. We can't and don't trust any of them. Maybe they're good, maybe bad. We haven't got time to bother with finding out, so to us they are all bad. That's the way it must be.

You know our main purpose is to protect bridges, so you and your father should know just about where I am since there is only one bridge we've taken. Wish I could be with you.

Love you kid, Doyle

Postcard of Burg Nideggen on the Roer

March 14, 1945

There isn't much news I can write about here. I'm sure you have read the news of this sector by now. Things are good and there's no danger. I wrote you that I was in Aachen. I have three postcards I got there. I saw the places, but they don't look like this now. It's all leveled. If you'll notice, it's called Bad Aachen. Bad in German means clean. It's clean now, clean to the ground.

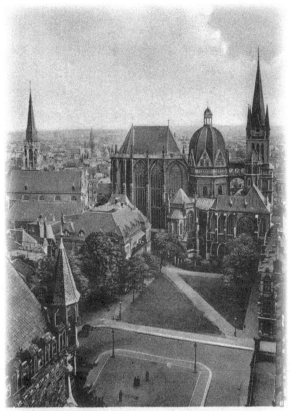

Bad Aachen. Dom und Katschhof.

Postcard of Aachen before bombs destroyed the city

March 18, 1945

"Is You Is or Is You Ain't My Baby" is on the radio now. You're my baby. Yes you are. Sure wish that I wuz with my baby tonight. There isn't much that I can tell you about here except one thing you can tell your father. I had a chance to look over the remains of a V-2 bomb. He's read about them I know. Honey, I'm seeing a great many spectacular things over here that I'm going to enjoy telling you about when I come home. There are some things that I can't tell just yet. Oh yes, I told you that I got one kid the Bronze Star. Well, now I have requested an award for two more of my boys. I hope they get it. They certainly deserve it.

The Battery D History, 639th BN *documents that from March 12 to March 18, 1945, the 2nd Platoon guns were on the right side of the Ludendorff Bridge facing interior Germany:* "This particular sector of ground was receiving a merciless pounding by 88s and the platoon communication lines were being cut to pieces." *Pfc. William Saul and Pfc. Louis Benedetti worked continuously day and night,* "... demonstrating unsurpassed courage and devotion to duty, keeping the communication lines in perfect working order" *[Battery D History, 639th BN]. The men were awarded the Certificate of Merit.*

"On 18 March 1945 [the day after the bridge collapsed] we moved across the Rhine River to Unkel, Germany, where our gun sections took up AA positions protecting the Pontoon Bridge across the Rhine" *[Battery D History, 639th BN]. See the letter of March 29, 1945, for an eye witness account of the bridge collapse.*

March 20, 1945

In Germany I have seen many nice things that I would just love to send you, but honey, I just can't. It's called looting. You won't have to be jealous anymore now that I'm in Germany. We aren't allowed to fraternize with the German people. If we are even caught talking with one of them, we are immediately fined $65.00 and court-martialed. So there's no worry.

March 24, 1945

I got three letters from you last night after I wrote you. Honey, they are so sweet. Your letters are all that keep me going. I'm still on the Rhine and it's really beautiful here. We took this sector so fast that there wasn't much damage to property. The weather here is wonderful. The sun shines all day, the trees are budding and the birds are singing. It's hard to believe that the enemy is just a short distance away. There's a peach tree in bloom just here at the end of the porch. It reminds me of Georgia and you. There are several fig bushes around the house that are budding. Just got news that the Ninth and Third Armies have crossed the Rhine. Maybe if all three armies start pushing, the war will be over soon. I want to come home to you.

I played a game of ball today and did quite well for my first game of the season. I played first base and made 18 put-outs, was in on two double plays and hit 3 for 4. Quite good, eh?

I just poured you a glass of captured wine, my sweet, and one for me. I drank mine after giving a toast to my quick return. I then smashed the crystal wine goblet. Your glass of wine is here before me now. I see your smiling face in the glass. As I drop my eyes to the paper here, your reflection fades away; as I look back at the goblet, your face emerges from the bubbles. I'll close my eyes and drink to you and to our being together soon. While I drink I will feel you near me. While my eyes are closed, I will smash the goblet against the cement railing around the porch. Honey, I might sound a bit over-romantic but I'm not. I'm just writing down my thoughts. Darling, I love you.

March 26, 1945 [in Unkel]

Honey, we found a beer brewery today, and it was full of good German beer. You should have seen the guys here in the CP. They took the hoses that came from the vats and had a beer battle with them. It reminded me of my younger days when I got into water battles with the kids in the neighborhood. There was a vat of sweet beer, a vat of not so sweet, and a vat of good bitter beer so we decided to fill up a barrel for each gun crew and take it out. You wouldn't think there was a war going on, would you?

My CP is about 1000 yards from the Rhine, and honey, from here you can see for miles and miles up and down the river. To the northwest you can see the seven mountains of the Rhineland. On them are the castles you've read about. It's most beautiful, honey. The towns along the Rhine Valley are very luxurious, but those in the mountains on either side are very poor. I think the towns directly on the Rhine must have been resort towns. There are some beautiful things in these towns that I would just love to send you, but we aren't allowed to loot souvenirs.

The next time you see Mama, ask her to find out in a tactful way what my cousin Ruth sent me. It was a #2 can of what I think was chicken broth. The boys in the CP and I had the best time trying to figure out what it was. The suggestions I got during the evening went from boot preservative to a new type of gun oil. I finally decided to heat it up and it wasn't bad when you tasted it, so I volunteered to drink a cup of it. The guy who told me it was shoe grease tried some of it on his shoes and he said it worked wonders. Please don't let Ruth know that I'm making so much fun of her gift. I did appreciate it a lot. It was nice to know that she thought of me. We had a lot of fun trying to figure out just what it was.

The Germans are admitting defeat now. They are running on all fronts. We'll keep them on the run too. Just you wait and see. Honey, I ran about 15 people out of a house yesterday and took the house for my CP. You didn't think I could do that, did you? Well honey, I'll tell you just how I've learned to do it. I have come to hate Germany and Germans to a point that nothing bothers me as far as they are concerned. I thought I hated them before I came over, but I really didn't until I saw some of the atrocious things they have done. They are no good until they are subdued. Then maybe I can sympathize with a few of them. They killed Jeep Hardin, James Goss and many others I know. So I don't worry about them. I haven't changed. I'm still just the same Doyle and the same loving husband as when I left you, but now I have hate for the Germans in me. They caused me to have to leave you for a while, and since I'm here, I'm doing my best to make them think twice before they start another war that will involve our sons and daughters. The civilians left here (most of them follow their armies) really hate us. They can be on the streets only two hours per day. At night we always travel in pairs. It's safer that way.

I have a Jewish boy in platoon headquarters that speaks Yiddish, which is almost the same as German. He does all my dirty work for me, like telling them to get the hell out of a house. I have a snapshot of him. His name is William Saul, and he's my switchboard operator and lineman. Pretty good kid. Plays the piano really well. When I'm around he plays "Georgia on My Mind" just to kid me. He also plays "Someday We'll Meet Again" at my request.

William Saul

I just sent Louis Benedetti to Paris for three days of rest. He will probably send you a card from there. He's a great kid.

I am still operating alone and doing quite well at it, but if I didn't have such a good bunch of guys I couldn't do it. They get all the credit. They really do a job for me. Tell your pop that we've gotten our share of German planes. I'm even surprised myself. Also at Honsfeld we got our share of V-1s. Then came the German counteroffensive. Oooooooo. It's a dream now. A bad one. The bastards are paying for it though.

March 27, 1945

Honey, I've got us a good German camera with a tripod and all. I'm sure it was looted, but I bought it from a kid so my conscience is clear. The only thing missing is a sight, but any camera company or camera shop can put one on for us. It has ten different shutter speeds and any lens adjustment that you want. It takes a large size film. We'll have so much fun taking pictures with it.

March 29, 1945

Honey, I think I wrote you about it, but maybe not. The bridge at Remagen was not destroyed as you seem to think. It did go down, but a long time after it had served its purpose. Our tanks went across and held off the enemy long enough for us to put pontoon bridges all up and down the river. Just before the first tanks went across, there was a small demolition charge set off that weakened the bridge so a train couldn't go across. After we had ensured the bridgehead crossing by creating pontoon bridges, the engineers started to work repairing the bridge for train passage. During the time the engineers were working, the Germans made every attempt to knock it out. They tried crash-diving planes on the bridge. They sent out high-altitude bombers. They tried to sneak in through the valleys. They tried to float demolition down the river. They sent swimmers out from 15 miles upriver in an attempt to knock it out, but they couldn't get in—my boys, mind you. I'm proud of them. We knocked planes out of the skies and shot to explode demolitions floating on the river.

On the 17th of March, the engineers were working hard to reinforce the weak point on the bridge, and in so doing probably weakened a girder with a cutting torch and she came down. Honey, I was standing not over 200 yards from the bridge and I saw every bit of it go from the time that it first cracked. It went down in about three seconds—a 300-yard span. It went down so very easy, just like a ribbon in the breeze. It was sickening to see it go. The worst part was that some 40 soldiers went down with it. I was standing in one of my gun pits. I immediately called Battery Headquarters and told them of the catastrophe and to send all available ambulances. Then I made a mad rush down the riverbank to see what I could do about getting some of the men off the span. Honey, it was rough. Some of the poor guys were pinned in the wreckage with broken backs, legs and arms. I stayed around doing the best I could until the medics came, and I left it with them. But please honey, don't think that the enemy destroyed it. The papers mess some of the news up sometimes. The bridge served its purpose. Germany is being badly beaten now and that's what we want.

Night before last we made a forced march from Remagen to some 40 to 45 miles east of the Rhine. Yes, I've been over the Rhine since March 18th, but recently the army I'm with started a drive so we were sent up with them. We went up and just kept going; then all at once our mission changed and we were sent back. Now we are more or less in a rest mission some 12 to 14 miles to the west of the Rhine [in Rheinbach guarding a weapons depot]. It is quite a relief.

We liberated a large group of slave laborers on the way over, and honey, it was amazing. They were so happy (both men and women). We didn't have time to stop in some towns because we wanted the enemy to keep on the run. All the houses had white sheets hanging out the windows. In the parks and on the edge of town were sheets on the ground showing the Air Corps that the town had surrendered. We passed up many prisoners because we didn't have time to fool with them. They were trying to give themselves up. The German armies seem to be destroyed. The

Russians and Polish and Czechoslovakians and Italians who were in the slave labor groups were taking anything they wanted from the Germans. It was funny. One Russian took a German's horse and when the German kicked about it, the Russian punched his nose. Did I laugh!

We were up only one night and one day before we came back across the Rhine to where we are now. On the way back, we traveled 12 or 14 miles on the Autobahn Highway and honey, it was beautiful. The moon was full, making it as bright as day. I closed my eyes and imagined you sitting beside me. Once or twice I even started to put my arms around you and pull you close to me. Then I would awake to reality. Darling, I love you and want you. I'll write again tomorrow.

"On the 17th of March, the old bridge at Remagen, which had been closed for repairs since the 12th of March, collapsed. Several soldiers from the 639th AW Battalion jumped into the river and rescued several engineers who had been reinforcing the structure when it fell into the river. But by then, two pontoon bridges on either side were accommodating all the traffic over the river." (Col. E. Paul Semmens, "The Hammer of Hell: The Coming of Age of Antiaircraft Artillery in WWII," *Air Defense Artillery Magazine* [ADA], 2010. Web. 21 Oct. 2014. Hereafter cited as Semmens, "Hammer of Hell.")

IN HIS FOOTSTEPS

April 30–May 3, 2010: *Ken and I explore the castle ruins of Burg Nideggen, stay overnight in Rheinbach, visit German forest battlegrounds, ride on the autobahns, visit a German cemetery, go through the cathedrals at Aachen and Erfurt, tour the excellent Peace Museum in the remaining towers of the Ludendorff bridge at Remagen, overlook the Rhine Valley from Unkel and Erpel (counting the castles we can see) and delight in the springtime blooms of fields upon fields of crops, enjoying their fragrance. We observe tall smokestacks and graceful wind generators in heavy industrial areas of Germany. We spend nights in Giessen and Kassel. We cross the Roer, the Rhine and the Elbe. We pass through the sad town of Weimer, tour the concentration camp that blemishes it and end up in Pölzig, where Dad was when the war ended. In all, we put 2000 miles on our rental car over a 12-day period in Belgium and Germany. We learn more about war, Dad and ourselves than we ever dreamt we would. And we feel him by our side.*

Second Platoon gun crew defending the Ludendorff Bridge
before its collapse

Doyle or another soldier in his battery took this and other original photographs he sent to Juby for their scrapbook. The battery history identifies the location of Battery D's 2nd Platoon as "100 to 300 yards on the right side of the Ludendorff Bridge as you faced interior Germany." *Ken and I were able to stand at this very spot and imagine the bridge in place.*

Western approach

M-16 half-track and crew

"The Luftwaffe launched air strikes that had an excellent chance to destroy the bridge, isolating the American units on the far shore and denying the Allies the huge psychological prize the bridge's retention represented. Instead the First Army Antiaircraft Artillery quickly established a solid defense and defeated the Luftwaffe. The AAA victory at Remagen was cemented in the first 72 hours. It was ... a victory for combat soldiers who rid themselves, once and for all of the 'Red Comforter Corps' label. The actions of the III Corps' 16th AAA Group and the AAA battalions assigned to it represented the culmination of a series of doctrinal, organizational and attitudinal changes that had been emerging since North Africa. ... Because it was the capstone event that marked the culmination of the many efforts which had been ongoing since the end of World War I, ... the Remagen Bridge ranks as one of the greatest Antiaircraft Artillery battles in American history" (Semmens, "The Hammer of Hell").

From Doyle's memoir [Titles in italics indicate the corresponding sections in the *Unit History, 639th BN.*]:

Through Herve-Aachen and Duren: The march order from Verviers came on my 28th birthday, March 5. Our living conditions during this move were reduced to tents. It was something awful to see, especially Duren. It was in this town that a large statue of Bismarck had been jarred 180 degrees by bombs and shells.

Defending and crossing the bridgehead at Remagen: The Germans were constantly firing 88s and larger caliber shells at the bridge. In the meantime, the engineers were extending pontoon bridges across the river at different points up and down the river. I saw the results of damage from two V-2 bombs. The Germans used JU 87s and the new bat-shaped 252 jets. I saw both models in action, including ME 109s. There was so much ack-ack in the area that planes were forced to fly too high to be effective. British soldiers brought in anchored balloons to prevent low-flying planes from reaching their targets. Antipersonnel bombs and destruction bombs were falling everywhere but caused very little damage. They could be seen dropping from the sky.

The defense of the bridge and final collapse: Our engineers were on the bridge attempting to repair the damage when the bridge fell. I saw a first aid medic cut a man's leg off at the knee with a pair of gauze scissors in ten minutes. Speed was necessary because the span that caught his leg was slowly settling down the bridge parapet. Two minutes after the medic and the legless soldier were lifted onto the parapet, the span slid into the river. I led the first AA platoon across the bridge to the east bank of the Rhine. We were presented one of the flags that had been raised on the ramparts of the Ludendorff Bridge.

In German territory: During the next move, a mad dash across Germany to Leipzig, we accumulated prisoners of war. Most of them were willing to be captured. They had no organization, and most of them were hungry and very tired. The winter was about over so they were no longer cold.

IN HIS FOOTSTEPS

May 1, 2010: *We leave Hotel Dorn in Rheinbach this morning for travel to Remagen. On the way we notice fields all around, solid with yellow blossoms. They are fields of rapeseed plants from which oil is made. Also impressive are acres and acres of apple trees, their limbs adorned with delicately beautiful blossoms swaying in a gentle breeze and reminding us of peach orchards in south Georgia. We pass through wine country and more fir forests. Later we break through to a dense hardwood forest, the canopy so thick that road signs remind us to turn on headlights. Yes, we are indeed in interior Germany today.*

Reaching the Rhine at Remagen, we easily recognize exactly where we are relative to Dad's photographs. The remaining towers of the Ludendorff Bridge on the west side of the Rhine have been converted to a Peace Museum, giving us the history of the bridge from its conception, construction and service to its capture and final collapse during WWII. The bridge was built during WWI as a railroad bridge for moving troops and equipment. In March of 1945, retreating German troops failed to destroy it; therefore, it was the only remaining bridge across the Rhine when American soldiers of the First Army's 9th Armored Division advanced, taking control on March 7. It remained standing long enough for troops and equipment to cross into central Germany and for pontoon bridges to be completed. For ten days, Germans attempted to destroy the bridge by any means possible. All available antiaircraft units were summoned to defend it and did. But on March 17, while engineers were attempting to repair it for rail use, the bridge collapsed, wounding many and killing 28 engineers.

Outside the museum are plaques honoring specific units involved in the capture and defense of the bridge. Among them is a tarnished plaque, appearing much older than the others. On it are the following words in German and in English:

"Built for war, destroyed in war, the towers shall always remind
Here fought soldiers of two great nations,
here died heroes from near and far."

On the topmost floor of the western tower, in an area which had housed German troops while they defended the bridge, we watch a 30-minute video that intersperses wartime film with accounts by veterans of both sides. The lead-up to March 17, 1945, is explained from each viewpoint. For the first time, I see photos and film of the immediate aftermath of the bridge's collapse and evacuation of the wounded. For a split second I see a man in a helmet at one corner of a stretcher that reminds me of Dad.

Medics at the collapsed Ludendorff Bridge at
Remagen (Bettman/Corbis Images)

After the collapse, 1945
(Corbis Images)

The towers that remind, 2010

Chapter 20: The Rhine at Remagen; The Ludendorff Bridge

In another room of the Peace Museum is a meditation area with simple square blocks as seats. On the surrounding walls are many individual blocks, geographically positioned, which name all of the wars, conflicts and skirmishes worldwide that have occurred and are still occurring since WWII. There are more than 200 since 1945, and the number continues to grow.

Upon a high rocky cliff across the river is a huge cross flanked by German flags. This memorial, on the east side of the Rhine, is directly above the opposite pair of towers. Since there is no longer a bridge across the Rhine here, we must drive an hour to Bonn in order to cross. (The Ludendorff was never replaced.) I remember Dad had written about going to Bonn just after it was taken and snipers were still about. After crossing, we drive along the east side of the Rhine to Unkel, a town diagonally across from Remagen. We ask about a brewery there, but can't find anyone who knows about it. However, a winery is touted as being old and famous, but now functions only on a limited basis and none of the wine is exported. We wish we had time and access to sample this special local product and find the winery, because this may have been the site of Dad's story about finding a brewery and showering in beer. However, there are many other wonderful things to find and enjoy.

In our encounters with Germans, the tone is businesslike but lacking in curiosity. People are friendly and helpful, but not enthusiastically welcoming like the Belgians. We do not find memorials, directional signs to battle sites or museums on every corner. Evidently the people and the government have made a concerted effort to move forward by refusing to memorialize a most repulsive part of Germany's past. A German friend tells me that the government has made it illegal to collect, display or sell Nazi memorabilia. The chief clientele for such material would be the neo-Nazi organizations of the world—not to be encouraged.

March 30, 1945 in Rheinbach

Tonight I'm writing to you of things that I dream about throughout the day and night. ... Day before yesterday I had other things on my mind. It was war. Of course I haven't forgotten about the war, but today it seems so remote. The night before last we made the road march that moved us well back from the front. The kids drove 62 miles blackout [using no headlights]. Honey we have a great bunch. They know the tricks of this game called war. They really learned fast. They had to. For almost three years, they were told to dig in when they moved into position. Well, this is something that could have been learned in five minutes because 88-millimeter shells are fast teachers. They whistle a warning sometimes, but when they come in close they travel faster than sound and you're hit before the sound reaches you. Only one man has been hit with shrapnel, and he wasn't hurt bad. From the looks of things, we won't have any more casualties because I really and truly think that the German armies have collapsed. We'll know in the next few days.

Honey, I'm sorry about one thing. Remember I said I was going to send home a stein and a beer mug set? Well the stein will be on its way tomorrow, but the beer mug set I had to leave because we had to leave for the front too fast. It disappointed me more than it does you because I wanted it for us so much. Oh yes, on the stein you will notice a list of names of an artillery platoon of the German Army of 1902–04 and the name of the regiment the artillery was attached to. Quite an interesting piece. Will is going to be so envious.

March 31, 1945

Well honey, it seems that I am set for the duration. You can stop worrying about me because I am definitely a rear-line soldier now. We have a mission that probably will be permanent. It's nice to have that certain feeling of security, yet it is quite a letdown. Most of the men are mad that we are so far back. But I am satisfied to bide my time until I return to you and complete happiness.

266

I can't write you things about the people I live with because in Germany we aren't allowed to live in the same house with civilians. We aren't even allowed to talk to them. I can tell you that I found about 100 films for the camera I bought from one of the boys in the outfit. They are all plates too. I took three time exposures last night and pictures this morning in the sunlight. I'm having them developed just to see what my mistakes are; then, honey, I'll take you many pictures.

Honey, I must stop now. I just got a call from Battery to report there. I'll see you a little later. ... Here I am, back again after paying the men and eating supper. We were paid in German marks this month. It really isn't German. It's like the invasion money that we issued in France and Belgium. One mark is 10 cents. Or ten marks is the equivalent of one sawbuck of American cash. Let me see now, first it was pounds and shillings and three-penny bits and crowns. Then it reverted to French francs and belgas (Belgian francs). Now it is marks. Maybe next it will be Czechoslovakian money. We have one hell of a time trying use the present type of money to pay off a debt that was made in some country way back. It is really funny seeing some of the guys trying to figure out the rate of exchange. Have to stop again. Will finish later.

Hello again, honey. The last time I was called away from your letter, I was informed that I will leave Monday morning for the Riviera down on the Mediterranean in southern France for a seven-day leave. I'll probably be gone for two weeks because it is quite a distance from here. You see honey, I have been operating with my platoon alone since December 26, so I guess I deserved the leave more than any other officer in the 639th. Only one can go, so I'm the one. I do need to go someplace and rest for a while. I wish you could meet me there. We'd go to Monte Carlo and other places together. Honey, it makes me feel awful to think that I am getting to see all of these places and you don't. Of course there are some things I have seen that I wouldn't have you see for anything in the world. They would be too gruesome for you. I'm used to such things now, but at first they bothered me a little. I was surprised at the way I took things as they came along. I really feel that I am a good officer. Of course my men have done everything for me, but you have given me the confidence I need to take the responsibility that I have had since I have been over here. Darling, I love you more each day and long for the day when I can take you in my arms and really make you know just how much I do love you.

Chapter 21

Rest and Recreation on the Riviera

April 1, 1945

Juby dearest:

Honey, I'm going to fly to the Riviera and back to the outfit when the seven days are up. It's the trip of a lifetime. We are leaving in the morning at 0900 by way of a Dakota (to you, a C-47). Two of the enlisted men in the battery you haven't met are going with me, Corporal Bracker and Sergeant Glick. Bruce Schwartz is burned up that I got the pass. He took a three-day pass to Huy, Belgium, about two weeks ago and that knocked him out of the chance to get this one. The only thing that bothers me is that you can't see the same things that I get to see. But honey, I'll do the next best and tell you about it in letters. It's only a four-hour trip by air, so when I get there I won't be at all tired. I am really thrilled over the trip—I guess I've earned it.   I'm yours, Doyle

Cannes, France

April 5, 1945

Here I am on the French Riviera elbowing at the bar and hob-knobbing with Lily Pons and her husband Andre Kostelanetz [American operatic soprano and actress; orchestra conductor and

The Carlton; X marks my room

arranger]. No kidding, sweet. I can't begin to describe the place in just one letter. But when you come right down to it, it's just another Miami.

I have taken some pictures with my new camera that I'll send to you soon. I'm in my room on the third floor of the Carlton Hotel in Cannes, France. It is only about 20 yards from the Mediterranean. I flew down from Remagen. We flew over Paris on the way. Somewhat out of the way, but we did.

I wish you were here with me. It would be heaven. I am sleeping, eating and swimming a little. Now and then I'll have a beer and cognac to be sociable with the other guys. The sleep on soft beds with sheets is the best thing. Honey, the war should be over soon, and then we can go to a beach together and really enjoy it. I'm not having much fun here. But it's nice. I may send a photo of Lily and Andre if I can see them when I have my camera. I had a drink with them the other night and a short chat. She isn't so glamorous off the screen and stage.

April 6, 1945

Dammit. Men should be given lessons on what to buy for their wives. The captain I room with asked me to go downtown and help him pick something for his wife. He almost drove me nuts. Would she like this? Would she like that? Hell, I didn't know what his wife would like. He may not have a wife as easy to please as you are. I saw many things you would like, but I can't afford to send everything I see. He ended up buying some postcards and that was all.

I just today got back some prints of the pictures I took with my new camera and the plate film I found. Honey, they are wonderful. Two of them I took by candlelight. They look like professional work. I'm going to send you an awful lot of pictures from now on, I can see now. You can't imagine what a find I made.

271

Self-portraits (eight-second exposure)

Honey, I'm already getting tired of this place. Sleeping and bathing in the sun and taking pictures. That's about all. An occasional drink, but drinks are too expensive so I have to ration it. But all in all I'm enjoying myself and trying to forget the Army for a while.

Day after tomorrow is our First Anniversary, sweet, and it's a shame that we must be apart bodily. But I know that our minds and hearts will be enjoying that anniversary together. We'll have many others honey, but I'm so, so very sorry that we can't be together for this, the first one. Darling, it seems only yesterday that I was preparing myself for the trip home to marry you. It has been very sweet this past year, even though we have been apart for over half of it. It is so nice to know that there is such a sweet, beautiful girl (who is my wife) at home loving me.

April 8, 1945

One year ago today, you and I became man and wife. Providence has caused us to miss that wonderful celebration of the first anniversary, but my sweet, you and I will make up for it a little bit later. I have found something for our anniversary that I hope you like. You asked me to send you matching cameos for earrings. Well I started out to find some, and to my surprise the first place I went had this beautiful necklace carved from tortoise shell with earrings to match. There are seven cameos on the necklace and one on each earring.

I am sitting at the Red Cross Lounge now overlooking the Mediterranean Sea. The water is just like a mirror this morning. Not a ripple on it. It looks as though you could walk out on it. Honey, again I say that I wish more than anything on earth that I could be with you today of all days, but alas we must finish our job. Then you and I will never be apart again.

Postcard of the Mediterranean at Cannes; "Not a ripple on it."

Chapter 22

Back to Duty

April 14, 1945

Dearest Juby,

Honey, I missed writing you last night because I hadn't slept very much in the past two nights. We left Cannes by air on April 11th and flew to Marseilles for gas. Then it took us six hours of flying across parts of France and Belgium and Germany to Giessen, Germany, where I took a truck back to Remagen, then to where I am now. I went through Kassel and many small towns on the way up. I'm some 60 to 70 miles beyond Kassel and may soon go farther.

Things are good now, as you probably know by the news from papers and radio. All of us were sorry that Roosevelt died. He did a great deal for us. I'm sorry he couldn't see the end of all this mess. He's a great guy. Kiss me darling, Doyle

April 20, 1945

Honey, for the past two nights I have been organizing and training men to work in my darkroom. You see, I have confiscated developing material and we have been experimenting with it. In my first attempt, the negative is too strong. We didn't leave it in the developer long enough. I'll keep trying. I'm going to send some printing paper home for our use. You can give some of it to Will if you like. He might like to try some home developing. But keep most of it for us. We'll have so much fun in the darkroom.

It is now clear that Doyle has a newly developed (ha!) obsession. Beginning with the "captured" camera he got before he went to Cannes, adding film and plates and lastly, developing chemicals, this hobby was off and running. Perfect timing, because he would soon enter a long period of boredom, frustration and homesickness. Teaching himself photography was an excellent diversion. His writings contain repetitive details of successes and mistakes in this endeavor. As he accumulates more cameras and equipment, he sends some of it home as gifts. After Juby receives a camera, he tries to teach her by giving basic instructions on light and speed settings. He'd ask her to take photos and have them developed to send to him, and then he would critique them by describing what she did wrong and how to correct it. This truly was "distance education." The family still has two of the cameras.

April 21, 1945 [near Worbis, Germany]

Yesterday I was out with three of the boys in the jeep just cruising around looking for German soldiers hiding out in the woods. We came up on a very old castle and decided we'd investigate. We went up the mountain, crossed the bridge over the moat, then went through the gate into the courtyard of the castle. We were greeted by Countess von Wintzingerode and her lady-in-waiting, a Swedish woman married to a German. The countess was about 70 years old. Her husband was killed in the last war and her only son in this one. The only male left in the family is a grandson who is ten months old. In the castle were beautiful oil paintings hundreds of years old. There were dungeons and torture chambers and beautiful pieces of furniture and china and hand-hammered brass and copper. It was a treasure. The countess asked me if I would like to see her hidden collection of old knives and guns. Of course I did, and honey, when I saw them I went crazy. She told me some of them were 600 years old and some were from the Napoleonic Wars. I tried to get her to give me two pistols and two knives for my den, but she wouldn't do it. She said that she was saving them for her grandson. Of course I could have taken them, but I just couldn't. You see, they aren't supposed to have knives and guns on the premises. But she had taken them from the walls and hidden them to prevent pillage. The Germans took everything they found wherever they went. I might go back and get myself some of them. They would be nice souvenirs. Her son was our enemy and she probably is too. We can't trust any of them. *[Doyle did not go back to confiscate the weapons.]*

I captured two prisoners after I left the castle. We're finding quite a few that have been afraid to come out of the woods and face us. But as they get hungry, they come out. Berlin should fall soon, and when it does our armies will only have mopping up to do. Then we'll start coming home a few at a time. Darling I think of you every minute of the day and keep hoping that soon we'll be together. ...

IN HIS FOOTSTEPS

May 4, 2010: *With considerable effort, Ken and I (with Michael's help) finally get our point across to the tourism information director in Worbis. We are searching for the nearby castle that Dad described. We are given directions to Burg Bodenstein, a thirteenth-century castle. There we find a plaque that lists previous owners including Wintzingerode. We learn later that the land was confiscated in 1945 and distributed. Countess Gisela Wintzingerode achieved a transfer of the castle to the Evangelical Church of the Province of Saxony in 1948. It is now a retreat and education center for the church.*

April 22, 1945

Just before I started this letter, I finished reading *Brave Men* by Ernie Pyle. Honey if you haven't read it, get it from someone and read it. It's exactly as war is. It is every soldier's expression of war. It's mine, but I could never express it as he has in that book. It only takes a short time to read. It's in the March *Omnibook*. Your pop will enjoy it. [*Omnibook Magazine was published from 1938 until 1957 and featured* "authorized abridgements of current best-selling books."]

April 24, 1945 [to Pölzig where ammo dump is being relocated]

I took a trip yesterday to within 15 miles of Leipzig. I'll name some of the larger towns I hit on the way to my destination: Worbis, Nordhausen, Eisleben, Halle, Merseburg and Weissenfels. I came back last night. I tell you this so we'll have a guide to mark the map that you want me to mark when I come home. I've been in so many towns, I can't possibly remember them all unless I tell you of them. Our children may be interested. Sure hope that I can get to Berlin.

Honey, I want to get a pass to Spa so I can go to Liège to a crystal factory and get you a set of Belgian crystal. If a check comes in from over here, you'll know that I cashed one at the Red Cross for the crystal. I can get it cheaper here and it's beautiful stuff. It rings like a bell when you thump it.

IN HIS FOOTSTEPS

April 25, 2010: *Ken and I visit this factory, Val Saint Lambert near Liège, 65 years after Dad wrote this letter. We purchase a goblet, haul it gingerly across Belgium and Germany and back and then present it to Mom from Dad for Mother's Day. It does "ring like a bell when you thump it." It is 24 percent lead. We pour some French wine we brought back, and the family toasts Dad.*

April 28, 1945

Honey, I got seven letters from you yesterday, ranging from April 1 to April 13. One from Mama and one from your pop. Honey, you seem to want to move into an apartment. You can if you want to, but I don't want you to live by yourself. Can't you get Frances to move in with you? If she would I think it's a good idea, but if she won't I'd rather you wouldn't move. I'd be afraid to have you living alone. About the items taking up space at your parents' home—why don't you move some of it and have it stored and insured? Or if you want, Mama would keep some of it for you.

You seem to have gotten the idea from one of my letters that I wouldn't be moving any farther up. Maybe at the time I thought that I wouldn't be on the front line anymore. Since then we've been pushing right along. We are now in the center of Germany, not

Lawn and gardens

too far from our goal. I'm going to send you some pictures of my present CP. We move into a town and take the best places for the CPs. The place I have now has two bathrooms and two kitchens, one upstairs and one downstairs. In front of the second floor is a sun porch. The first floor has another sun porch with a garage underneath. Out in front is the lawn. I'll send you a picture of this too. It's an idea for our lawn [also described in letter of May 7].

May 1, 1945

Hitler is reported dead, I don't believe he is! He's pulling a fast one. … You wrote about talking to the sergeant from AA that was hurt at St. Vith. Did you find out his name? We had a sergeant that was hurt there named Muzzilo, a staff sergeant. What outfit was he with? I probably have been with or near his unit. AA really caught hell during the Von Rundstedt drive (Battle of the Bulge).

May 3, 1945

Honey, there is no news from here except things you heard about as soon as I did. Hitler reported dead, Berlin garrison surrendering, Italian front surrendering. The thing that pleased us most was the downfall of Berlin and the capture of Von Rundstedt. He caused us the trouble back in December and January, and I think that outbreak started his downfall. The thing that has beat Germany is the blood and guts of Yanks and gasoline. Kid, I never knew that Germany could have so much equipment. I have seen thousands of airplanes that were in perfect condition, but there was no gasoline for them. The ration of gasoline in the States has really paid off. It licked Germany. Now if the Japs will fold up soon, things will be lovely. It will be just a matter of time before we start coming home.

Honey, I'm enclosing a pair of Nazi patches in the national colors. You might want to open and close my stay in Germany with them in our scrapbook. I wish I was at home so you could show me the book. [See image of a Nazi patch in the color gallery.]

Honey, I've got to make another trip today. I get so tired of going places. I do want to take a trip to Czechoslovakia. I'm not too far away. I was through Jena the other day. Wasn't that the town where Napoleon had one of his big battles? Never thought I'd be so far from home. I've seen quite a bit honey, but I'd be glad to forget it all just to see you. We've got so much to do when I get back. Loving, going places, seeing things, doing things, buying clothes for me. Remember honey you haven't seen me in civilian clothes yet.

May 3, 1945 [second letter]

Just got back from my round trip of 140 miles. I had to go to a court-martial. I got the kid cleared, and I'm certainly glad because he's a good kid. He's from another battery, but I know him quite well.

May 4, 1945

I got two letters from you today. One was written the 24th, the other the 25th of April. You said you had sent some [lieutenant's] bars for me. Honey, I'm glad because I can't get any over here. I have only three bars to my name and one set of those belongs to Murphy.

Honey, the German armies are surrendering as we expected because we really gave them hell after we crossed the Rhine. It seems like a bad dream now, almost forgotten. We laugh about the narrow escapes we had back there, but it wasn't funny at the time. In fact, we really can't imagine that it's true now that things are so quiet and peaceful. All we can find here to shoot at is deer and there are plenty of them. Your father would get a big kick out of being here. I have killed three deer myself in the past five days. The meat is good too. Ask your father if he would like a venison steak. If he does, tell him to come to Germany, but he must bring you.

I'm going tomorrow to see one of the many concentration camps that I am sure you have read about. Some of the stories are very atrocious, but not any more so than some of the things I have seen

281

myself. Tomorrow night I will tell you of the things I see there. It's near Weimar, Germany, well back from where I am now. I'm going to take some pictures and send them to you. We've been fighting to put a stop to the things that have been going on over here. I don't ever want to forget the things I've seen. It's so easy for us, as Americans, to forget that there are people who will commit such crimes and have been doing so for the past seven years. I have no pity for the German people, because it has been proven to me that the German people permitted these things to go on. The few that objected or in any way showed that they didn't like what the State was doing were sent to concentration camps. These camps weren't hidden in the caverns of large cities or in the Black Forest or the Harz Mountains or in the remote districts of south Germany, but were located in and around the small communities of Germany where the rank-and-file citizens could see it all. They deserve no pity whatsoever and get none from me or any of the men in my platoon. That's enough of my opinions and such.

I'm going to send you a print of all my gun sections to include in our scrapbook. I sent you something lovely today. There are four separate china figures. One is a woman in Colonial dress. The other three pieces are a set. One figure is a jester playing a concertina. It stands some 10 inches high. The other two are dancing girls. They are 6 or 8 inches high. I hope they don't break. They are so dainty. I packed them well, but you know how things are treated at customs in Atlanta. *[The two dancing girls had arms and hands broken; the "Colonial dame" had her head broken off. They have been glued and re-glued many times. The jester is still intact. They all are displayed in Juby's home. See image of the jester with dancing girls in the color gallery.]*

I was going to send a rifle home for our kid, but honey, I'm sick of guns now. I've had enough of them. I may send one home later, but at present I'm not in the mood.

Chapter 22: Back to Duty

The war is about over here, but there is another one to end on the other side of the world. If the Army says that I must go [fight Japan], then I must. So honey, if I have to serve there, just be patient. I'll be coming home soon. Now don't be upset because I might go to that theatre. I just want you to realize the possibility.

Chapter 23

Victory in Europe
Tour of Buchenwald

May 5, 1945

Dearest Juby:

There is no jubilance here. The armies of Germany are surrendering day by day. Only one sector in the south is emitting any organized resistance. Yet we soldiers who helped bring about the long-awaited collapse of the German armies can't feel or display any degree of jubilance. We only breathe a big sigh of relief when we hear of the unconditional surrender of some of the armies. We thought we'd be very happy when it came, but somehow we aren't. We are happy, but we don't celebrate because there are some who aren't as fortunate as we are. The war has been over some time for a great many, and they will have no homecoming. Yes, that's why there's no shouting and blowing of horns. It has been a tough, rough road and some were not able to finish the grind. They are the ones we and the people back home should be very grateful to for having been in our army. Their job is done and done well. I imagine that back home everyone is shouting and waving and raising a ruckus in general over the news. We are only thankful, and to show it we say to ourselves, "We're lucky." No one can have this feeling but the men that have been in it. All of my men have been in it. I know because I was with them. It has been rough staying away from you. But honey, it's going to be so good to be able to tell our son that I fought and helped to suppress a nation of sadistic, maddened killers.

I saw today a concentration camp. The worst part of it had been cleaned up, but I'll tell you about what I saw and learned. The guide was a Polish prisoner in the camp before it was overrun. He could speak English.

The camp was Buchenwald Concentration Camp. We were met at the gate by the guide. We walked across a large assembly area which covered some three or four acres. On three sides were buildings that housed the prisoners. After their liberation on April 11th (less than a month ago), the prisoners dressed up the buildings with improvised flags of their respective nations. There were Polish, Russian, Czech, French, Belgian, Danish and other flags hanging here and there. In the center of the assembly area near the front entrance was a huge billboard painted with Russian, American and British flags.

Flags of the liberators

We walked across the area into a building. It was the crematorium, housing a huge blast furnace with 15 or 20 doors. Inside the doors were grates just like in a coal furnace. The fire came up through the grates and bodies were thrown on the grates. It was awful. Underneath the grates I saw ashes—human beings' ashes. One child, a boy ten years old, told us he saw his father and mother burn there and he was to be burned but escaped through a window. He was caught and taken back the second time to be burned and again escaped. We went to a room that contained the gas chamber. It was so gruesome to hear the guide say, "Any prisoner that entered this room never came out alive."

Crematorium ovens after liberation, April 1945;
ashes and bones within (National Archives)*

*"Bones of anti-Nazi women still are in the crematoriums in the German concentration camp at Weimar, Germany, taken by the 3rd US Army, Prisoners of all nationalities were tortured and killed." Pfc. W. Chichersky, April 14, 1945. 111-SC-203461 National Archives OPA Electronic Record (ww2_182.jpg)

Crematorium, May 2010; roses now replace the ashes and bones

At liberation (National Archives)*

---

*"These are slave laborers in the Buchenwald concentration camp near Jena; many had died from malunutrition when US troops of the 80th Division entered the camp." Pvt. H. Miler, Germany, April 16, 1945. 208-AA-206K-31 National Archives OPA Electronic Record (ww2_178.jpg)

We went to the kitchen where nothing could have been cooked but potatoes and stew. It contained 25 or 30 one-hundred gallon caldrons and that was all.

In the barracks and the hospital, "beds" consisted of five-deck bunks made of wood. No mattresses, just a few blankets. Each six-foot square bunk could accommodate five men or ten children.

Barracks and bunks, May 5, 1945

Honey, it's terrible to tell you of all this, but I want you to know the situation here. It wasn't just a few in Germany that we were fighting—it was against all of what Germany stood for.

On the door of one of the hospital rooms was a sign saying, "40 to 80 men died daily in this room." We were shown a room where men were taken for castration.

As we went out the other end of the room, the guide said, "On that concrete platform, some 50 bodies were placed each morning and a truck came daily and carted them to the crematorium for disposal."

There were from 60,000 to 80,000 prisoners in the camp. The camp was overrun on the 11th of April and we learned that on the 10th, 3000 prisoners were executed. Plans had been made to execute all of the prisoners on the 12th. Again I say, my sweet, I almost feel ashamed to write such to you, but I know that our families think that sometimes what the papers have to say is propaganda when they publish these atrocious acts of the German people, so I thought you might like to hear of it firsthand. You've read the result.

As you know, the war over here is about over. But until we get a view of the Statue of Liberty or the nation's capital, we can't get a thrill out of it. Darling I love you more and more each day. I'll never realize any excitement until I see you. Then I'll be happy. Love you kid.

I'm yours completely, Doyle

One of the stories Dad told us is not mentioned in the letters or his memoir. He spoke of the "Bitch of Buchenwald." Legend holds that one of the supervising SS officers had a wife who requested that tattooed skin from the Holocaust victims be made into lamp-shades and other macabre décor. When I searched for information, I learned of Buchenwald's second commandant, Karl Otto

"To Each His Own"—from within the camp looking out
the front gate, May 3, 2010

Koch, whose second wife, Ilse Koch, is known as Die Hexe von Buchenwald (the Witch of Buchenwald) due to her exceptionally cruel brutality. She was tried and convicted of her crimes after the war. Soon after Buchenwald was liberated, tales of the atrocities committed there were widely publicized, including those of misuse of human skin. Recent articles have questioned the validity of some of the claims.

IN HIS FOOTSTEPS
May 3, 2010: *On this first cold, cloudy, windy day of our trip, Ken and I tour Buchenwald. The horror still hangs here. Arriving before the information kiosks open, we are alone for more than an*

Site of inmates' living quarters

hour, self-touring by reading plaques. We appreciate the solitude and dark chill as fittingly depressing. We are speechless, each of us coping privately with the oppressive reality. Built in 1937 and operated as a forced labor camp for the armament factories nearby, Buchenwald was also a medical experiment station. SS records document that 33,462 persons died here. Estimates based on secret documentation by former prisoners put the total at 56,545. Most buildings have been razed, but their foundations are marked by blackened gravel and their purposes explained by signage.

The biting wind sweeps across acres of unholy ground where barracks once stood. We are able to tour the remaining prison, where political prisoners were tortured on entry, and the infamous crematorium, both still standing and serving as memorials to those who died within.

Prison hallway

Crematorium

Gatehouse

Fresh wreaths of flowers have been placed at many points along the way; fresh rosebud stems even grace the ovens of the crematorium. A film shows us the camp as it was when liberated by the Third Army on April 11, 1945—hard to watch, but a necessary lesson. Buchenwald was not an extermination camp like Auschwitz, but many died from being shot or hanged for minor reasons, or just for meanness. Illness, starvation and experimentation killed many others. Late in the war, many who had survived thus far were sent by rail to Auschwitz for the "final solution." The film presents aged survivors who share specific stories, such as seeing starving men fight to the death over rotting, discarded potato peelings. We learn that Jews and homosexuals were treated especially worse than others, being isolated and starved in an area known as the Little Camp. I am surprised to learn that for every one of the infamous camps across Germany there were dozens of sub-camps. A series of stones gives visual meaning to the numbers. According to the visitors' guide, Buchenwald alone had 136 sub-camps.

Among the structures of extraordinary malice is, incredibly, an enclosure that had been a small zoo for the children of the SS who controlled the camp. I find it appalling to imagine children playing so near unspeakable misery and death.

We stay in this gray place for nearly three hours. We are reminded by a now-wilted wreath in the Little Camp that President Obama visited here just a few weeks earlier. We also remember Dad's visit on May 5, 1945. Two days hence marks exactly 65 years since he was here. His pictures and descriptions have some-what prepared us for our experience today. The horror is real to us now, much more than described in history books and shown in movies. It hangs in the silent, cold, damp air of this overcast day, and it will stay in our hearts. We choose not to walk to an area where a bronze statue of American liberators overlooks three stone rings enclosing mass graves. We have had our fill of this eerie place. From here we use the autobahn. We can't get away fast enough.

May 7, 1945

Honey, things are so very quiet around here now. If I didn't have my darkroom work or magazines to read, I think I would go crazy. When I don't keep myself occupied I think too much of you. There's so much speculation about whether the troops going from here to the CBI [China/Burma/India] will go through the States or go direct. If I have to go, I sure hope we go home first. I don't know if I could take it if I didn't see you first. I don't believe I could carry on.

All the troops of our common enemy have given up here but for just a few in Czechoslovakia. They are expected to surrender anytime now. They might as well; they haven't got a chance.

I was back in Erfurt again yesterday. It's some 70 to 80 miles back from where we are now. I went in to defend some guys on a fraternization charge. They were guilty, and there was nothing I could do about it. The fraternization law is one law that is going to be enforced to the letter. We don't want our men to have anything to do with Germans. Our law is that they can't even speak to a German, only in the line of duty. Remember, they are conquered—not liberated as was France and Belgium. I don't want to have anything to do with them. I've seen too much. They are all treacherous. No good. *[See images of antifraternization posters in the color gallery.]*

Honey, I find it very hard to write you any news now. There is none that you can't get in the papers. I don't do anything all day but work on photography and visit the gun sections or read. I have a 15-room house for my CP. My office is the largest room in the house, and it has a bay window with my desk in it. Tomorrow I'll send you pictures of the front of the house. I just this morning took them.

IN HIS FOOTSTEPS

May 3, 2010: *Ken and I use Dad's picture to find the house that served as his CP in the small town of Pölzig, Germany. It is well kept and unchanged. We are humbled to be in the place where Dad was in the days leading up to V-E Day 65 years ago. We feel*

Command post in Pölzig, 1945 and 2010

his presence as we stand together under an umbrella outside the gate. A gentle rain provides the only sound accompanying our thoughtful reflections.

In the near future, I'm going to send a group picture of each one of my gun crews for our scrapbook. I just sent one of the kids off to Brussels on a three-day pass. Every time they go on pass, I have to give them a fatherly talk on the dangers of sex relations with strange women. Then I give them some tangible protection just in case they forget my lecture. You never knew that I had this to do every time they leave for pass did you?

Gun crew

Well honey, I was dreaming of you so I had to write and talk to you for a while. The news just said that Churchill was standing by the microphone to announce at any time the end of hostilities in Europe. We might stay as occupational troops or we might go to the CBI or we might come home. No one knows yet. I hope I can come home. I have had enough war. If I have to go to the CBI I have to go, but I don't want to. You can't blame me can you?

Chapter 23: Victory in Europe; Tour of Buchenwald

May 8, 1945

Well honey, just as I said yesterday—the war is officially over today. It makes me a wee bit angry to hear the broadcasts about the great celebrations in the large cities of the world. Here we are, still in Germany. All I could do for my men today was call in all but two men in each section and play ball with them. I bought ten cases of beer and we had cheese and crackers here in the CP. Nothing was said about the end of the war. The conversation was about the Japanese war.

I have six cameras now and four more lenses and mechanisms with bellows I can have fixed when I get home. You and I are going to have more pictures than you can take care of. I have the cutest little job for you. It's an Agfa with a 6.4 lens, 1/20, and it has six shutter speeds. You'll just love it. I have another one for me. It's a 6/16 but I'll have to change the case on it. It only takes slides now, but it'll be easy to change. Then we have two 9/12 plate cameras. And the 6/20 that is so very cute. When you drop the case open, the bellows unfolds as the door opens. On the 1/20 you have to pull the bellows out after the door is open. There is another one that is a 6/16, plate and roll camera. Now let me see is that all? Yes to date that's all; only six.

You asked me for money from the countries I've been in. I have sent some coins in letters all along, and I sent currency from each country. Most of it was invasion money or money that the army issued to take care of the payrolls. Oh yes honey, I have us a microscope that I'll bring home when I come. You'll see me looking through it in one of the pictures. One of the kids took it one night, and I was presented with this picture the next day. They now call me Doctor (the lights went out). See you later.

Honey, after the ballgame yesterday I'm a little sore. We are playing again this afternoon, so I will work out the soreness. I think

"Doc" and his microscope

Notice the pictures of Juby on his desk.

I will play ball with one of the Textile League teams when I get home. Would you want me to?

A letter from Mama told me James Whittenburg was due to be home for the wedding in about two weeks. She said he had already reached the States. I'm sure glad that Harriet is one of us now. She's a swell kid and has proved that she's a wonderful girl by her patience in waiting for three and a half years. Give her my best wishes for happiness and extend my congratulations to James. He has had enough of being away overseas. God, I don't see how he stood it. But now he's back and that's something. They have my best wishes for as happy a married life as ours. I love you with all my heart.

James Whittenburg, Doyle's first cousin, served with the 208th Coast Artillery (AA) across New Guinea's Papua Peninsula to Buna. A medically discharged soldier from the unit, Harold O. Bertz, who had served 28 months in combat, returned to the States and lobbied officials including Congressman Ranulf Compton, President Roosevelt and his Secretary of War, Henry L. Stimpson, for relief for the "forgotten men" of this unit: "This small group of men has been marooned in the South Pacific area under constant attack for nearly three years without relief. Is there anywhere in the world greater heroes than these boys who have fought the Japs and the jungles and the gnawing agony of homesickness for 34 months without complaint and without relief?"—Rep. Compton.

From a letter by Bertz to President Roosevelt: "The 208th was badly shot up and as a consequence it was dissolved and the surviving members were transferred to other units where they have become the 'forgotten men.' ... Somewhere someplace, there had been a slip-up in the records and they have been put on the shelf by mistake." *The above information is taken from news articles saved by James Whittenburg. A handwritten note signed by James says,* "After 3 years, 2 months and 6 days I got out of this hell hole to come home. It took 5 weeks to get to Rome, Georgia, and Harriet! I shipped out from Frisco on February 18, 1942 weighing 180 lbs. Came back in weighing 140 lbs. on April 6, 1945."

I never knew James and Dad trained together until after they were both dead. The clippings were in an envelope marked "James Whittenburg, WWII" among Dad's papers.

1941 Ft. Eustis training photo
Cousins James (1) and Doyle Whittenburg (3)
with an unidentified sergeant (2)

HEADQUARTERS
639TH AAA AW BN
APO 230 US ARMY
VICTORY MESSAGE

1. Today the war in Europe is ended, and one phase of our war-job finished; with other free people over the world, you will pause to be thankful that Nazi Germany has crumbled around its own militaristic foundations. This war, born in Germany from the seeds of greed and aggression, has come home to Germany to die. Add to your thanksgiving today a solemn prayer that out of San Francisco the United Nations will bring the machinery to prevent the rise of another national beast to threaten the world's peace and freedom, ever.

2. Through France, Belgium and Germany you have met DUTY face to face wherever it appeared and each time you have emerged a credit to yourselves, your People and your Country. I am immeasurably proud of you.

3. Whether the next phase of our war-job will be here in Germany or in another theatre, it will be no less important than the last. Other battles have to be fought and won and the peace has to be secured. Whatever part you are called upon to play, I am confident you will do it well. When we return to our homes from this war, let's carry the assurance that neither we nor our children will return for another one.

W.A. CAUTHEN
Lt. Colonel, CAC
9 May 1945

A STORY FROM THE GERMAN SIDE

While preparing this manuscript and related trip, I visited a local frame shop owned and operated by Renate Corbin, a very community-involved, longtime resident and business woman in Rome. I knew she was a German immigrant who had married an American soldier and come to the States in the 1950s, but I didn't know her age or her history. She casually mentioned that she would soon be taking her annual trip to visit her family in Germany. I told her of my project and intended trip across Germany during the upcoming spring, hoping to follow my dad's path in WWII. I sensed that this would open the floodgates of discussion and it did. I was fascinated.

The Third Reich was a reign of terror for rural Germans. Renate remembers from her earliest years hearing the propaganda from Hitler's Minister of Communications pouring out of radios anywhere her family went. She remembers being scolded by her mother for making the remark, "Why is that man screaming?" while in a store. Her mother was terrified the storekeeper would turn the family in as anti-Nazi. All information to the public was carefully controlled. As the war progressed, she remembers being wrapped in blankets and taken to sleep in the basement every night because of constant air raid alerts.

The family fled from eastern Prussia by train as the Russians advanced in late summer 1944. Her mother, with three children of her own as well as four of Renate's young cousins, made it safely to an uncle's farm near Stargard, where they remained relatively comfortable and self-sustained from September 1944 until March 1945. Forced to flee once more, her parents and uncle had to hitch an old wagon to a tractor and make their way with the seven children across the northern edge of Germany near the Baltic Sea. They traveled cross-country and only at night and hid in the forests, sometimes being shot at or caught in bombing raids.

During the night they had to siphon fuel from downed planes in order to continue. This horrible journey took four weeks. Now they were truly refugees, and the government assigned them to be housed on an estate in Kiel. Renate remembers harsh resentment from the estate owners, which she did not understand at the time.

German economics and politics were collapsing. The family had to sneak into fields at night, stealing the milk from the cows to nourish the youngest children. Her father taught them to do this only during desperate times, never for profit. They would scavenge for potatoes and rutabagas that fell from trucks. Renate describes her mother as a miracle cook who stretched meager ingredients in order to feed the family.

Renate was eight years old when the war ended. She remembers hearing the rumble of tanks one day. Her mother was bathing the younger children. A soldier opened the door and spoke in English, telling them the war was over. Outside were tanks with white stars—a blessing because it meant the tanks were not Russian, bearing red stars. They were British. Renate said they felt numb and so very glad. Relief soon became available, distributed through the churches, but not the Lutheran church to which the family belonged. The father was adamant that they not join another faith to get supplies, so it was some time longer before they were able to begin their recovery.

Renate said most British and Americans were kind to them, but the Russians were brutal in the worst of ways. I was humbled to hear this story from the other side.

Chapter 24

The Aftermath and Mopping Up

Pölzig, Germany

May 9, 1945

Dearest Juby,

Honey, this is the second time today I have chatted with you. I was sitting here after an afternoon of softball, volleyball, touch football and a trip by jeep on which I shot a six-point buck—how's that for an afternoon of varied sports? I had fun shooting at buck rabbits with my combine and my .45 automatic. It's funny to see one start out across a field some 200 yards away and watch the dirt fly around him. We have to do this to more or less keep the men's morale up. It is a lot of fun and we have "bocoup" [*beaucoup*, very much] ammunition. Don't know what will be the outcome of our present situation. We're just sitting tight and letting things go as easy as possible.

Tell your father about the buck I got today. I gave it to one of the gun sections to eat. I have had enough venison for a while. Too much is sickening. ... I love you, Doyle

From Doyle's memoir:

Today is January 1, 1992. This morning Juby and I drove our two grandsons to a game preserve where you can observe deer herds. We were riding slowly, peering through the leafless forest. A meadow opened up beyond a hedgerow, and a deer was grazing on the far side. We stopped. The kids got out and crept to the hedgerow, and lo and behold, another deer appeared, and then another. Four or five does came into view, then a huge buck came bouncing out. He was a pretty animal. My grandson said, "That's what a buck does—sends the does out of cover first." Then he, having received a hunting bow for Christmas, made a motion as if he was aiming his bow at the buck.

When he did that, I had a flashback of several incidents that happened during the Bulge. My jeep driver and I were going from La Gleize to Spa one morning, and a deer ran across the road in front of us. It turned parallel to the road and was running alongside the jeep about 30 to 40 yards away. I had the idea to take my .45 pistol and see what I could do with a moving target. I fired three shots at about 45 yards. The third one hit the deer, causing him to jump in the air and crumple to the ground. I really didn't expect to hit him. We picked up the carcass, returned to the CP and prepared venison. The meal turned out to be no more than a lump in our throats.

Over the years I have had more genuine remorse for killing that deer than I have had for outright killing two soldiers I did not even know. They were men only acting as soldiers, as was I. One of them, along with his tank crew, had been shooting at me and others for a day and a half. The other one and I met face-to-face coming up out of separate bomb craters, both of us in full battle gear with guns drawn. Thank goodness I fired first. I still wonder if he would have dropped his gun. At the time I was not a gambler, nor did I have time to make another choice. I have remorse for the helpless deer, but only regrets for my action concerning the men.

There is another story Dad told through the years. We remember it as a source of angst for him. During the Bulge, a grandfather and grandson were captured while signaling the location of American troops to the Germans. They were brought to the CP, and Dad instructed a soldier to take them to headquarters. It was very cold and deep snow covered the ground. Soon after the door closed, he heard two shots. He opened the door, and the two prisoners lay dead in the snow. The soldier said that they had tried to escape. Dad believed that the man just didn't want to be inconvenienced by the trip in the cold to HQ. The pain and pathos stayed with him, but this story is not told in the letters or his memoir.

May 10, 1945

Honey, I'm getting lazy. I do nothing in the mornings but get up, eat and sit around. I hear that the first boatload of men have already left the ETO for the CBI. Hope they miss me. We are doing nothing now but cleaning our equipment and playing a lot of sports. If you were here, you and I could travel all over this part of Germany in my jeep. You'd love it, honey. The country is so green and fresh and neat-looking. Of course most of the larger towns are torn to hell, but at one time they were beautiful. You can get on the Reich autobahns and travel for miles and miles. These are really eight-lane highways. They have a break in the middle for shrubbery and are really pretty.

I sent you a picture where the first American troops hit the North-South Autobahn. (I was there.) Dangerous at the time too. But that's over now. *[Evidently General Eisenhower was also impressed with the autobahns. During his two terms as president, he supported the Interstate Highway System, creating jobs and increasing interstate commerce. These great highways now join the lower 48 states in all directions.]*

Honey, I'm sending you another beer stein for our home. It was owned by a German sailor, so it will go with the one I already sent that belonged to a soldier.

May 11, 1945

I got a kick out of what you said about what people ask you. Just tell them that I like to send things to you. That's all. It is a pleasure honey, and it's the least I can do for you to try to make you happy in my absence. As I see things that you'll probably like, I'll send them if I have marks at the time.

May 12, 1945

Honey, just yesterday I went on a trip that was 550 miles. I was tired when I got back at 0130 this morning, but it was a beautiful trip. We traveled the autobahn all the way but for short detours. The entire length of the autobahn is just like a drive in a park. The trees are so very beautiful and so well kept. I enjoyed the trip down, but it was a back-breaker on the way back. We went down to find quarters for the men.

If you'll check your map and travel from Gera on the East-West Autobahn to a town just northwest of it, you'll find Giessen where I landed when I came back from the Riviera. To the west of Giessen is Wetzlar where I went yesterday. You see, I drove some 200 to 225 miles just to get a letter from you. But when I got here, the mail orderly was asleep. When I got up this morning, he had gone for more mail and hasn't come back yet. So I still haven't gotten the letter I drove so far to get.

May 13, 1945

My prayers each night for the past several months are plain and simple: "God, permit me to get safely home to Juby, and permit me to get all my men safely home to the ones they love. Amen." That prayer will never change, honey, regardless of how long it takes to get home. My men and I have been through some rough days and nights, but they're still with me and we are thankful to know that we will get home even though we have to wait for a while. So please honey, just remember those prayers and know that they'll be answered. Things are safe now. The only part unanswered is actually getting home. Darling I love you.

From Doyle's memoir [written December 17, 1992]:

Last Sunday morning I arrived late for worship service. The usher led me to a front row seat, the only one he had to offer. The seat was facing the table that held the candles for the Advent celebration. I was only three feet away. In fact my feet were almost under the table. When the time came for the candle lighting, the young man lit the first candle and a strange feeling came over me. When he lit the second candle, I realized what was happening to me. My imagination had covered me with a pup tent. I was alone. I had a match in my hand and was lighting a candle. I found myself reliving a memory. I lit the candle for warmth and light to write a letter to my wife. Snow is 30 to 40 inches deep and still falling. A single candle warms up the two-man tent in a few minutes. The falling snow insulates the canvas but also closes air passage into the tent, creating the need for a vent hole. Thus began my experience in continental Europe, December 1944. Remembering the misery of conditions on the battle-front, the loneliness, the helplessness of being in such a situation and not being at home brings deep sadness.

My wife and I had only been married six months and had been together four to six weeks of the six months before I went overseas. I wrote her over 400 letters while we were separated. The only prayer I uttered over there was that He allow me to return safely to my wife. I did not ask for safe duty, but I did ask for protection from harm. I truly received it. I had the honor of going overseas with 68 men that I had trained with for three years here in the States. I also had the extreme pleasure of returning to the States with the same 68 men. We helped each other earn three battle stars. After the danger was over, we all agreed that it was a miracle. The prayer I prayed many times during those long, difficult months had been answered.

May 17, 1945 [in Asslar and Wetzlar, towns near Giessen, Germany]

I didn't get any mail from you today so instead of listening to you, I'll talk a while.

You probably already know most of what I have to say here, but to clarify my past letters I'll tell you again what I have done in the ETO. We took off from Camp Kilmer on September 29, 1944. We came over on the SS *Chitral*, were in route for 11 days and landed in Greenock, Scotland. There we took a train to Aldermaston, England. We were there from October 11 to November 27. We then loaded our equipment "combat load" and proceeded to Southampton, England. The next day we were loaded on Liberty ships. Mine was the *James Nelson*, I believe. We docked at the mouth of the Seine River for seven days until we got channel priority, then up the river we went to Rouen.

About 12 miles from Rouen, we pitched tents and lived in the rain for two weeks, then drew ammo and moved out, traveling by truck convoy. We spent the night on the side of the road—one night near Mons, Belgium, the other at Theux, near Spa—then to Honsfeld, Belgium, for four or five days where our primary mission was shooting at V-1 buzz bombs. The bombs would fly over, but we couldn't see them for the first three days because of the fog. When it lifted, we shot down three of them. It was dangerous work but a lot of fun. After the fifth day, we (being very green combat troops) learned that the Germans were only 1000 yards away and also learned by my ignorance that they were massing for a counterattack. Yes, like a dope I went for a joy ride and ran into more trouble than I expected. I saw German artillery, tanks, infantry and all the rest. Luckily I saw them first and whizzed back with the information. As usual, it was slow getting to Army HQ. Sixteen hours later the Germans struck.

Dad often recounted that early one morning he and his jeep driver went out to explore the icy roads cut through the nearby forest. Approaching a clearing, they came upon a German tank directly in their path. The only option was to drive around the tank to head back in the direction they came. He described the slow turn of the tank's gun toward them. He attributes the slow reaction of the crew to it being so early in the morning that the men had been fast asleep. The jeep sped away into the forest and made it back to safety.

In the meantime we made two evacuation plans. We knew that unless reinforcements or support came soon, we'd have to withdraw. Like fools, we stayed there until the last minute. Only after the Germans hit us with all they had—artillery, infantry and tanks—did we receive the order to withdraw, but it was too late to evacuate all of our equipment. If we had had a dozen tanks and 200 doughboys as support, the Germans never would have come through. We were dug in and they had their artillery zeroed in on us. My men's gun pit parapets were leveled. But not a man was hurt, thank God. We pulled out at 0330 and the Germans came into Honsfeld at 0400. The bastards were afraid. German paratroops were dropped in the path of our withdrawal, but with God's help, we slid to the north of their drive. We regrouped at Malmedy and then moved into Spa to set up antitank positions.

Honey, that drive of the Germans was costly in equipment for the 639th, but we only lost one man and he was from another battery. It was worth a million dollars in experience. Our men were turned into rough combat troops overnight. It has paid dividends on many occasions since then. Boy, they're really good. They're as mean as hell when they have to be, but right now there's not a one of them that is at all hardened because of the battles they've fought. They're good men that have done a good job for the world. I'm proud of them.

From Spa we moved steadily south as we closed up the Bulge. It was in Francorchamps that I had the closest call of my life. A plane dropped a bomb about ten yards from my CP and we were simultaneously strafed. They got Kenny there, but he's back now. From there we went to Stavelot and La Gleize and Malmedy. I was about 200 yards out of Malmedy, then occupied by our troops, when our own bombers leveled it. I hadn't been out of town over three minutes. We had to go in and get our own soldiers out of the wreckage. Dead, mangled and dying. That explains my outburst about the Air Corps around that time. *[This action occurred December 23–25, 1944. Ken and I visited Malmedy and saw the memorials near the cave where civilians hid under deplorable conditions during weeks of battle. In the churchyard, stone tablets bear the names of the some 200 civilians of all ages that were killed in this unfortunate incident.]*

Just before St. Vith was retaken, we were called back to Battalion Headquarters at Verviers, Belgium. We stayed in Verviers from about January 20th to March 1st. From there we moved to Duren, Germany, for three days, then to Nideggen on the Roer, Bonn and the Rhine at Remagen. ... It seems like fun now. But then!! We were the first AA outfit to go across the Rhine. It was dangerous, but we were very proud to be the first to go. No casualties—I have smart combat soldiers with me. They know how to operate. God was on our side too.

We left the Rhine and went east to some small town that I can't remember and the next night we made a forced march in blackout back across the Rhine to Rheinbach. From there I went on my leave to Cannes. I left from a landing strip near Unkel on the east of the Rhine and flew to Marseilles. The plane gassed up there and flew on into Cannes. Eight days later I flew to Giessen and was trucked to Bad Godesberg just down the Rhine from Remagen. I caught our battalion mail truck to Marburg. From there I went to my platoon at Breitenworbis with Bruce who was just then moving his platoon from Rheinbach west of the Rhine. We stayed at Breitenworbis for about two weeks, captured 79 prisoners, and that's where I got my cameras.

From there we moved to Pölzig, a town just northeast of Gera. It is about 25 to 30 miles from Czechoslovakia and about 50 miles south of Leipzig. That's where we were when the war ended. Day before yesterday we moved back to a town near Giessen. I expect to be here for the next few months or at least in the general area. So now I have expanded on my travels during this war in such a way that by using some of my old letters (if you keep them) you might be able to understand my situation. I was expressing my emotions when I wrote you during the trying moments of the war that has just ended.

You are the only one I have to shower my thoughts and feelings on, my sweet. You were the one that gave me the inspiration to do the job I did and, not boasting or bragging, I say I did a good job. I brought my men through some close calls, but they are the ones to credit. As for you honey, I'll have to wait until I return to show you my appreciation for your being my wife. Darling, I love you with all my heart. Now you talk for a while.

From Doyle's memoir:

I remember when we were bombed by our own planes near Malmedy because they were bombing as briefed by radio (so they said). We radioed back that if their bomb bay doors opened on the next wave of planes, they would be met with unfriendly friendly fire. The second wave approached with open bomb bay doors. We opened fire and downed two or three planes. Not a crew member was hurt seriously. We picked up the crews, gave them a meal and transported them to Battalion Headquarters. The front was not static. The plane crews had been briefed for the bombing run on the assumption that German tankers would be located at that point. We were still there instead. Our temporary roadblocks had stopped the German drive. We almost signed our death warrant because we were "hanging so tough" in the defense.

From the unit history of the 30th Division MPs: "Despite the frantic efforts of the 30th Division to convince Army Headquarters to the rear that friendly forces occupied Malmedy, the American medium bombers again bombed the town. Our antiaircraft knocked down an American fighter plane strafing the area and the pilot was bewildered to learn that American troops occupied the area." [30th Infantry Division, Old Hickory, "Bombing of Malmedy." Web. 7 July 2013.]

From the unit history of the 120th Infantry Regiment: "The valley of Malmedy looked like a Christmas card. Two hours after noon December 23, the buzz of planes was heard. ... B-24s dropped bombs which neatly leveled the main square and the central part of town, the once busy and unharmed Army rest area. Various company and platoon CPs in town including that of AT Company were hit directly and left many soldiers buried beneath the debris. Fire consumed many of the buildings and whole blocks lay in heaps of rubble. There were many Army deaths and civilian casualties." [30th Infantry Division, Old Hickory, "Bombing of Malmedy." Web. 7 July 2013.]

May 18, 1945

Honey I got two letters from you last night. You seem to want to know just when I'll be coming home. I'll be in Germany for three or four months. After that, if MacArthur needs some AA in the South Pacific, we may go. The outfit is on the borderline. Our CG said the outfits here before January 1st would probably go home within the next four months, but some of those that came in just

On Foreign Soil
Aldermaston

Aldermaston Court near Reading, England, 2010

Fireplace and carved banisters

Secret door

Clock tower and smokestacks

Pet cemetery

The churchyard and the village church

The locked door

Lord and Lady Forster

Miscellaneous

Ration stamps

"Shines like a new penny" 2010

Vintage copper tub on display

Dragon's teeth of the Siegfried Line, 2010

The farmhouse in 1945

The farmhouse in 2010

Photograph from
the scrapbook

Poster in Ensival
Historical Museum, 2010

"Always loyal to the 639th"

Well-earned hardware

Souvenirs

Nazi pins

Jester with dancing girls

Cupid bowl from Oberheil, Germany

Nazi patch

German dress sword

before January 1st might have to finish the other war. It is good to know that General Timberlake is batting for us.

Honey, you haven't sent me a notice of the bank account lately. By now you should have the $1000.00 that you tried so long to get. You once said that you didn't think you could ever reach the thousand mark. By the time I get home we should have $2000.00, don't you think? We'll have a nice start, won't we sweet?

May 19, 1945

You asked about the ring. It is a gold ring with an agate setting. It's really pretty. I got it at Nideggen on the Roer. I'll tell you how I got it someday. Can't just now.

May 20, 1945

I was asked to take a regular army commission yesterday, and I turned it down because now I have more to consider than myself. I told them I wanted to get out because I had a wife who would go ahead and make herself like the Army, but neither she nor I could live the normal life that we had planned for postwar living. The way I see it honey, army life just isn't for us. So I told them "No." My only ambition in life, my sweet, is to make you happy. I'm at your disposal. Anything you want you shall have.

May 21, 1945 [Asslar, Germany]

I'm sorry to hear Luke is slated to go to sea. Just yesterday I wrote Mary a letter kidding her about sending her husband over with a boat to take me home. I felt bad about it today when I got a letter from Mama that included a letter from Mary explaining why she might have to come home. I sure hope that Luke can make a deal to stay with Mary.

Honey, I am now set up in Asslar. It is about four miles northwest of Wetzlar which is about ten miles southwest of Giessen. We will be here a few days and then move to Wetzlar to take over a Russian misplaced [displaced] persons' camp and a French and Belgian prisoner of war camp.

During my visit to Buchenwald, I learned about many sub-camps across Germany. I later learned that the prisoners who had been liberated had no means of basic sustenance, let alone transportation to their home countries. I began to realize that the camps of horror were by necessity converted to these so-called "displaced persons" camps—refugee camps of sort, managed by the occupying armies. In essence, they remained custodial camps, though better food and medical attention were provided. They were not the horrific, nightmarish compounds as before, but distressing in other ways. It is such a camp that members of Battery D and other AA personnel were assigned to guard now that there were no more enemy planes to shoot at. Doyle incorrectly labels these "misplaced persons" camps in his letters. Henceforth, the error will be corrected.

These people over here certainly have funny standards of modesty. Some of the men in the outfit can't get used to the way women show their bodies. They think nothing of undressing in front of us. It's certainly a good thing the nonfraternization law was passed. This mass of people is a mess and a great problem for us. I can't see why, since their liberation, France and Belgium can't send after their people. Hell, they sit on their fannies and let us do everything. I just can't understand it. But why beef about it, it won't help.

I like this particular picture because I have a faint suggestion of a smile and also because it was taken on V-E Day. At the left you will see two clips of 40mm ammo with a helmet on top. How do you like the way I sling my pistol?

Doyle on V-E Day

Mustard gas shells*

From the *Unit History, 639th BN*, Chapter XI, Occupation:
 "The job of Security Guard called for protecting vital installations, setting up road checks to see that the population did not
violate regulations about movement, searching for hidden arms
and ammunition and maintaining roving patrols to discourage the
conquered 'supermen' from attempting to start trouble. By this time
we were assigned to the Ninth Army, the First having left for the
Pacific via the States. Our chain of command was really a dilly—
Ninth Army, XIX Corps, 70th Infantry Division, 49th Antiaircraft
Artillery Brigade and 11th Antiaircraft Artillery Group. We did not
lack for a higher headquarters! Little trouble developed and that was
usually from Allied Displaced Persons or released Prisoners of War.
At no time were we required to use force to quell any disturbance."

On the back of the picture: "We were prepared for possible German use of poison
gas. There are thousands of these in the ammo dump we were guarding."

Chapter 24: The Aftermath and Mopping Up

May 22, 1945

Thought I had better tell you I am now attached to the Ninth Army. We are still First Army troops and can be called at any time. I am telling you this because of the radio announcement this morning about the First Army being on its way to the Pacific Theatre via the US. It hasn't been settled and probably won't be for several months. I sure hope we can come home when we do make a move. I can see now your beautiful face, your smile, and hear your mature, experienced laugh. Yes, I remember every little thing about you and I'll never forget it. Never. Darling, I love you.

Honey, if you don't mind and haven't already done it, don't try to mark your big map until I come home. I will do it for you. We'll use colored pins and colored string showing the routes. We'll make a nice map to hang in my den or in the game room. I sure hope you won't have to send for a map of the other side of the world.

I just heard Kay Kyser's rendition of "Accentuate the Positive." It's really cute how Dolly works up to the number and the number is good. This afternoon I'm going to see my first movie since I saw *Going My Way* in Reading, England. That's the only movie that I've seen since I left the States. May get to see more now that things have quieted down.

May 23, 1945

Honey, I wrote you that maybe the outfit would get two more battle stars. Well, we did. One for the Ardennes and the other for the crossing of the Rhine. Now I won't be ashamed to wear my ETO ribbon. I'll have three stars on it to show I did something in the war and, by gad, I did and I'm proud of it. Murphy and I were talking tonight about the past months of combat, and both expressed our thanks that not one of our men was killed. That's what an army officer hopes and prays for throughout his command. We had plenty of chances to get them killed too. *[See image of well-earned hardware in the color gallery.]*

Of course the men are the ones that deserve all the credit. I tell them they are good, but when they start trying to get by on their laurels I jump on them with both feet. They are highly disciplined. For example, as soon as the war was over they came out of foxholes and started shining shoes and washing clothes and saluting like recruits that were afraid they'd be court-martialed for not saluting. That's what you call soldiers—men that can adjust themselves to any situation on the spur of the moment. It's a pleasure to salute a bunch of men like that. It really takes a few battles to make someone feel as I do about my men. It would hurt me deeply to see one of them hurt in any way. I guess that that is the way every officer should feel about his men. They have done a job and done it well. They knocked down 14 German planes at Remagen one day, 12 the next and 9 the next. During the Bulge they got 17 planes and helped in stopping five tiger tanks, plus some smaller armor, plus quite a few SS troopers.

That's pretty good for an outfit that never sees frontline duty. Ha. Yes, it makes me laugh when I think of the jerks in the States telling us that we'd never see frontline action. Oh yes, the kids got three buzz bombs. A very dangerous and nerve-racking mission. But you know honey, not one of them cracked under the strain of it. I'm a part—a small part—of a damn good outfit.

I went to the movie yesterday. It wasn't too good. It was *Hangover Square*, a British picture filmed just like *Jane Eyre*. Remember the shadow scenes?

From the *Unit History, 639th BN*, Chapter X, The Last Lap:
"Many of us believed the Battalion earned a Unit Citation in the Ardennes Campaign, but it was not in the cards and so

we content ourselves with the knowledge that there isn't a better combat outfit in any of the armies. We wear the First Army 'A' and our three campaign stars with the justifiable pride of seasoned fighting troops."

THE RECORD					
	Planes		V-1s		POWs
Battery	Cat I	Cat II	Cat A	Cat B	
A	4	1	2	0	122
B	1	0	0	0	17
C	1	1	1	0	34
D	8	11	3	0	103
HQ	0	0	0	0	19
Total	14	13	6	0	295

Chart detailing combat results from the *Unit History, 639th BN*

May 24, 1945

Honey, I received three sweet letters from you today. I'll have to admit I burned with jealousy when you told me of your war bond drive assistance. But I can't blow my top if you have Mama backing you up. ... My points are: 57 plus 10 additional points for combat stars. I hope that I won't get any more. They aren't worth the danger. I've been very lucky so far, and I don't want the opportunity of earning any more.

War bond drive
Juby, secretary in the Human Resources Department at
Tubize, types job applications for factory workers.

Chapter 24: The Aftermath and Mopping Up

May 26, 1945

Honey, I am enclosing pictures of your latest piece of china. It is without a doubt the loveliest piece I've sent yet. You can see the two little cherubs holding a latticework bowl. The cherubs are six inches high, and the bowl is about ten inches long. I imagine that it is a fruit bowl. Notice the primrose vine running on the latticework. Honey, the leaves of the vine actually stand out and are so thin that they will cut you. The petals of the blooms are as thin as actual petals. The stems [stamen] that hold the pollen are even there. It's most beautiful. When I saw it, I just had to buy it as a token of my love for you, my sweet. *[See image of the cupid bowl in the color gallery.]*

I saw something the other day I had never seen but in the movies. It was a stork with its nest built on a chimney. There were two young ones in the nest. Maybe that's why there are so many babies around here. Damn, every girl you see from 16 on up is pushing a baby carriage—kids that probably someday will fight our sons. But I sure hope not. If ever our country suggests that we arm to stop an uprising like the present one, I want you to give it your wholehearted support, regardless of how many sons we might have and might lose doing it. Roosevelt wanted to start an army before he did, but the public wouldn't let him. It will save a great many lives to be prepared next time. Honey, I love you with all my heart and do so much hope to see you soon.

May 30, 1945

Honey, I took a ride down to Frankfurt to get photographic supplies this morning. The city is really torn up. Picked up some developer, fixer, more paper and two rolls of film—all the film they would give me. You asked me where the picture of the tank was taken. It was taken on the East-West Autobahn at Gera. Have you a map that shows Gera?

US Sherman tank with rocket launcher on East-West Autobahn at Gera

Pölzig is the farthest I got into Germany. I am now in Wetzlar. Day before yesterday our CP was in Asslar. A battalion show visited us this evening—our own D Battery band that I organized back in Aldermaston. They played for two dances there before we moved on to continent, and now the battalion has taken it over for entertainment. They have just now started playing again and have made quite a hit over here too. They aren't playing for dances because we can't get any women due to the nonfraternization rule.

There are no rumors as to what will happen to us. The Army moves slow, but when it does move it moves fast.

June 2, 1945

In one of your letters yesterday you said something that made me love you even more than I did. You told me regardless of what happens, don't let it get me down. Honey, all these months I have been trying to prepare you for a possible trip to the CBI after the European war was over, and at the same time I neglected to prepare myself for the possibility. When I read that letter, it meant so much to know how you felt about it. Honey, a love as strong as ours can't be touched by any physical separation regardless of how long it might be. Darling I love you, and when I do come home, it will be worth the waiting.

June 3, 1945

Honey, I am sending to you a German camouflage suit for Jack. It is a two-piece affair. The jacket has a hood on it and a drawstring belt. The thing is padded with cotton and quilted. It is reversible. The one side is white, and the other is like the jungle suit I gave him. I also have a couple of sterling lockets with chains that I'll send soon. The front is made of onyx. I'll send one in each letter I write the next two days. They would be nice for any daughters we might have.

June 4, 1945

I was in the battalion yesterday and played some volleyball with the officers. I had a few drinks of cognac, and Shepp, Murphy and I just finished a bottle of champagne. It was pretty good. Made in 1937. Wish that you could have helped me drink it.

"Me and Shepp share a bottle"

We are having some beautiful weather here now, and if it wasn't for the present war with Japan, I couldn't see any reason why you couldn't come over and stay with me. You could see Germany and all the countries between here and the States. Maybe after the Army of Occupation is picked, they will let wives come over. Really honey, it wouldn't be bad to live over here for five years if you could be with me. It would be just like a five-year honeymoon because Germany is a beautiful country.

June 5, 1945

I have spent most of my time in my darkroom of late, and now I'm even fed up with that. This afternoon Shepp and I went over to the battalion to practice softball. We have a game with the 563rd tomorrow. As usual the Colonel has money bet on the game. After winning him $100 yesterday, and if we can win that much tomorrow, maybe we can expect a drink or two off him. Did I tell you that Captain Hooper is at the Riviera on leave? He has been gone four days. He deserves the trip. He has done a good job.

June 6, 1945

Today is the anniversary of the storming of the Normandy beaches. It has been declared an army holiday by our Supreme Commander General Eisenhower. Only necessary army duties are being done today. Day after tomorrow is our 14-month anniversary. It's been wonderful, my sweet, to have you as a wife these 14 months.

We played a volleyball match yesterday that netted our colonel 1,000 marks. He had it bet on us. This is 100 bucks. Now he has bet on us in softball so we better win.

Honey, my present mission is guarding a Russian and Polish displaced persons' camp. I'll tell you one thing—the Russians are certainly a mess. They are the filthiest people that I have run across anywhere. We found a fully developed premature baby out back of our CP yesterday morning. It had been thrown over the fence out of the Russian enclosure. Of course the baby is better off dead because of the living conditions and the food situation. We have been trying to ship the Russians back to their country, but we have to force them on the trucks with fixed bayonets. I guess they haven't got much to go back to. *[Doyle had no knowledge of the harsh reception given returning POWs by Stalin's regime.]* The Italians also are waiting for us to transport them home. Hell, I'd walk. Honey, you can't possibly picture just how lucky we Americans are. We have everything. Even the Germans admit that we have everything.

Some of our drivers say when they stop for a rest while hauling Russians, the Russians pick up stones and sticks for the purpose of stoning returning German soldiers and breaking shop windows along the way. One big husky Russian gal had a stick, and every time our driver drove close to a German along the roadside the Russian babe would lay them cold with it, probably killing some of them. Boy the Russians are tough, but they are afraid of us. They have been our chief problem since the end of hostilities.

June 7, 1945

Honey, I'm having trouble keeping my men from fraternizing. You know by now that everything that enlisted men do, right or wrong, reflects on the officer in charge. I have planned to talk to every man in the battery today, and if the talk doesn't do any good, I just don't know what I'll do. So wish me luck. I think they will play ball with me, however. I've always played fair and square with them. We just can't do much about a man when women are concerned, I guess. As for me, I can't forget the fact that not too long ago these girls' brothers were trying to kill us all. I have no sympathy or love for any of them. But some of my men seem to have forgotten that the German people are our enemies until we change their Nazi ideas.

June 8, 1945

How are ya kid? Just had to talk for a while. I played softball last night, and as usual the boys came through for the Colonel. Our battalion officers played the officers of the 563rd AAA AW Bn. The first four innings I played first base and participated in three double plays. Then they asked me to pitch. I have never pitched in my life, but I went ahead and pitched for three innings, and they didn't get a hit off me. The Colonel is proud of us. The score was 4 to 2. I got two doubles for three times at bat. Not bad for the first game of the season. I scored two of the four runs and batted in one of the others. I'm still thinking about playing ball on one of the Textile League teams.

After the game was over, the commanding officer of the 563rd had us down to the officers' quarters for a drink or two. I had about six drinks of cognac and a glass of beer then went to Battalion Headquarters where I had a big glass of wine. When I left they gave me a bottle of wine for helping to win the ball game. I got back to the battery, and 1st Sergeant Shepp and I drank the bottle of wine. I got to bed about 2200 and during the night I had to get up four times for water. The wine really made me dry. Honey, will you send me some cigarettes? The cigarette situation, now that the war is over, isn't so good.

Honey, I'm going to send a poster made by the First Army. It has the names and insignia of all the major units. The 49th AAA Brigade is the one we were in. It is signed by General Timberlake, our 49th Brigade commander, and by Colonel Newton, our 11th Group commander. Timberlake was in command of the defense of Washington when the Truman Committee made the investigation. He used wooden guns because the war lords were sending all the weapons to the fighting fronts. He used the dummy guns as a bluff, hoping that soon he could get some guns that would shoot. He was a colonel at the time but was made general after Truman finished the investigation.

HEADQUARTERS
49th ANTIAIRCRAFT ARTILLERY BRIGADE
APO 230
Germany

SUBJECT: Commendation on Performance of Duty in the Ardennes, Rhineland, and Central European Campaigns

TO: Commanding Officer, 639th AAA AW BN, APO 230, US Army

1. At the conclusion of our victorious campaign through Europe, I want to express my deep appreciation to you, and through you, to the officers and men of your battalion, for the outstanding drive, tenacity of purpose, and aggressiveness with which the 639th AAA AW Battalion performed all combat missions in the Ardennes, Rhineland, and Central European Campaigns.

2. Narrative.
    a. The 639th AAA AW Battalion was initially committed in the P. A. C. Belt east of Bullingen, Germany, on 12 December 1944, with the primary mission of destroying P. A. C. over German lines. On 16 December 1944, when the Germans launched their Ardennes Counter offensive, the 639th AAA AW Battalion found itself astride the main axis of advance of the 12th S.S. Panzer Division, and upon withdrawal of elements of the _____ Infantry Division [blank in original document] on 17 December held the Butgenbach shoulder of the Ardennes Bulge with support against fanatic enemy

infantry and armored attack until the arrival of the 1st US Infantry Division on 19 December 1944, and then fought shoulder to shoulder with the Infantry troops of this Division on the northern shoulder of the Bulge in the counter-attack which converted the "Ardennes Bulge" into the "Ardennes Bubble."

b. The 639th AAA AW Battalion successfully provided AAA defense for vital rear installations in the FIRST ARMY zone of action until the seizure of the Remagen Bridge across the Rhine on 8 March 1945, when the Battalion was rushed forward to participate in the impregnable AAA defense of that historic crossing.

c. When the FIRST ARMY broke out of the Remagen Bridgehead and raced to the Elbe River, the 639th AAA AW Battalion moved aggressively and progressively forward, finding itself upon the termination of hostilities, providing AAA defense for Leipzig, deep in the heart of Germany.

3. The fighting instincts, esprit de corps, and outstanding tenacity of purpose of the officers and men of the 639th AAA AW Battalion, who chose to stay and slug it out, shoulder to shoulder with the Infantry, in the most critical battle of the European campaign, redounds to the glory of their Battalion, their Brigade, and their Army. The forceful leadership, high degree of personal courage, and technical and tactical skill of the officers and non-commissioned officers who led this hard-bitten battalion in the greatest military campaigns of all time, is directly reflected in the outstanding achievements of the 639th AAA AW Battalion when the chips were down.

s/E.W. Timberlake
t/E.W. Timberlake
Brigadier General, US Army
Commanding

From another letter to "All Officers and Men of the 639th AAA AW Battalion:"

> "The termination of the fighting in Europe does not remove the opportunities for other outstanding and equally difficult achievements in the days to come. In many ways the immediate future will demand more fortitude than has the past, for without the inspiration of combat, you must maintain, by your dress, deportment, and efficiency, not only the prestige of your unit, but also the honor of the United States. I have complete confidence that you will not fail."

> —E. W. Timberlake, Brigadier General,
> US Army Commanding

June 10, 1945

Men will be men, and they are fraternizing to the fullest. I'm not trying to stop it; I just don't want anyone else to see them messing with German people. You see, when a Yank goes with a German girl he usually gives her a ___ (you know what I mean). They think that's what the German people deserve, so what can you do? I only ask them to be very careful and not let anyone catch them. Then everything will be OK. I really don't understand what the nonfraternization law is for. They tell us that we must teach the Germans our way of life. How in hell are we going to do it if we can't talk to them? That is one to answer. General Eisenhower has said that there will be severe punishment for fraternization.

I heard something today that was encouraging to say the least. The rumor is that we are to go to the CBI via the States. It takes about one and one-half months to get home under the present situation. We would have 21 days at home, then train six to eight weeks with First Army and then go through POM [Processing for

Overseas Movement]. By then the war in Japan would be over. How does that sound to you? I'll let you know when I find out if it's true.

I told you I would tell you about the ring later. I'll tell you about it now. It would be better if you wouldn't tell anyone about it; they might not understand. It came from the finger of the first German soldier I saw go down, and honey, he wasn't too far from me. I took it as the first and only souvenir I have wanted. You can see why I didn't want to tell you before. Maybe I shouldn't have told you even now. I felt a little funny after my first encounter, but I soon found that it was the "survival of the fittest" and my chicken-heartedness toward the Germans soon dwindled. Remember, they killed James Goss and Jeep Hardin. Honey, don't get me wrong. I'm not a killer at heart, but when there's an enemy that will kill me, it's different. We guys over here haven't changed one bit unless it's in a way to make us appreciate home life more.

I was the host of a couple of American girls yesterday and the day before. What do you think about that? They were the violinist and soloist of an all-girl orchestra in Camp Shows, Inc. from the States. They were on their way to Wetter and stopped in for lunch. We had chicken and ice cream for them. It was the first ice cream they'd had since leaving the States. It was the first that we had had too, but I made them think that we had it every other day. They came back the next day (that's yesterday), and all we could offer them was apple pie.

Captain Hooper is due to return tomorrow. I'll be glad to have him back because Murphy is acting CO and he's afraid of his shadow. I can talk Captain Hooper into doing things, but Murphy is afraid to do anything unless ordered from some higher-up. I guess that proves he is a good soldier. But the Remagen Bridge was not taken under orders. The general that took it seized the opportunity and over the bridge he went. That's the way things are done. Use every opportunity that comes to hand.

Friend "Jeep" Hardin in front of Doyle's boyhood
home, killed in action (KIA) in Italy

There's no excitement in the ETO any more, like air raids and artillery shellings and bridges falling and the like. How do you expect me to write you an interesting letter? I know that I'm not a writer, but at least I've taken up some of your time and I just love to take up your time.

June 11, 1945

Captain Hooper has just arrived from the Riviera. I haven't talked to him yet because he was called to the battalion as soon as he got back and I was out lecturing to the men about what happened from D-Day to V-E Day. I talked to them for an hour. Using their own picturesque GI language keeps them more interested than perfect English. That's my excuse and alibi for swearing so much.

Things over here are going to get organized pretty soon. The war in the ETO ended six to ten months ahead of schedule, so as time rolls along, things will shape up and more of us will come home to the ones we love. Your sister Frances and girlfriends of yours have husbands that have been over much longer than I have, and I have done more to end the war than most of them. Yet the job they had was just as essential as mine and maybe even more so.

Frances's husband, Henley, in India

June 11, 1945

Honey, this is the second time today that I have written to you. I started this last night, but just as I finished the first sentence the Sergeant of the Guard came in, and since I was the OD I had to go with him and settle his problem. Two lieutenants from Group Headquarters had entered the Polish camp on what they called official business. Of course the Sergeant of the Guard thought that it was highly irregular to have official business at 2330 at night. So he came after me to investigate. Well, one of the lieutenants turned out to be a kid that I gave basic training to at Ft. Eustis and I asked him what the score was and why he was there. You see, they could have been there checking up on my guard.

After I got there, I knew that they were there to possibly do a little "pole-ing" with the Poles. So I parked myself where they had left their jeep and let them go ahead with their alleged "official business." When they returned and learned that the Officer of the Day wanted to talk to them, they were very embarrassed. They gave me some song and dance story that I took with a grain of salt and I pulled them away from the enlisted men of my guard and told them that if they wanted to fraternize against existing regulations to please not do any of it in front of my men because I was having enough trouble with them as it was. By right I should have reported them, but there is a gentleman's code amongst us.

Well honey, I just got a job assignment. I may be on my way to France in the next two or three days. Don't know what to expect from there, so please honey, don't get your hopes up. I am going to Marseilles. I'll keep you posted as to further developments. Keep your chin up and remember: you are my baby and I love you.

IN HIS FOOTSTEPS

May 5, 2010: *We make a U-turn heading west out of Germany, having accomplished our goal of following Dad's path through England, Belgium and Germany. We leave the Cannes and Marseilles portion of his experience to a later time. Perhaps a Mediterranean cruise someday. Back in Erezee, Belgium, as guests of our guide Michael, we watch a spectacular red ball of sun drop into the forested valley below. For this last evening, we sleep in a 300-year-old castle. A perfect way to end our tour. Days later we are able to walk Mom through our journey day by day with pictures, pamphlets and souvenirs. When we are done, she says, "Well, I feel like I have been there." Mission accomplished!*

PROJECT REPORT

July 12, 2009: *When Dad talked about his overseas experience, he most often told stories about combat. Now, as I learn there was time for sports and photography in the days following V-E Day, I am beginning to grasp that the postwar months before homecoming were long and agonizingly boring. He spent more months struggling to stay busy while waiting to be shipped home than he spent in early transit and subsequent combat duty.*

After hostilities ended, Dad seemed comfortable in Germany, where his outfit was assigned to deal with prisoners of war, guard ammo dumps and (later) guard camps for displaced persons. During this time, he "liberated" some abandoned German photography equipment and taught himself how to use it, accumulating a collection of cameras. He gradually sent them home along with darkroom supplies, intending to continue the hobby. Reading detailed descriptions of his efforts and realizing the extreme interest and fascination driving the process, I thought he should have become a photographer. I commented to Mom about this, and she said that, once he got home, all of the overseas experience and everything associated with it was put aside.

Every time I reread Dad's letters, I discover more threads. One of the most important is the thread of confidence vs. the lack thereof. As he related the hurdles of Officers Candidate School, he lauded his own leadership skills. Yet he always anticipated some mishap that could block his commission—particularly in the academic portion of the training. But soon after becoming a second lieutenant, he lost all confidence and wrote agonizing letters of despair. This depression almost caused him to abandon his romantic relationship with Mom. After their reunion and subsequent marriage (overcoming his "better" judgment, which to him meant waiting until after the war), his confidence returned. There would be no more whining about his job until the long wait in Marseilles when he couldn't see how his assignments were helping the army at all.

After the surprisingly intense introduction to combat in Belgium, Dad gave Mom credit for making him a good officer. He also bragged about the performance of his men, giving them full credit for a job well done during dire circumstances. His confidence was there during OCS, bottomed out shortly after, returned with the marriage and grew thereafter through the assignments in the ETO. Full cycle.

Another thread is the relationship between Dad and Captain Hooper. Early on, just after orders of deployment for the 639th, Dad said disparaging things about his CO in D Battery, and a number of times during the overseas assignment he referred to animosity between the lieutenants and the "higher-ups." But he also referred to playing cards, tennis and other recreational activities with Captain Hooper, especially after V-E Day. At one point, Dad finally admitted, "He did a good job." Obviously their relationship and mutual respect came full cycle.

Dad's letters also contrast the wild V-E Day and V-J Day celebrations at home with the reaction among the troops still stationed abroad: "There is no jubilance here." His reaction is no more optimistic when anticipating their future homecoming: "People will have forgotten all about it—hero today, gone tomorrow." Indifference seems to be the case today as well, perhaps because during a decade of war, fresh troops routinely replace returning soldiers without a "winning moment" in sight, although many groups are now trying to improve public awareness of returning veterans' needs.

Spending these last few months studying Dad's journey, I couldn't help but compare his story with that of soldiers in more recent wars. Dad's letters often mentioned the possibility of "becoming hardened" or changed, but he assured his bride that it would not be the case with him. As far as I can tell, he was right. I think the long delay between combat duty and the return home helped moderate the transition.

Soldiers who leave an intense combat zone directly for home and family seem likely to experience far greater reentry problems than those who have a chance to decompress. Murder and suicide rates among recently returned veterans continue to increase despite today's efforts toward identifying and treating post-traumatic stress disorder (PTSD). In WWII, soldiers were deployed for the duration, however long it took, and often came home long after the job was done, knowing their commitment was over. It would be difficult to know how many suffered PTSD, since the condition was not recognized at the time.

I think back to the return of my friend (later, husband) from his Vietnam (VN) tour. His tour was split: six months in VN as infantry platoon leader and six months in Okinawa as assistant legal officer. I have letters describing rain and mud in the field, cellulitis, dysentery, a fire-fight and the death of his radio man in his stead. From Okinawa, letters describe "the good life" with golf and football, but also racial tensions and drug abuse. There, his job had to do with the prosecution and legal representation of violators. Looking back and comparing his situation to Dad's, I think they both had an advantage, though it didn't seem like one, of having time and space (due to a safer assignment) between combat and the trip back to "the world." They were able to leave "over there" what happened over there. Afterward, they forged ahead and lived their lives. Dad talked often and with pride about his experiences. My husband lauded his Marine Corps experience as the best service he could have chosen. Many servicemen of the VN conflict were not as fortunate.

The long-term effects on current military personnel who face repeated deployment to foreign combat zones, thus shifting between two very different environments—home life and hostility—are yet to be fully comprehended. These soldiers are living an entirely different story. Will their history be documented as was Dad's, now that e-mail and other electronic technologies replace the traditional

339

letter? I hope so, because all those who come after them need word pictures to be able to appreciate the day-to-day sacrifices their loved one made in the name of service.

Now, after taking this time to reflect, I shall eagerly continue transcribing. I am anxious to see this officer home and discharged!

Part III

The Overseas Story
Southern France

Of Post-Combat Assignments and the Agonizing Wait for Passage Home

June 19, 1945, through November 15, 1945

Chapter 25

Whither Hence and When?

Marseilles, France

The remaining chapters cover a period of uncertainty, frustrating boredom and anxiety about getting home. Dad never talked about this extended and dissatisfying time. Again, letters reveal his innermost thoughts about his experiences: reflections on the war itself, vexation with the army over perceived disorganization and unfairness, disgust with the French port city environment and social behavior. He doesn't hold back in expressing his opinions. Additionally, he has more time for photography, sports, selecting and sending souvenirs, letter writing and drinking. This is the inglorious part of the story, but valuable in its own right. The pressure of separation intensifies and is as hard to survive as was the battleground.

June 19, 1945

Dearest Juby,

Well honey, now I am at Marseilles, France. I came through Frankfort, Hamburg, Nancy, Macon, Lyons and Valance. We are bivouacked just outside of town.

343

Boy, Marseilles is just like you would picture it. You can see anything here. I've been into town for the past two nights, and I have never seen such a mass of humanity. We have been given a detail here. How long it will last I don't know, but I don't like the setup. We are too available here regardless of what we might be doing. We could be ordered to the CBI overnight.

I am really getting sick of the Army. The public newspapers convey the idea that everything about the point system is a square deal, but in reality some soldiers are getting a very raw deal. We of the 639th have learned that it doesn't pay to plan on a damn thing. The Army moves slow until it starts moving, then it moves very rapidly.   I love you and miss you, Doyle

June 23, 1945

For the past four days, all I have done is come to Marseilles with a pass convoy. After I get here, there is nothing to do but go to a bar someplace, have a few drinks and read. Honey, if I am told that we are to go back to Germany as Army of Occupation, please forget what I said about you coming over because I wouldn't drag you into this mess for anything. The people over here are rotten. The French people are charging us prices that will pay their war debt. It's preposterous, but we GIs can't do anything about it. We have to grin and bear it. Our money is given to us at a rate of 2.5 cents per franc, and a franc is worth 1 cent according to the NY Exchange, so we aren't getting full value for the amount we draw here. I am sending a wire today requesting $50.00 to aid me in getting back on my feet. While I was in Germany, I spent most of my money on things for you, and the trip to Cannes made me suffer financially. I need a money order to pay back a debt or two that I have. I'll try not to let it happen again, sweet. Please don't think I am a spendthrift because I really have done well with what I draw for my own use. And honey, don't expect too many gifts

344

from me from France because the French are taking advantage of us, the blasted vultures. I hate them.

Honey, today I want you more than I have wanted you since I left. My last picture of you was you lying sleepily in bed there in Wilmington not realizing that I was leaving for quite some time. When I left that morning, I did the hardest thing of my life. I didn't want to leave you. I like to remember you lying there in that room where we had spent our last eight days together. You're my life, sweetheart.

June 24, 1945

Honey, I am still very, very disgusted with the situation here. We are living in pup tents out in a dusty field that is as hot as blazes. Of course it is a hell of a lot more comfortable than it was last December and January when we were in pup tents in the snow, but it is still miserable.

My opinion of the Germans has been boosted a great deal since I returned to France. I can say this for the German people: they are clean. These French people are nothing but pigs. The women are dirty-looking and filthy. Some of the tales that the boys tell about their dealings with the French babes turn my stomach. In the town of Marseilles, it is a known fact that 90 percent of the women are infected with syphilis or some type of venereal disease. We will probably have more venereal troubles now than we had with fraternization. At least fraternization with German women didn't leave the men open to injuring their health as much as now. Some men must have their women regardless of the danger facing them. I was standing in the Red Cross Club last night watching some officers dance with French babes, and a major said to me, "I wouldn't dance with one of those lousy French babes for anything." Well a Frenchman heard him and became very offended, expressing it in a way the major didn't like. The major immediately floored the offended Frenchman. More fun, the Frenchman produced a knife in his defense and the major proceeded to make him eat it. It was fun while it lasted, but it didn't last long.

The other night a Frenchman took a couple of pot shots at one of our boys from a window with a pistol. As a result, about a dozen of the boys beat the hell out of every man in the town. They did a good job, too, especially on the one that they thought did the shooting. We aren't hard to get along with, but we don't take anything off them. They are out to get all they can off us, and if we have anything to do with it, they aren't going to get by with a thing.

Darling since I got started with this letter I have received two pieces of your heart. The two letters were so sweet. You're my life.

We're moving about 40 miles away tomorrow. It will be better because we have built our own camp. We are using seven-man squad tents and we have our own flagpole and all. Battalion is setting up here in Marseilles, so we will be by ourselves. I like it better like that.

June 25, 1945

Darling, if you keep sending me little pieces of your heart, you won't have much left. But keep it up, my sweet. I love it. I'll bring your heart back to you soon.

I'm going to send you two cameras. One of them is for you, so you must send me some pictures of you. Remember this: for best results on a sunny day, have a shutter opening of 8 and a shutter speed of 50. In exceptionally bright light, you can close the shutter and also speed up the shutter to 125. Darker days reverse the procedure. Understand?

June 27, 1945 [Mirimas, France]

You mentioned in one of your letters that the Ninth Army was coming home. Well honey, I am no longer in the Ninth Army, so I missed the boat again. I'll catch one pretty soon however. It will come before either of us knows just what is happening. At present we are pulling MP and guard details around some QM dumps [Quartermasters (supply)]. It isn't hard work at all. We raid houses of prostitution, and honey, a French prostitute is the filthiest thing in the world. All of them are diseased. I can't see why an American soldier would want to go in one of the places but they do. We have caught them there.

June 28, 1945

This is the most boring place I have ever been in. We are out some ten miles from any town, and the one closest has only one café in it. What I am doing is so nonessential to the Army that I could just stop doing anything and the Army would never know the difference. I could come home, and it wouldn't hurt the Army at all. But it seems the Army thinks they need me. There is nothing you or I can do to change their idea. We will just have to wait until they are through with me. Honey, did you know that I am located within two miles of an airport where planes take off by the dozens each day for the States? Yes, I am only 36 hours from home. It makes me burn to think that I am so close to you and yet so far.

June 29, 1945

Honey, you continue to send little bits and big chunks of your heart even while you are vacationing. Yes, I got four letters mailed from Daytona. One contained the pictures of you in your new suit. Wow!

Juby at Daytona Beach, Florida*

On the back of the picture: "The back of the suit is red, the front, yellow. I had a yellow bandana on my hair. Hope you like it. June 18, 1945, Daytona Beach, Florida"

July 1, 1945

I have found out no officer will be transferred from one branch to another. So there isn't much danger of being placed in infantry, which relieves some of that dread. The WD [War Department] has found it more confusing than helpful; it is better to make commissions from the ranks.

July 4, 1945

Today is a holiday for all men not actually pulling some type of duty such as guard, KP [Key Personnel], MP or the like. I have brought some 25 men into Marseilles for a holiday pass. The Red Cross is serving free doughnuts and coffee in celebration of the 4th. ... I sometimes wish we were still in Germany. I don't like the French people. There is more dirty, filthy debauchery going on in this country than any I have been in.

July 5, 1945

I got back from Marseilles about 0200 this morning. One of my charges got lost and we had to hunt for him. He is a rather rattle-brained guy. Very brilliant but absent-minded. I had to take the same guy by the arm and lead him to a truck when we escaped the Honsfeld trap. But that's the Army, I guess. It takes all kinds.

Honey, I am sending two boxes tomorrow. One contains nothing but printing paper for our proposed darkroom. You can open the case or box but don't open any of the small boxes or packages. It will be ruined if exposed to light. In the other box is a German paratroop helmet. ...

The top of the stein wasn't bent when I sent it, but packages really take a beating in shipment. Was the German blanket in that package? If so it might make a beach blanket for us. Golly I sure hope that the china dolls and the bowl aren't broken. I was sure

German paratroop helmet

that nothing would happen to the beer stein. It was packed better than the other cases. Damn, you just can't win it seems. If the dolls are broken, I'll just die and I know that you will too. They're so dainty and pretty. The very thing for a music room.

Please don't expect me until you hear from me. As you say, the Army operates very strangely at times. As far as I can see now, we'll be here until all troops and equipment are disposed of in this section of France. Of course we are very, very available. We are ranked very highly as combat troops, so if there is a flare-up of Japanese offense we will probably be sent. Keep this in mind my sweet.

About what I paid for the items. Don't worry about it kid. I didn't pay money. I paid for them with cigarettes and candy out of my rations I buy each week. You can't imagine just what value these items have in Germany, France and Belgium. It's called black market, but to me it's a way the soldier can equalize the tremendous difference in exchange of French, Belgian, German and American money. I call what the French are doing to us highway robbery.

Chapter 25: Whither Hence and When?

July 8, 1945

Bob Hope is on now. He's in Paris. He will put on two performances at Calas Staging Area tomorrow night. It's about 15 miles from here. I might go to see him. He's terrific. He can really cut loose over here. He doesn't have to pull any punches when he isn't over the ABC [American Broadcasting Company] or the MBS [Mutual Broadcasting System]. He really pulls some raw ones, and the boys love it. So do I, and so would you if you heard him.

I went over to a lake nearby today for a bath. It rained in the mountains at the source of our bath stream and it is too muddy to take a bath in, so we drove about two miles to wash up. The water was nice but the rocks hurt our feet. Just a minute while I check on the mail situation.

I had two letters from you. They were short but sweet. One was written on June 17 and you were really down in the dumps because you had heard the Ninth Army left Marseilles for the CBI. I thought I told you, my sweet, we are back to the First Army, assigned directly to DBS (Delta Base Section). We are service troops of the staging area and port here. Don't worry about it honey. I really believe that we'll be home by October. By the way my sweet, I've done something I know is inexcusable but I've forgotten when your birthday is. Tell me please. It's the 10th of some month I think. Gosh I'm embarrassed. Also send me Hess's and Wilbur's address. We're starting a history of the 639th and we want to include them in it.

In one of your letters, you mentioned something about a surprise for me. Honey you really caused my curiosity to come out. I can't imagine what you have up your sleeve. I bet it will be good though. Is it pictures or what? I can't guess. Tell me what it is. Come on now, please tell me.

July 9, 1945

You say that your family likes me. Well I sure hope so because I think that they are swell. Every one of them. Honey, I must stop now because it's getting dark, and since we are living in tents it's hard to write after dark. That's why I'm not sending you very many pictures lately. I can't set up my darkroom.

July 10, 1945

I just got a book from the airport nearby. ... Golly but I'm getting bored here. Wish that you were here. There's the nicest officers' club at Mirimas, and all I can do when I go there is sit and listen to the music and drink rum and coke and think of you.

July 10, 1945 [second letter]

Got a letter from you today written on July 5. Mail is really coming through. That's five days from home to here. How long is it taking my letters to get to you? I got a letter from Mary. She seemed to be so happy that Luke won't have to go to sea. (The news from the Japanese Theatre is good. I just stopped to listen to it.)

I was at the club for a while last night. Had three cuba libras [Cuba Libre—rum and Coca-Cola with lime] and got disgusted with my loneliness, went back to camp and slept. There's much to do and see here, but it isn't fun to do it alone. There are beautiful blue lakes to swim in, swimming and boating on the Mediterranean Sea, bull fights in Marseilles, rodeos from Spain and dancing. Anything you want to do you can do here. But if you come, it would mean a five-year stay for us.

We have a beautiful camp built now for just our battery. We have a street with tents on each side and out front are our baseball field and volleyball court. We put our flag pole up today. We're going to have our formal flag raising tomorrow. I'll send you pictures of the ceremony when I can get them developed. I may try to make a roll of negatives tonight, but operating in a tent is so inconvenient.

Street of tents

I haven't heard any good rumors to pass on to you. One thing though, our combat record has followed us here. Some of the high-ranking officers of DBS have commented on our record and told us that the Negro troops here (and there's *beaucoup* of them) are really afraid of our MP squads. They look at the three stars and the First Army patch and say, "Boy I don't wan nutin' to do wid dem combat troops from de First Army." It's really funny. One camp had an average of two murders per night. Since we took it over, there have only been three murders in all. We have a rough bunch of boys who are also damn good. Real soldiers. *[Another indication of postwar violence, prejudice and pent-up frustration.]*

July 11, 1945

I played three games of volleyball today with the boys and had two baths out in the irrigation ditch that runs by our camp.

Then I went over to the airport to steal a couple of lengths of pipe to make us a wash rack. That's all that I did today except dream of you.

July 13, 1945

I played ball today, and during the game I slid into third base. Since I only had on a pair of shorts I burned the nicest strawberry on my hip and knee. A "strawberry" is a skinned place inflicted when sliding without slide pads. It really hurts when it starts healing, so I am in for a bit of pain in the next few days.

I'm going into Marseilles tomorrow to an officers' meeting about I and E [Information and Education]. Ugh! The Army is making great plans for educating its GIs. The plan is to use officers as teachers, and you know that I am not a teacher. I am only a GI wanting to come home to you. I try to imagine what you are doing. I can see you flitting around getting ready to go to work. You were always so cute sitting there at your dressing table in your slip. You put on your dress at the last minute. You didn't think I would remember that, did you? I remember every little thing. When I hear beautiful music on the radio, I can see you dancing to the rhythm of it. You move as if on a cloud. My thoughts and dreams of you are what keep my spirits up. Until we are together again, we will continue to make love on a piece of paper, as you put it. But honey, this paper represents me because I try to write every thought that comes into my mind.

The mail just came in. I got three letters, one from Mama and two from you. Just a minute. I have letters to read. ... Mama said that James Whittenburg was back at the gas company. No one ever told me he was discharged. Find out and let me know where James fought. I'm curious to know if they met with any Japanese aircraft.

July 14, 1945

I have sent another package of photographic equipment. More paper and the camera I used in Cannes. Also there is a tripod for cameras, a paper cutter and a microscope. The microscope is 500x and 1000x power. There are two lenses for it. It's nice to have. Our kids can use it in their high school biology classes. *[Ken and I both ended up in careers that involve microscopy, no doubt due to the opportunity to play with one as we grew up. I was very young when Dad pricked his finger and let me see the magnified blood cells; then he allowed me to prick mine. I was captivated.]*

We are now in Category 4. That means that we are to be broken up. If I am lucky, I'll be put in an outfit that is coming home. I'll have 79 points, and 85 is the officers' critical score. I still don't know which way I'll go, but honey as soon as I find out I'll let you know. If I am to go to the CBI and censorship is in effect, I'll put Dearest Ruby instead of Juby and you'll know. Remember that now.

Honey, I saw the biggest mass of milling people I have ever seen today. Today is Bastille Day in France. I had to go to Marseilles, and the streets were packed with a parade of people walking 12 abreast as far as you could see. It took me 30 minutes to walk a block. The people of France are to celebrate three days. There will be millions of gallons of wine consumed, and the prostitutes are doing business free in Marseilles today.

July 16, 1945

You have asked for pictures so, by golly, I'll be sending more than you'll want. These were all taken at Camp Murphy today. Remember Captain Murphy? He's our Battery Commander since Captain Hooper went to battalion. As you know, RHIP [Rank Has Its Privilege] so our camp is Camp Murphy. Some of the guns have swastikas that we are authorized to paint after knocking down an enemy plane.

Keeping track of downed enemy planes

The ones of me are rather beaten up because I tried to make them myself. The boat I have by me is a three-man assault boat we acquired since we got here. We use it when we go to the lake nearby.

"Assault boat"

"Catch of the day"*

On the back of the picture: "How's this for two hours of fishing? Three of them. Show this to Will. He'll be envious I know. The fish are pickerel. Very 'game.' What beautiful 'gams' I have! Wow!"

July 18, 1945

The envelope I am sending with this letter contains about 50 negatives of pictures I took coming down from Germany.

Tent life in Germany

July 29, 1945

Honey, you should be here. Our nine-piece battalion band (six of which are from D Battery) is making history here in southern France. One night they play at the Red Cross at Aix, one night at the Red Cross at Mirimas, then one night at the officers' club at Aix. The other nights they come out to the battery camp for a jive session. Boy, they really make the house jump. They are really hot. I started the band at Aldermaston. The pieces include two trumpets, sax, clarinet, piano, guitar, bass viola, base horn and drums. They imitate Johnny Cong and Tommy Dorsey mostly. I really enjoy listening to them. The 639th really has a lot of talent in it. But when the time comes to fight they are right there, Johnny-on-the-spot. Good men all of them.

I got the bowl in Oberheil, Germany. It is a small town near Wetzlar. I got it for three bars of candy and two packages of cigarettes. I could be charged with fraternizing for making the deal, but now that it's lifted (I mean fraternization), I'm safe. It's too bad I'm not still there. Now that the nonfraternization law is rescinded, I could get some lovely things for you. I took the chance on a few items and got by with it.

THE BAND WAS IN BIG DEMAND THROUGHOUT THE AREA

Photograph and caption from *Unit History, 639th BN*

July 20, 1945

I shoot the bull with the guys who are also writing their wives and girlfriends. The guys are about to crack under the strain. The monotony is too much for them. We passed seven fast months when we were tactical, but now we have too much time to dream of people like you and it's tough.

July 21, 1945

I sure hope that the war with Japan keeps progressing in our favor because as soon as the Japs bring on a counteroffensive, if they can, more troops will be sent to the CBI. When General Von Rundstedt started his offensive in December, I remember every excess medic was given a berth in the infantry and every quartermaster in the rear was sent to the front to help stop it. From seeing and knowing this, I know that if the Japs break loose the same thing might happen to us. When things happen, the Army moves fast regardless of who they might hurt.

My 79 points might get me out of this man's army faster than I expected. I have been told that more officers volunteered to stay in than were expected to, so the standing 85 point critical score for officers may be lowered. It might not be long before we will be civilians. I mean you and me because you're as much in the Army as I am. It may take me a couple of months to get used to being a civilian again, but it's going to be fun learning to be one with you.

Chapter 26

Staging Down

July 22, 1945

Dearest Juby,

I have done very little since we got to France. All I've done is try to make our little camp here more livable. We are set up as nice as anyone could be in tents. Tomorrow I start to work putting in a shower unit. We will have six showers to start with and add more as we get them.

We're turning in all of our guns next Tuesday. It will be nice to be rid of them because we won't have to clean them. The guns served us very well. Eight guns knocked down 27 planes and kept hundreds from getting to their targets. All we'll have left is our rifles.   Wanting to be with you, Doyle

July 24, 1945

It's the same life each day. Very little work to do. Only an occasional trip someplace to secure lumber, nails, paint, etc. Lumber is really scarce around here. We have scraped up all available wood for construction. There's such a great difference between this part of France and the parts of Germany I was in. Up there we could get anything we wanted; here it is really rough. But in time we'll have a good camp.

I'm going to enclose some negatives of some shots of the camp. You'll probably have to tell the photographer to wash some emulsion off the negatives. I didn't take time to clean them well. All I did was "fix" them. Let me know how you're coming out with the 35mm negatives I'm sending to you. Send me a sample of an enlargement sometime.

I'm going to send some links from an SS trooper's necklace. The necklace was worn in special formations. The small chain that goes around the neck is what I'm sending to you. Every other link has a swastika, and the ones between have an eagle. It is made of brass. All the boys are wearing bracelets made of it.

Collecting lumber

July 27, 1945

Honey, enclosed are a bunch of negatives showing scenes of the camp here. One series is Retreat—the lowering of the flag in

362

the afternoon. It shows the method of folding the flag so that only the blue field shows. It's folded into a triangle shape. You probably notice the star made of cracked field rocks. A German prisoner of war made it. It's very pretty don't you think? The scenes of the beach swimmers were made at a nearby lake. It's a GI beach, so don't have it enlarged too much because some of the men don't have on trunks.

Rock star made by German POW

GI beach

July 27, 1945 [third letter]

I told you I'd be back again before the day was over. I just had to talk to you again. I got a letter from you today telling of the receipt of the camera and the sword. I'm glad Jack liked the sword. *[See image of a German dress sword in the color gallery.]*

I got a letter from Mama today. She wrote about canning, a little about Luke's possible discharge and a story about Mrs. Arnold catching a soldier having fun with a girl on the ground at the end of her porch. Mama thought it was awful and I guess it is. To be caught is bad.

The Japs are taking a beating now. I hope it keeps up. They offered to quit, but dammit they still want to remain armed. We want it unconditional. No ifs or buts. We want them beaten and they'll be beaten.

July 29, 1945

Hot, hot, hot. This has been the hottest day yet, but thank goodness Captain Hooper asked me up to Aix to play tennis, and after tennis we swam in the pool there. It was so nice. I had lunch with him at the club and then went back to the pool. I laid down on the edge of the pool in the sun, and as I dried off I would roll into the water and it made me brown faster. Captain Hooper had to return to Battalion. He was Duty Officer there.

July 31, 1945

Honey, you keep asking me what division I'm in. I'm not in a division. You know that AA units are separate units. We are still First Army reserve and attached to Delta Base Section until redeployment. If we last through August, it's a sure thing that we will come home. But it still will be October before we come. Time is really going to drag until I can see you. I may be a little bit fidgety at first until I settle down, but outside of that there won't be any change in me. I know it. I thought for a while that the condition that one gets after a time in combat would stay with me, but I'm completely over it now. So don't worry about any change in me. *[Reentry issues crop up more frequently as a possible homecoming approaches.]*

August 3, 1945

You told me that you got the First Army operations maps. I think that they are very nice don't you? If I ever have a den, I'm going to frame one of them and place it there. ... I have about forgotten that I was ever in combat. It's funny, back then I saw so much blood, mutilated bodies, limbs, head wounds, etc., and I wasn't bothered at all. Not the slightest suggestion of sickness from the sights I saw. I guess I was prepared for it. To get to the point, yesterday one of the men here cut his finger and I almost got sick. It's hard to explain.

August 4, 1945

I took some pictures of the black market in Marseilles today. You see, when a pass truck comes into town, hundreds of people crowd around to buy anything the GIs might have. They pay 100 francs for a pack of cigarettes, 250 for a German radio and 50 cents for Pfc stripes. The crowd is just a small part of the terrific black market going on. The people in the pictures are only small operations. The people are of all races. In the center of one of the pictures is a Moroccan soldier. He has on a high, red felt hat. On an enlargement it'll show up good. And there is a picture of an outdoor knick-knack shop—the table under the umbrella. This is a typical scene in any large French town. *[These photographs are of very poor quality, no doubt due to inexperience. Though enhanced, there is little improvement. Even so, I am including them to complement Doyle's descriptions.]*

"Knick-knack" shop   Moroccan soldier

August 5, 1945

I was in Aix again today and played three sets of tennis with Captain Hooper. Beat him every set. They were 6–2, 6–4 and 6–1. I think he's getting peeved now because he hasn't beat me a single set. Honey, I still play a fair game. We'll play some when I come home.

August 6, 1945

"A Lovely Way to Spend an Evening" is what they are playing on the radio. I wrote you a short note last night just before I went on patrol, just riding around checking on things such as houses of prostitution and other clip joints. Bruce and I have been offered 2000 francs per day to leave one house alone. That's over $40.00. That's not hay, but I wouldn't be bought by these lousy French people. They are no good whatsoever. I haven't seen any of them do a day's work yet. All they do is dance and drink. That's why the Germans came in. I'm so glad that I have fought a little bit for our country. It's a great country. Don't ever let me contribute to French relief. They don't deserve it. I don't know why I'm even talking to you about these people, but they make me so damn mad.

On this day on the opposite side of the globe, an American B-29 bomber named Enola Gay reached its drop zone, the center of Hiroshima, Japan.

Chapter 27

Definitive End—The A-Bomb

August 7, 1945

Dearest Juby,

Honey, I will attempt to write to you now, but I'm afraid it will be a mess. I just broke my little finger playing volleyball. It hurts like the very dickens, but if you can read what I'm writing I can endure the pain.

The news came to us this morning about the damage that an atomic bomb causes. It's terrible, but the Germans had things that were as terrible on a smaller scale. If the Japs had any sense, they'd quit, but I'm afraid they won't until it's too late. Germany tried to last, and I've seen the results of their mistake. Total ruin. Now we have even more to give the Japs. They started it at Pearl Harbor. We'll end it in Tokyo. I hope this new weapon makes them see the light.

There is no news about when we'll be coming home. We're still pulling security guard and MP duty. Just routine pick-ups such as drunks, speeders, small-time black market operations and the like. At first it was interesting, but now it is getting to be very boring.

Your Doyle

August 10, 1945

There's a rumor going around that the Japs want to surrender. I sure hope it turns out as the German war did. It will save them a great deal if they quit. Honey, you can't possibly conceive the damage that our Army can do to towns and cities. If Japan wants to survive, they had better stop before it's too late. The atomic bomb is terrific. I've seen the immediate results of the V-2 and from what I hear, the atom bomb is a thousand times as destructive.

We are having a battery party for the men tonight. We're having beer and sandwiches and the band is coming in to play. We tried to get girls, but at the last minute they changed their minds. The French people just can't be depended on. We'll have a good time drinking beer and eating and shooting the bull. You should hear some of the stories some of the guys have to tell. ... Darling, I love you with all my heart. "Dreams" is being played now. All I do is dream.

August 11, 1945

It's morning now, after the boys' party. We finally got about 25 French girls to come. We had sandwiches, and the girls really ate. They like the Coca-Cola we had too. It was really a nice party. We're planning to have another one in two weeks.

Betty Hutton was in Istres night before last. Istres is only a little over a mile from camp. She sang until she couldn't sing. Most of the entertainers that come over here do a wonderful job. I talked to Mickey Rooney one night just after he'd finished a performance, and he acted just like the average GI. He asked me if I knew where there was a "cathouse." He also wanted a drink of cognac. He's a regular guy.

We're all waiting to hear just what the powers that be say about the Japanese peace proposal. I'm of the opinion that if they accept, it will include a condition. I think if another atom bomb or two is dropped, they will omit the condition. It has always been the consensus of opinion that, when Japan capitulates, the Emperor will remain as a symbol although we will have our own military government. If they offer to surrender "if so and so," there is a new light on the subject. We've fought this far, and we don't feel that anyone can tell us what to do.

Honey, I still feel that we'll be coming home in October. If the Pacific war ends, there will be a slackening in troop movement unless public opinion speeds it up. The Army works slow until an emergency arises. It will be left up to you people at home to speed up our return. The Army can do things, but they have to be forced at times.

August 13, 1945

Honey, the Japanese still haven't answered our offer of ruling through the Mikado. Of course it's only 0830 now, and they expected a six-hour deliberation by the Japanese government heads. I sure hope that they accept because I don't want them to use the atom bomb anymore unless the Japanese choose to fight further. Then I say use it.

Honey, where will I find work when I come home? Sometimes it frightens me to even think of it. But let's not worry about it. We'll have a long honeymoon vacation and talk over where we will live when I get back. Under the army demobilization plan, I am to go to Camp Gordon [in Augusta, Georgia] to await discharge. This means that when I return to the States you and I can probably meet in Atlanta, Macon or any place in middle Georgia.

August 14, 1945

The Allies have an answer from the Japanese now, but it hasn't been announced yet. The announcement is expected from the four Capitols at any time now. I sure hope it ends the war. That doesn't mean I'll be home any sooner, but it will save the lives of the men fighting the Japs in the CBI. Gosh, I hope they quit. I'll really feel like celebrating then because I'll know, as will every other soldier, that we are the superior nation and we have proved it to the entire world. No one can catch us in development. I hope they never again catch us with our pantaloons sagging as they did this time.

Honey, it's the next morning now. I had to quit last night and go on a patrol, and we ran into a GI that was bloody from head to foot. We picked him up and took him to a hospital where we learned that Frenchmen had beat him over the head with bottles. Had about 14 stitches in his head. I got his blood all over me, so I guess you had better send me another $50.00 money order to buy new trousers and a shirt.

Well honey, the Japanese have quit. The men that are home now are being rescued. I bet when the 639th comes home people will wonder what we're doing in uniform. But that's the way with war. Hero today, gone tomorrow.

August 15, 1945

The following letter was transcribed from a handwritten note sent to Juby by the wife of a soldier friend from the Wrightsville Beach days:

Dear Juby,

Today is a wonderful day for us all isn't it? Juby, aren't you thrilled to tears? Just think, this mess is all over, and soon we will all be back together leading a normal life. We are having the day off today and although it is quiet around, everyone is so happy that they are practically speechless.

Paul will be in Germany for quite a while yet I believe, but as long as he is safe, that is what counts most. Juby when the boys come home, we will just have to have a big reunion. I still feel as though I belonged to the 639ers, even though we are no longer in the outfit.

The things that Doyle sends you must be absolutely lovely. Isn't he thoughtful to do it Juby? Just think how proud you will be of them when you have your own home and can really show them off to best advantage. Write soon.   Lots of love, Ruth

August 16, 1945

From what we hear over the radio, you people at home are really celebrating. I'm glad that there is celebration, but we over here can't celebrate until we can come home. Yes, a legal holiday was declared for today, but we can't enjoy ourselves because we don't know when we'll get to come home. We aren't doing very much these days. We're just marking time until we can get a ship home. A year ago yesterday this part of France was liberated. They celebrated yesterday and again today. All they do is celebrate. They never work. I know that.

August 18, 1945

Received a letter written on August 10th. You wrote about the possible Japanese surrender. However the peace terms have not yet been signed. The Japanese emissary is to depart from Tokyo tomorrow for Manila. You were right in thinking that we might go to the CBI from here. We were slated to go sometime in October. At present we don't know how we stand. All we know is that all troop movements have been cancelled for the present. I can't say just yet how fast they are going to ship men home. They say 3,000,000 men will be discharged in one year. There's no need for a nine-million-men army if peace is signed and Japan is disarmed. I'm happy for those fighting and those scheduled to fight, but until I'm home and with you I can't do any celebrating or be very happy. When I come home I know that you and my immediate family will be the only ones to welcome me. Most people will have forgotten the war within months. I guess it's the nature of Americans to forget aggression. I'm not feeling sorry for myself because I know I'll be greeted with open arms by the only one in the world for me. I love you darling. You're my inspiration, you're my dream. A flower in my desert of loneliness.

August 19, 1945

I really don't feel like writing to you today because about 500 letters came in and not one was for me. I'm really a bit peeved. I get less mail than any man in the battery. I realize that you are doing your part of the letter writing but even yours are getting to be routine letters. You don't write about yourself anymore. You're all that I think about, and thus you are all that I care hearing about. Please honey, don't stop writing. I'd go crazy if you did. I felt so bad when I found out there wasn't any mail for me from such a stack of mail. You can't imagine what it's like. You get set to read a nice letter, and when you don't get one you just can't believe it. It just seems impossible. But there wasn't a single letter for me out of about 500. Bruce got twelve, Murphy got eight, Shepp, four, and me not a one. I realize I don't write anyone else very much but I write to you every day, sometimes twice a day. I write Mama about once per week. But I don't get mail very often. It's heartbreaking too.

August 22, 1945

Honey, it is very sweet of you and Mama for being so considerate and thoughtful to buy me a suit, but you were right in not wanting to pick my clothes. I'm not home yet, and it will be some time before I'll be there to wear it. So I'll thank you and Mama for you wonderful gesture and ask you to have Esserman and Co. return said suit to stock. If they want, they can keep the ten-dollar deposit. It's OK. Don't worry about the clothing situation, my sweet. If I have a pair of pants and a shirt to start with, I'll be OK. I am not as fastidious as I once was. You say that you picked out a brown suit. How could you, sweet? Four years now I have worn khaki and olive drab, and you and Mama pick a brown suit? I know that you knew better, but you were only trying to keep peace in the family by agreeing.

Honey, there isn't any news from here. All shipping lists have been cancelled for the present. We're having another party here in our mess hall for the men this coming Friday. Our chief task at present is keeping a high state of morale. It's hard in peace time. When we were fighting, the men kept our morale high.

August 23, 1945

Honey, I went to the movies last night at the Officers' Club. We have movies there every Wednesday night. It was such a good show. *Without Love* with Kate Hepburn and Spencer Tracy. They were so cute. Lucille Ball was good too. I enjoyed it. It's the first show in about four weeks.

August 23, 1945 [second letter]

Honey, we've finished our battery history, and in the next day or two I'll send you a copy. It is filled with personal stories by the men, as well as dates of sailing and such. It will be nice for us to keep for our children. It will give their history classes a personal insight on a part of the war that I'm sure they will be studying. Also there is a roster of the battery, giving addresses of all the men.

Chapter 28
The Waiting Game Intensifies

August 24, 1945

Dearest Juby,

The *Stars and Stripes* says that the Air Corps officers of 35 points or less are the ones to be discharged. The reason they give is inexperience. Hell, they should be transferred into other branches so some of the high-point ground force officers can be discharged. It is really screwed up now. The point system I mean. The organization Veterans of Foreign Wars proposed this: all men with two years of service in the Army, as well as those serving under two years but with overseas service, be discharged; those in the States with less than two years be sent as occupation forces. If this is carried out, I'm in pretty good shape to come home and be discharged. I have over four years, with almost one year of that in foreign service, including five months on the line. One of the divisions in the States set to be redeployed as occupation army in Germany beefed to Congress that they had 135 days on the line before returning to the States. Hell, we had 155 days on the line and haven't even been home. I'll be home in time though, I know. It can't be much longer. If they would only get more ships over here to send us out. They had better hurry because the French government is going to want the Marseilles port soon because it's their main import and export port. We might have to ship out from LeHavre or Rouen up on the Atlantic Coast. I want to ship from here so I can travel the Mediterranean and go through the Straits of Gibraltar. Probably would get a look at Spain and Portugal on the way. Another thing, I don't care to take a convoy across France again. It's hard work.

Your Doyle

Stars and Stripes *is an American newspaper reporting of and to all military units. Begun during the Civil War, it now operates under the Department of Defense though maintaining editorial independence.*

August 25, 1945

The EM party was another hit last night. We had a lot of mademoiselles, a lot of mamas and a lot of children, but that's OK. The guys had a good time dancing. You and I would have had a most wonderful time. ... One of the boys just came in and told me he just received the first letter from his wife in four months and she was requesting a divorce on the grounds that she had found a man she loved more than she did him. He had tears in his eyes. It's really pathetic. I told him to give it to her and start trying to forget it all. That's what he's going to do. He's the sixth man in the battery that has received such a letter since we've been over here. It's a shame these things happen, but I guess it's good they find it out. However my sweet, these men haven't been true to their wives so they haven't any right to say anything about their wives' actions. They ran around in England, France, Belgium, Germany and France again, so it serves them right. But it is a shame.

You've said that you have some more pictures for me. I wish they'd come. I always like to get pictures from you of you! Remember

378

when I told you that I didn't like pictures of people? I was crazy then. I was beginning to love you then.

Wearing a new hat and the onyx locket

August 26, 1945

One of the men in A Battery was killed day before yesterday. He and two more men were on MP patrol and started chasing a stolen jeep. They were driving so fast they lost control of the jeep and it crashed into a concrete post. He was buried today with full military honors. It's a pity that it happened. He had fought with us all the way, and then a lousy GI steals a jeep that causes his death. But that is life I guess.

August 28, 1945

You asked about what I'm doing with the photos you're sending me. Well, I have every one of them but one. I lost it at Remagen while diving for safety in an artillery barrage. I had two of my favorite snapshots of you pasted in my helmet with adhesive tape and sometime during a barrage one of them came out and was lost. So, my sweet, you were lost in combat.

Don't worry about my family's suggestions as to what I must do when I come home. They think that having been in combat has changed me for the worse. I'm changed all right, but not for the worse. I am more independent than ever now. I appreciate their thoughtfulness, but you and I can make it alone. As you say, you have a job of reconversion to do on me. But you won't have any trouble. Mama's idea of thinking I want to travel is all wrong because traveling during my army career has made me a home-lover. Your home-lover. I want to come home to you every night. Not on weekends as I did at Camp Davis and at Fisher. Ft. Jackson wasn't too bad, but even there I missed some nights. I want to have a job where I know when five o'clock comes I can quit and go home to you. I never want to be rich, just comfortable and secure. I'm sure that you feel that way too.

August 31, 1945

Honey, I am very tired tonight because I have been running all over the place trying to get the men paid. I have been up since 0600 and had to go to Marseilles after the money. I'm shaking like a leaf now, so if I cut this letter short you'll know why.

I am afraid I won't get home before Christmas, my sweet. We might be told to ship sooner than I think, but I'm afraid not. I'm going crazy too. Oh how I want to come home to you. Because of my desire to see you, I am getting nervous. I think that is what made me so tired tonight. I just don't want to work anymore until I see you. You're all I have, sweet, and I want you with me. I've just got to come home soon. Honey, I guess after you get this letter your morale will be low, but please write me a good letter. I haven't had one from you in four days.

Our outfit was saluted tonight over the radio. I hope you heard it. It came from Munich. It was a very good salute. My sweet, I must stop now and go sleep. Maybe it will help me. I'm still shaking. I'll be all right in the morning, and then I'll write you a long letter. I wish you were here to help settle my nerves. *[Could this sudden shaky nervousness be due to the soldier that was killed in a jeep accident two days before, leading to a panic attack about getting home safely?]*

September 1, 1945

At the present time, I'm having quite a few bad days. It is so boring now. Nothing to do. I like to dream of you, but honey I get so darned homesick when I dream of you hour after hour. If I could keep busy, the time would go faster. Much faster. ... Murphy left this afternoon for home. He has 104 points. He found out this morning at 0200 that he was to ship home and he's already on his way, so I might be wakened some morning with the news that I am to go home. I think I will come home with the 639th because most all the men have from 55 to 70 points. If they keep up shipping as they have the last two days, it won't be long.

About the clothing situation. I guess Mama doesn't realize that I can go to New York and have Earl Sams fix me up from the factory. He's the president of Penney's. I don't have to worry about it at all. I know the clothing heads. *[Doyle was employed as a retail salesman by the J. C. Penney Corporation when he was drafted in 1941.]*

September 4, 1945

You asked what we'd do with my uniforms. We'll save most of them for our boy. He'll get a kick out of wearing them to masquerade parties when he's about 18 years old. Our boy is going to be a lady killer. Our girl is going to be a heartbreaker too. I know she will if she's like you and I'm sure she will be. *[Ken did wear the uniform to school for his history class in high school. As far as I know, I haven't broken any hearts.]*

September 6, 1945
   We have men in the battery with well over 85 points, and nothing is being done about getting them home. It's a shame too. Every day the *Stars and Stripes* and the radio tell us that 85 pointers are going home, and we know for a fact that they aren't. Maybe the reason for it is because Congress won't leave the War Department alone. They continue to make suggestions, and in so doing, the Army can't settle down to any definite plan.

September 6, 1945 [second letter]
   Bruce is now battery commander and I am his executive officer. Max Shepp is with us as 2nd Platoon commander. He helped me during the war for a while. He's a good officer. He's the one who got a battlefield commission.

September 7, 1945
   You know honey, I got a letter from Eleanor today thanking me for the camera you gave her. It's the second letter that I have received from her during my army career. The other one was a request that I invest $50.00 of hers in a crap game. She sent me the request after I sent Mama $325 that I had won. I am smoking a cigar now in honor of Jack and Betty's child. Eleanor put in a P. S. that I would probably be an uncle again before morning.
   I'm sorry to hear that Henley is so low on points. It seems impossible to have been overseas that long and have such a low score. Of course I must realize that the 639th saw more combat in a short time than did any outfit in the ETO. We were looking

for trouble and on three occasions found it, but God was with us and we came through with five points from each of the three occasions.

September 8, 1945

Gosh! The 69 Pennsylvanians are playing and singing "Take Me in Your Arms." If I could only take you in my arms, we'd start off as if we had never been apart. I know we can. I'm kinda glad that we didn't have a baby because I want to watch our baby grow from the day it's born. I'd feel funny coming home to a year-old baby. I'd have to become accustomed to being its father and it might take a little time to do that. Take Harold for instance. He has missed the happiness and heartaches of bringing a child through the infancy stage. I want to share that with you. Everything has worked out swell for us, hasn't it my sweet?

September 10, 1945

Honey, another one of the men in the battalion was killed night before last. He was taking a drunk merchant marine to his ship, and when they got to the boat he slipped and fell off the gang plank, hit his head and drowned. It's really a pity. Just like the boy in A Battery, he finished the war and then lost his life. It's a rotten mess. That's two now in three weeks' time.

September 14, 1945

Let me tell you about our new house here. It's a big tent for four of us. We boarded the sides up about five feet and screened it in up to about seven feet. In one end are the office, sitting room and dining room. Our bedroom is in the other end, and we have built-in wall lockers for our clothes. We have a radio in the bedroom and we're going to run a loud speaker to the sitting room. We have burned the walls with a blow torch which gives a knotty pine effect. I'll take some pictures and send them to you. A place like this would only cost about $100 and it would make a wonderful mountain cottage or beach cottage. A bar could be installed, and it could really be a livable, homey place. We are proud of it because we made it ourselves. We have bed lamps and three low-hanging lights above the desk. There are three desk blotters on the long table, and Bruce sits at the small desk. Very businesslike. I sit right next to him because I am the executive, and on my left are Lt. Frasea and Lt. Shepp. We built up the perimeter tents for the men too. There are five or six men to a tent. You should see the chairs and tables they have built. Some are really nice. We've done this in about ten days. Our next project is our mess hall.

Our new house

September 15, 1945

Honey, I want you to teach me to dance so we can have a good time when we go out. I know I can dance if I could just relax, but somehow or other I just can't seem to get in the groove with my feet. My heart is in the groove, but my feet won't follow suit. I've only danced once since I left England, and that was about two months ago at our first battery party. The guys wouldn't dance with the girls so we had to get them started. At parties since then we haven't had that trouble. I don't think it will take me long to learn to dance the way I want to.

I've got to go down to Mirimas now and inspect the MP detachment. You should see it, honey. Half of Mirimas will be there to watch. They think the Saturday morning inspection is wonderful. We put on quite a show for them. It's held on the main street in front of the Provost Marshall's office. Bruce is Provost Marshall.

September 19, 1945

Honey, I got a letter from Mama last night and she gave me hell for having you return the suit. She said that I should have thanked you for being so considerate and when I got home I should have raved over the suit that you picked. I would have done just that if I had thought it was your idea, but you told me that it was Mama and Will meddling in our business. Mama seemed to think I had broken your heart when I had you return the suit. I'm sure you didn't mind.

Mama also gave me hell for feeling sorry for myself. I guess she's right there. I'm unhappy but there's no need to grieve my heart out because as she said, "It's a known fact that you'll be home soon, so why worry about it?"

We had another battery dance last night. When we have dances, the entire family comes to them. We send trucks to the neighboring towns after having dance posters out for a few days. We had about 80 French people here last night, and they ate 450 sandwiches and an equal amount of cokes and beer. It's really funny to watch them. Because of the shortage of food, they really dive in. Some less needy are embarrassed at their fellow countrymen's actions.

September 24, 1945

Honey, it is Monday morning and I am very tired already. I played tennis with Captain Hooper yesterday, and last night I went up to the club to see *It's in the Bag* with Fred Allen and Jack Benny. It was a screwball show. Only a lot of ham acting, but I enjoyed it.

In the next two weeks, we're going to move to St. Victoret Staging Area. Now don't get elated over this because we aren't going there for purpose of staging ourselves. We are going to take over the camp and stage other units for return to the States. I'll say this: every indication is that I'll be home by January. Now this is only a proposal, and there are many things that cause delays. Such as boats for instance. If the War Shipping Board doesn't get the boats over here, not much can be done about swimming the Atlantic.

I'm all confused about the war and all. It's so hard to understand. The war seems to have been so futile now that it's all over. All we have now is a right to say that it's our country and our world. It was our country and our world before the war, but it means a little more to us now because we had to work to keep it our country. An example on a simpler plane is this: You don't like your ready-made dresses half as much as the ones you make. In other words sweet, you and I have worked and kept our country a free, democratic country. We have killed and exterminated the moths that were slowly eating holes in our ready-made garment of democracy and freedom. We now have the right, as did our forefathers, to have children to enjoy the fruits of our hardships, mine and yours.

Honey, I just got a sterling silver identification bracelet and I had a German POW engrave my name on it. On the inside, he engraved

"Juby." It's so pretty and it only cost me $4.00. I've wanted one a long time but not bad enough to pay $11.00.

September 25, 1945

Well honey, it seems that things are happening here. I have written you about moving to St. Victoret Staging Area. We are going there as house troops. We are to process troops for return to the States. I am being transferred to A Battery within the next two weeks. Bruce and Max Shepp will have a part of D Battery to themselves. The mission that A Battery has requires one more officer, so I'm the one. I don't mind the transfer but for one thing—I will leave all the men that I've been with for over two years. Of course it won't take me long to get to know the men in A Battery.

September 27, 1945

There is no word about shipment home. We have started moving our camp to St. Victoret. I thought for a while today that we were going to have to leave all of our winterized tents here, but we ironed it out with the higher brass. Bruce and I might get reclassified over it. Two colonels and two majors bore down on us and told us to leave the camp as it was. We argued with them and finally they weakened a little, so now we can break camp and move out lock, stock and barrel. I imagine this mission we're taking now will be our last. It is my lot to be here, and I've become resigned to the fact that I can't be discharged just yet. ... It is very cold here now and a 50-mile wind is forevermore blowing. It's miserable.

September 28, 1945

I'm enclosing some snapshots that you might want. They are of Pfc. Seavella washing his fatigues in our irrigation ditch. I'd like to have them in our scrapbook.

Army wash day

September 30, 1945

   Well honey, tomorrow we finish moving to St. Victoret Staging Area. We've been on the job for three days now, and the only men left here are those I used to wreck and load the camp. We don't know how long we'll have the detail there. I wrote Will a short V-mail the other night. I'm trying to get him to write me. He hasn't written me for three letters now. Maybe he's still mad at me. I have come to realize that people that weren't in this war are rather self-conscious about it. Maybe I had better stop kidding him. He might have wanted to be in the war. Maybe I have gotten his goat. I don't know.

Honey, the pictures you sent made with the Agfa were bad because (1) the shutter speed was too slow, put it on 1/100 of a second; (2) the shutter was too wide, put it on 8—try that and see what happens; (3) don't take the pictures so far away. You can move in to about four meters. If you move that close, don't forget to set the range. A meter is about 39 inches, so if you judge distance in yards, you'll be almost right.

October 2, 1945 [St. Victoret Staging Area]

I don't know what kind of entertainment we'll have here at Victoret. There is an open-air theatre here that shows movies every night, and now and then they have a stage show. I contributed 500 francs toward making a battalion officers' club. I guess I can buy beer and drinks there when they get it set up.

I just finished writing Anne a short note, and I enclosed a set of rosary beads from Lourdes, France.

October 3, 1945

Honey, it's getting cold here, and it isn't too comfortable in the tents. It's going to be worse very soon. We have to take showers out in the open in cold water. It isn't too bad now, but when the cold air starts blowing in from the Alps it won't be so comfortable.

October 5, 1945

I hope you liked the flowers I had sent to you on your birthday. They weren't much of a birthday gift, but honey, it's so hard to get things here. I decided to send a money order to Ransom Florist. I didn't want to bother any of the family because they all seem to be so very busy lately.

October 7, 1945

Honey, I didn't write you last night because Captain Way, Max, Bruce and Lesser had a party here in our tent. We drank two quarts of whiskey and then fried bacon and shrimp. We had a very good time. I know I should have written before the party started, but you know how those unplanned parties are. You don't expect anything, then all at once you're in the middle of a party—before you know it you couldn't write a sensible letter if you wanted to. I was busy all day yesterday, and I had planned to write you last night but the party hit me square in the face.

I got a short letter from you yesterday. Honey, your letters do wonders to me. They are all that I have to go on besides memories. ... When the war was on, I hardly ever got really angry with the Army did I? Well now that things are over, I find myself getting more and more on edge. Seven of our enlisted men left today and were assigned to units staging here in Victoret. They will ship in the next four or five days.

We finished our showers in our new area, and they are really nice. Hot and cold water, and air tight. It's unbelievable what our men can do.

October 10, 1945

Happy birthday, my sweet. I sure wish I was with you today. We'd really celebrate your birthday, champagne and all. Darling, I love you and want to be with you, but at present it seems that I just can't seem to get on the shipping orders. In fact, eight boats are loading tonight and tomorrow for shipment to the States. Lesser, Watts, Morotta and Schaffer left today. Colonel Cauthen leaves tomorrow for Paris where he will pull duty. He has 134 points and doesn't want to go home. More power to him is all I can say. He can have my part of Europe. I've seen enough of it.

For two days there hasn't been a piece of mail to come into St. Victoret Staging Area. No one can explain it. The postal section doesn't understand it. Maybe tomorrow. Tonight I'll listen to the last game of the World Series. I want Detroit to win. *[They did, 9–3 over the Chicago Cubs.]* ... Honey, here's my heart on your birthday and every day.

October 11, 1945

I'm wondering why there's no mail and so's everyone else in camp, but I guess that the longshoreman's strike is what's causing it. Damn them anyway. They are holding up redeployment, but I guess we can't kick because while the war was going on they stayed on the job. That's more than I can say for some of the unions. I stay in camp all the time now and have seen a couple of movies, *Salome, Where She Danced* and *Johnny Angel*. It was more or less a seafaring mystery. Clair Tervor and George Raft were in it. I really started out to see *Weekend at the Waldorf* but went to the wrong theatre, and when I realized I was at the wrong one the jeep had already gone. The theatres here are all open-air. There are three of them. "GI Joe," "Ernie Pyle Memorial" and "FDR Memorial."

Open-air theatre at St. Victoret

They usually have the best, but this week they have second-rate pictures. Frequently they have stage shows for us. The only one that I've seen is the Copa Cabana Review which was very beautiful, but that's all you could say for it.

October 12, 1945

I played bridge last night and late this afternoon, and honey, I'm learning to play the game quite well. It's a pretty good game for old people and men, but where you're concerned I think we can find more interesting things to do. *[They ended up in participating in couples' bridge clubs for decades. Juby was still in two bridge clubs at age 86.]*

October 13, 1945

There is no news of interest around here but for the fact that England is calling in all their big troop ships which will slow down redeployment quite a bit. It seems everything is happening to keep us apart for a little while longer.

October 14, 1945

Just got back from Marseilles. Bruce, Max and I drove in to see a movie. It was *Out of This World* with Eddie Bracken. It was quite good. Did you see it? I'm going again tonight to a show here in camp. It will be *Guest Wife*. Don Ameche and Claudette Colbert. Should be very good. Next Sunday I am going to a bull fight. They have them every Sunday and I haven't seen one yet. They aren't as glamorous as they were before the war, but from what I hear they are quite interesting to see just once.

As long as I have to stay, I hope I can stay with the 639th because I have a feeling that by December 1st the 639th will ship home—that is, if the boats ever get there.

October 15, 1945

The bottom seems to have dropped out of everything here. No boats, no mail and no loving. The loving is what I want and from you. The war is over, and here we sit. It didn't take long to get us over here did it?

October 16, 1945

If I can be with you Christmas, I'll believe in Santa Claus again.

October 17, 1945

Got a sweet letter from you today. It was written on your birthday. Glad you liked the roses. I wish that I could have gotten you something else but honey, my heart was in among those roses. Did you find it? Well, keep it for me until I come home. ... Today Bruce called me to the side and said, "Whit, I'm going home." I said, "Bull___." He only had 57 points. He said, "Yes, it's an emergency leave." I was amazed. I didn't ask him what the emergency was because I was afraid to. He then said, "If I can't straighten out the trouble when I get home, I'm going to ask to be returned to ETO or CBI, either one." Well, I was speechless. I couldn't say a word, and I was afraid to ask him about his trouble. I thought it might be Vivian, but I don't know. Now honey, not a word about this to anyone.

October 18, 1945

Things might happen faster than I expect them to, but I learned long ago that it's better to be surprised than disappointed. If I could have you with me for Christmas, I couldn't possibly ask for more. I've been away from you 13 months now, and I don't want to be away from you one minute longer than I have to. I was talking to Captain Hooper this morning, and he still thinks it will be December before he gets home. He comes over practically every day. Says he gets lonesome. Bruce is supposed to leave Saturday. He said that it probably would take two months to get home after going through all the replacement depots.

October 20, 1945

Well, I said before that Bruce's trouble might be Vivian. But now I'm beginning to wonder. He and I went out last night and he got slightly inebriated. During the evening he started talking about how he hated to leave the outfit and he said, "Maybe my mother will wake up someday." So from that I changed my mind. He's an only son, and maybe she's making herself sick worrying about him or something, I don't know. But anyway, he leaves Monday night for Le Havre to ship home. He really doesn't want to go, but he says that it is a case of necessity. If he gets home, he can get discharged if he wants to.

We were in Aix last night. Our band was playing the dance there. Bruce and I moved our chairs right up in front of the band stand and led the band. We made ourselves very obnoxious, but we had a good time. The band just loves to have us lead them. They play their hearts out for us officers of the battalion. By the way, the boys have had recordings made. If I can get one I'll send it to you. No kidding honey, they are terrific.

Well honey, there is no news to tell you about this place called France other than tomorrow is election day. The questions put to vote are: 1. A new provisional government with De Gaulle and 2. A new provisional government without De Gaulle. Sign boards are covered with *Oui-Oui* or *Oui-Non* meaning Yes-Yes and Yes-No. It's very confusing but since I can't vote, why get involved in politics?

October 21, 1945

We just got word that 12 warships are coming to the ETO to relieve the pressure on redeployment. They will take away 21,000 ETO veterans when they all leave. Maybe that will speed up my return home, but as yet there is no word about it.

Boy, are you and I going to have fun when we get our home built. How do we know where to build honey? I don't even know where I'm going to work yet. Do you have any suggestions as to where you would like to live? Maybe while you and I are on our vacation honeymoon, we can find a place that we'd like to live. What I'd like to do is find some old fellow with an established business that wants to retire and have him turn the business over to you and me to run for him. That would be nice wouldn't it? Something like a hotel or a large restaurant. I think that you'd make a wonderful hotel hostess.

There are many businesses that I'm interested in, and the one that I'm least interested in is the one that I was in before coming in the Army. I haven't got the slightest idea that I'll go back to Penney's, but I must keep contact with them. I might have to go back there but I don't want to.

Indeed, Doyle's first job immediately upon his return was with J. C. Penney in retail sales. Companies were mandated to rehire returning veterans after the war. In spite of his other preferences, reality dictated that he accept the position available to him.

October 23, 1945

Honey, I got a letter today, and you tried to make a joke of feeling sorry for yourself because I'm not home. But honey you can't kid me. I know this waiting is getting the best of you. Frances's husband has been away from her well over two years. I think she has done remarkably well. It won't be much longer before you'll have me. Bruce left tonight and will be on a boat on his way home in 60 hours. In a way he's lucky, but I sure hope whatever his trouble is isn't serious. I hated to see him go. He and I became very good friends over here.

The 66th Division started for home this morning. After they leave we don't know what we will do. It is rumored that we will break camp here at St. Victoret. We will take down tents and turn all our equipment in.

I got your attempts at printing today, and you do fairly well for a beginner. You're giving too much light. We'll practice together when we settle down honey. Have you tried to use the glass plates yet? They are fun to develop. I guess you had better wait until I come home before you try any of those out.

Honey, that bacon and eggs the guys are cooking smells so damn good that I must go get some. I heard one of the guys say that he is now eating his 12th egg, so I had better hurry.

November 1, 1945

Honey, I am so glad you finally quit work. I can tell in your letters that you now have a peace of mind you haven't had in quite some time. In fact, you haven't seemed so cheerful in any earlier letters. If you can stay cheerful and happy for just a little while longer, it will make my stay here much more pleasant. When you write that you're getting sick from worrying about when I'm coming home, I feel like jumping a boat.

I was up at Aix last night. Our band was there and it was Halloween night. The ballroom looked so good and they had straw all over the floor. They (the guys in the band) thought that since I was from Georgia I could call a square dance, but I've never been to one so I couldn't call it. So they didn't dance a set of square dancing. Everyone seemed to enjoy themselves. ... I got the books you sent, and they have been read by me and all the officers here in our quarters.

November 3, 1945

Listened to the band again last night and had two dances with a nurse. My dancing is improving honey, and with a little help from you I think you and I can really knock people's eyes out on the dance floor. When we were having dances for the enlisted men, there were always girls there that the boys wouldn't dance with so Bruce, Max and I kept the dance moving by dancing with the wall flowers. Since I found myself dancing with various types and styles of dancers and also since I probably never would see them again, I started trying a few fancy "jit" steps. Now I am quite a "swing-a-roo-ster." Everyone seems to insist I dance with their girl when I go to Aix. If you could be there, we'd really put on a show for them, wouldn't we? Marollo, the professional dancer in D Battery, is in our band and he has asked me on two different occasions if he could be my manager. He said that he could give me some polishing up advice and make a terrific dancer out of me. He said that I was really built perfectly for a show dancer. So my sweet, you might as well get set to have your feet danced away because I like to dance more than anything else now.

November 5, 1945

We are contemplating a move to Marseilles soon to take up duties such as traffic directing. There will be little for me to do because it is a job for the enlisted men. We will have 18 traffic posts and three or four jeep patrols. We'll have the most beautiful quarters to stay in. Palm trees all around and mountains in the distance. … Boy are we going to have fun when I get back. I want you to catch up on your dancing. I know you love it, and I have acquired a liking for dancing that I didn't have when I left. I was self-conscious, but I have overcome it and have learned to dance. In other words, my sweet, I now just let myself go. With a little help from you, the two of us will be able to put on an exhibition for the younger set. *[And they did! On their 60th wedding anniversary, no less, in 2004. We—their children, grandchildren and great-grandchildren—are witnesses.]*

November 6, 1945

Honey, at last I have some news for you. If things move as expected, I will be on my way home by the time you read this. I am to join the 195th AAA Battalion in the next few days, and they are to leave between November 15th–20th. I may get to come home on one of the carriers that are leaving the States tomorrow. If I get on one of the carriers, I'll be home before December 1st.

I've been disappointed so many times that I still am a bit leery about believing things will go as planned. We move into Marseilles day after tomorrow to take over as traffic MPs. Maybe I'll miss that move. If my orders are in tomorrow or the next day, I won't go in trying to get billets for the men. Today I got a large chateau for some of them. Oh yes, all the boys with 70 points or more are in the 195th so I'll be coming home with quite a few of them. There are 26 from D Battery already in the 195th AAA.

I didn't get any mail from you today because there wasn't any mail at all. I'll continue to write you up to the day that I sail, and you keep writing me until I can tell you for sure that we are to sail. Don't worry kid, I haven't changed. You won't have to worry about what you should do, say or wear. I just want to see and be with you forever once I get home.

Chapter 29
Homeward Bound

November 7, 1945

Dearest Juby,

Honey, I receive my written orders sometime tomorrow to go to Calas Staging Area to join the 195th AAA. I don't know just when they will ship, but they are ready now and just as soon as the port gives them space in a ship they, including me, will ship home. I don't think we can possibly get out before November 20th, but at least something is happening and that's better than it was yesterday.

I love you, Doyle

November 8, 1945

Well honey, by the time you read this letter you can stop writing me because if things go as they are, I'll be on my way home while you are reading this. Honey, nothing interests me anymore, so until I see you my letters will be short. Time is really dragging now that I see my return to you in sight. Gosh, it's going to be a grand and glorious day for me when I first see you. I get more excited by the minute. I probably won't be able to say a word, but you'll know that I love you by just looking at me. Darling I love you and will show you how much soon. I love you.

November 15, 1945

Honey, I'm sorry I wrote you such a definite answer on my return home. There is no change so far, but tomorrow or next day will be the deciding days as to whether we'll be delayed or not. You see DBS keeps us guessing up to the last minute. On the 17th, day after tomorrow, we are supposed to start staging. Seven to ten days later, we will board ship and be on our way. I know as soon as I get on the boat I'll be so excited that the trip home will seem like an eternity.

I haven't had a letter from you in three days now. I'm now at Calas Staging Area and it's really cold over here. At Victoret we made ourselves comfortable before winter came, but now we haven't got time to build up our tents. At present I'm visiting in the lounge of my old quarters at Victoret, and my driver just came to take me back to Calas. So I must go.

Epilogue

$\mathcal{D}$oyle's last letter to Juby from Europe was dated November 15, 1945. We do not know the name of his ship or exactly when he embarked for home, but according to a note Juby wrote on the last page of the Battery D history book, he arrived in New York on December 5. Recounting the event in 2009 at the age of 89, she remembered sitting by the telephone for days, waiting for him to call. Reluctantly, she accepted an invitation to a short party for another returning soldier. It was during this brief absence that Doyle placed several calls to her. When he finally made contact, his first words were "Where the hell have you been?"

More waiting was in store for Juby. Brother Will pulled strings to get her a room at the Richmond Hotel, so she took the bus to Augusta, Georgia. The town was swarming with returning soldiers being discharged from Fort Gordon. For three days, Juby waited alone in her room while Doyle was en route to Augusta. She received a telegram from Camp Patrick Henry, Virginia—"Will leave here 15 hours. All my love, Doyle." She waited yet again while he was being processed for discharge. She went out to see a movie to pass the time, but a soldier came and sat next to her and put his arm around her, so she left and went back to the room.

Doyle was finally discharged on December 10. Juby needed a change of scenery, so she decided to go down to the lobby to wait.

When she opened the door to leave the room, there he stood. He was in uniform and accompanied by a bellhop and grip. He grabbed her, lifted her up off the floor (he is 6'2" and she is 5'3"), held her and hugged her for the longest time without saying anything. The bellhop stood there grinning. The embrace finally paused long enough to give him a tip.

First meal together, December 10, 1945, not alone

Heading out for a meal, Doyle and Juby ran into another dischargee and wife that Doyle had known while working in Lake City, Florida, prewar. They spent the whole evening with this couple, not alone together as they had planned. This photograph that marked the occasion allows us to see them reunited at last. On December 15, they left Augusta and came to Rome. They had their first child, a girl—me—in September 1946. You do the math. The rest is family history.

PROJECT REPORT

October 30, 2009: The typing of 411 letters penned by my father more than 65 years ago shows me his layered truth. His story reveals themes aplenty—the making of a soldier, the making of a man, the adjustment to the unspeakable horrors of wartime, the awakening to global realities, the expression of inborn and lasting qualities of faithfulness, honorability and compassion, the yearning born of lengthy separation from home and the completeness of a steadfast love.

There are also hopes and dreams for the future: a custom-made house and children to fill it, travel opportunities, a successful business of his own that would support each dream. There are family squabbles executed by long-distance—innocent statements become misinterpreted and lead to lengthy volleys of petty give-and-take across half a world.

And there is romance, oh, the romance. His ability to put intense emotion into words on paper, his determination to communicate his thoughts and feelings daily even under dire circumstances, his desire for constant dialogue despite sporadic and unpredictable mail schedules kept the connection alive and the love growing between him and his bride. He would write as if she were in the room with him. She was always by his side, giving him respite from warring and solace from loneliness. Some of the romantic passages read like a screenplay. They "paint a word picture," as he would say. He holds nothing back. He calls her letters pieces of her heart, and he pours his heart out to her in return. I find it uncanny how completely he can express his feelings, and then analyze them with amazing insight.

This correspondence covers so much time (from Nov. 26, 1942, through Nov. 15, 1945) because Doyle and Juby (Mom and Dad) were apart through their entire courtship. He was in the US Army, and they could only see each other when he had leave, which was not often. Then, when they were married in April 1944, it took

403

several weeks before she could join him at his duty station; even so, they only saw each other on weekends. They were actually together only late May through the first week in July before they were separated again, when she had to go home for a six-week recovery from appendicitis surgery. By the time she rejoined him in North Carolina, his deployment was imminent. He left Sept. 8, 1944, and returned to her Dec. 10, 1945. I'd say that the entire basis of their relationship for three years was the written word.

Through his letters I get a day-by-day account of the activities of a soldier in training. I get a list of the entertainment provided the military during war years—from songs on the radio to performances by stars like Ella Fitzgerald and Mickey Rooney. I get a description of the countryside and people he encountered along the way. I even have postcards of the places he stayed, sent to document his specific itinerary—which I plan to follow myself someday.

Due to censorship regulations, he does not describe actual combat episodes at the time they occur. As the censor for the men of his unit, he knows the censorship requirements: never identify the unit of assignment or location until the unit has been moved away from that location for two weeks. Therefore, during an assignment a letter will contain only family chatter, humor and romance. Or he may say vaguely, "I'm sorry I didn't write for a couple of days. We were busy." Weeks later, he gives a description of "busy" as he remembers it—being strafed by Luftwaffe, attacked by tank divisions, shooting down buzz bombs, moving by night in blackout conditions.

Having completed my generational journey guided by Dad's words, I find I have progressively uncovered raw truths and reached my own emotional core. These things I learned: the written word is everlasting and an open heart is undying. The end of my pilgrimage also marks a beginning. I will continue learning, and I hope my footsteps henceforth will encourage a bridge between the past and future in my family as well as in the families of others who may read and enjoy this story.

Author's Notes

MY CHAPTER: How This Book Came to Be

I belong to the baby boom generation, born on the leading edge of the famous population explosion that began as victorious young soldiers came home to start families and careers after WWII was over. The US Census Bureau considers 1946, the year I was born, the beginning of the birth rate surge. According to the CNN Library, there were nearly three and a half million babies born in the US that year; that is 9,345.2 per day or 6.49 per minute.

As sons and daughters of these WWII veterans, many of us were exposed to our parents' war stories as we ourselves came of age. We saw war movies that supported the stories and we accepted the historical truth, but we barely comprehended that truth's power and the impact it had on our parents and on us. Decades later, we learned that we are children of the "Greatest Generation." Now, as our own generational tasks are near completion (raising children and maintaining careers), we have time to look back to our own origins, analyze our birth decade and learn how we came to exist.

The death of our parents often leads to unexpected discovery of things that happened in their lives before we were born. Cleaning out trunks, closets, rooms and houses full of memorabilia reveals heretofore hidden information in the form of photograph books, souvenirs and letters from an era when our parents were young, tender and coping with turmoil. I always had access to such items, even when my father was alive, but time was the missing ingredient. My dad's death was the first of successive events that left me with plenty of time: I retired after thirty years as a biology professor, then happily saw my nest empty with the marriage of my daughter. I needed a new passion and mission in order to fill a great void. I looked to the unfinished business of Dad's war.

I would start with my own memories. I realized I had been prepped for this mission all of my life. As early as I can remember, Dad would refer to "When I was in Europe..." or "During the war...." He told snippets of battle stories and key between-battle experiences repeatedly. As youngsters, my siblings and I didn't know how much credence to give these stories. We only vaguely recognized how Dad was influenced by the experiences he related to us, but knowing about them made us proud. When the opportunity arose in the classroom, we would brag about Dad and what he had told us. Given history assignments, we were able to shine. We had unlimited access to his war souvenirs and the scrapbooks Mom had thoughtfully and skillfully created from photographs and postcards he sent. Without my parents' keen appreciation for the history they were living and their urgently detailed documentation of it, we would not know the story as we do.

Later in Dad's life, the war stories became all he wanted to talk about. The repetition made us roll our eyes. He kept hinting that I use his letters for some grand purpose. He knew they were important, but I thought all that could be said had been said and all that could be learned had been learned. I was wrong. I am still learning, and I am increasingly awed by the service of veterans in any era.

In 2009, shortly after my daughter's marriage, I asked my mother if she wanted me to work with the letters. She went straight to the closet and got them for me. They were enclosed in a brown vinyl legal-sized file folder, cracked and split at its folded edges. I took the folder home and began.

The pages were yellowed and the envelopes had been discarded long ago. Pages from a single letter had been stapled together and Mom had written the date she received the letter at the top if Dad had not dated it himself. The letters were placed in chronological order, written on very thin paper except for those reduced for V-mail. Because my house was being re-roofed at the time, constant staccato hammering from many directions at once should have been a terrible distraction. Not so. The simultaneous reading and typing, the total immersion in a present that had taken place over 60 years ago, the daily discovery of facts, emotions, intimate thoughts and gut-wrenching decisions about life and love—all this kept me mesmerized to the point that I no longer heard the sounds assaulting my ears.

As I began my new road to discovery, I knew my heart had been given a special treasure—a window into the youthful souls of the people who would be my parents. Having heard Dad's stories through the years, I expected to validate what I knew about his military experience. I did, and was surprised by the added richness of reading those same stories freshly written. Also surprising was how much "in between" material was newly revealed. Dad was not afraid to express his emotions. He held nothing back. He allowed Mom (and now me) into every corner of his soul. I was astonished at that.

As the weeks progressed, I experienced Dad's military training as well as his courtship of Mom. I experienced his transition toward a combat soldier. I experienced his trepidation about each step as well as his curiosity and awe in new surroundings. As I went with him to Europe via what he called his "word pictures," a desire to retrace his path awoke in my heart and mind.

I let my mother read the entire unaltered transcription. She returned it to me with certain (predictable) passages blacked out. The censorship of authority continues! She said, "Those words were for my eyes only." I agreed with her. I was surprised and thankful that these deleted sections were relatively minor, considering the full body of work. By Christmas, I created gift copies for distribution to family members so they could share the joy of discovery as I had experienced it.

I now turned my thoughts toward the idea of a trip. Creating an itinerary based on Dad's assignments in 1944–45 seemed daunting at first. But things I never thought possible turned out to be. I offered my brother Ken the chance to go with me. We made plans to travel in April 2010, and did. Along the way, we were able to get to know each other better than ever as we shared our thoughts and feelings about this great adventure that had so much personal significance for us both. We accepted and appreciated a new bond between us. Together we were better able to share the experience with our mother and sister. Our travel experiences are documented in the "In His Footsteps" sections of this work.

Ken comments: "The letters are a fascinating look at my father from the perspective of young adulthood, his love for my mom, his dreams for them together and his service to his country. They are a personal time capsule, penned from the hand of just one of the Greatest Generation who also happens to be my dad. With great anticipation, I agreed to go to Europe with my sister. Our itinerary, like Dad's, was essentially planned by senior WWII military officials. I was a complete novice on this pilgrimage, prepared only with a sense of sentimentality and wonderment for my dad in a period of his life before mine began. The journey was for me an almost unbelievable prospect."

Dad was with us all along the way. We felt his spirit so very near. More than ever I wanted him to know that the places and things he admired and wrote so eloquently about are still there. His descriptions were meant to help Mom experience the same things he did, with the same awe and wonder. If they had attempted to make such a journey at the time they were rearing and supporting a family, they would not have been able to visit some of the best places. For example, the Aldermaston Manor only became available for public use in recent years. Nor would they have had access to the relatively recent phenomenon of Internet connectivity. The Web allowed me to communicate freely with our Belgian guide in advance of the trip, leading to contact with the Jamar family as well as finding the location of the Spa Thermal with its copper tubs. Living in modern times was in our favor.

As I began this project, I thought I would learn more about the war, but instead I mostly validated stories I had heard before, coming to understand them with a new freshness, but still yet not fully. The first time I heard about Peiper, I was having breakfast in a lodge near Malmedy, listening to a lesson by our guide Michael Baert on WWII in the Ardennes. I wondered why I'd not heard of Peiper before. Later, when I combed back through Dad's letters and rechecked his unit and battery histories, his favorite sources, I found no mention of Peiper, yet he led the SS Panzer units that crashed through Allied-held territory beginning December 16, 1944. Indeed, Von Rundstedt is the only German leader mentioned by name in these limited sources, which most often refer to the Germans as "the enemy" and "Jerry." Since Dad never mentioned Pieper in his stories, even when describing the Malmedy Massacre for which Peiper accepted responsibility, I assume he never tried to find out who he was up against during those dangerous days. Only in his last few years, after Tom Brokow published *The Greatest Generation,* did Dad begin to accept his role as a hero. Even so, I don't think he ever knew just how great a feat he and his men accomplished in the defense of those small towns in Belgium against the final push by Hitler's elite troops in mid-December 1944. Or perhaps he knew full well, and I was the one who didn't know until now.

One aspect of fighting a war has become somewhat clearer to me—those long periods of downtime, boredom and apparent non-productivity between combat assignments and engagements. Dad refers to the US Army's "hurry up and wait" pattern. It is during the wait periods that he shows keen interest in his surroundings and paints the clearest pictures.

I had never heard anything about the long period after V-E Day during which there were too many soldiers and not enough for them to do. Dad spent the first few months of this trying time in occupied Germany, guarding ammo dumps and camps for displaced persons while wondering whether his unit would be sent to fight in the Pacific. Later they were moved to the Mediterranean coast to serve as needed until passage home came available. This period seems to have been the most agonizing and painful of the whole experience—feeling useless and having too much time to yearn for home. I was surprised at the vehement hatred of the French that Dad developed at this time, and surprised by the prevalence of violence around him. I remain somewhat intrigued by Dad's take on European women and his perception of general debauchery. Was it really that bad or was he rather prudish?

I learned much about separation anxiety, maintaining a deep connection through the written word and true commitment. Early in Mom and Dad's courtship by letter, it appears that each played the jealousy card, trying to manipulate each other as their relationship developed. Putting together the maturing bond revealed by Dad's letters with the relationship that I saw between the pair as I was growing up, I find myself envious of the strength of devotion and faithfulness that eventually evolved. The ability to form such deep, true and lasting bonds seems elusive in today's world.

I learned that Dad was boisterous and given to braggadocio, but he had underlying insecurity. He held back nothing in expressing his fears of failure to Mom before he was deployed. I learned that he could be judgmental and suspicious, assigning ulterior motives to the actions and behaviors of those around him. I'd known that he had similar trust issues in subsequent decades. I'm not sure where it came from—maybe the Great Depression, maybe being raised without a father. After the war had ended,

410

he bragged about his leadership, but gave credit for his success to his men and to Mom.

In his tireless effort to keep the home fire burning, Dad made good use of popular love songs. From beginning to end, I enjoyed his many references to these songs and also to movies and books—all things he and Mom could share despite the distance between them. My daughter used iTunes to purchase original broadcast recordings of songs my parents had so enjoyed. She made me a personal CD, which she labeled "Granddaddy's Soundtrack." Included are key radio broadcasts, such as the BBC report of the Americans crossing the Rhine at a bridgehead "somewhere south of Cologne" and the first reports of the British liberation of one of the concentration camps. And finally, Truman's voice announces the end of hostilities in Europe. I get chills when I listen, even yet. At the end of this personal playlist, she included "The War Was in Color" by one of her favorite music groups, Carbon Leaf. The lyrics describe the pain behind old black-and-white war photographs found by veterans' descendants. I wish I could afford to produce such a collection, but that is unlikely. I suggest this to older readers like me: ask your tech-savvy children or grandchildren to use Internet sources and create a playlist for you!

All my life I have seen and appreciated the items that were sent as gifts—love offerings—from Europe, especially the delicate china pieces. Reading about where and how Dad obtained each piece, including his excitement as he prepared to send each of them home, makes me appreciate them all the more. I do wonder why he kept choosing such fragile items after the first few did not survive their journey halfway around the globe. His attempts to safely package such things improved, but none arrived in perfect shape. Nevertheless, these objects have always been treasured, and even now each has its place of honor on a breakfront shelf in Mom's living room.

Encouragement to pursue the publication of this work came from many sources. There is a wonderful group of women that I regularly hike with, six or so miles at a time, on local mountain trails. These hikes are not just about the exercise. They are therapeutic in many ways, and we all treasure our time together as we unburden stresses from many sources. From the beginning of this project, I have shared with this group my excitement over each discovery. These dear friends helped foster the thought of eventually publishing a book.

To move in that direction, I needed experienced help. The husband of a friend of mine is a history professor who has recently published a book. He agreed to read the manuscript and tell me what was important from a military history standpoint. Another friend read it and made reassuring comments on the general interest and personal aspects of the story. I talked about the project any time I was out and about in social settings. I always received encouragement, but specific direction was elusive. I attended writers' workshops, joined writers' groups and quizzed local authors. Again, I'd get encouragement and general information, but no specific assistance.

A crucial question for me was how much to alter Dad's words. Dad writes in stream-of-consciousness style; or, as he put it, "I just write down what I think." He was likely to place a period at the end of a perfectly good sentence and then continue to add phrases as more thoughts occurred to him. As written, many letters are lengthy, rambling and repetitive. There are errors in grammar and spelling. My urge was to correct and shorten, but I didn't know whether doing so would invalidate the authenticity of the work. I yearned to streamline his words but felt it might be cheating. For a while, I redirected my efforts and began collating visuals and auxiliary information with the text: I scanned photographs and postcards from scrapbooks, made new photographs of existing souvenirs, found supporting information in the battalion and battery histories and in relevant news articles, elicited clarifying comments from my mother and selected "then and now" photographs from the trip.

I was ready to invest money into expert direction, but I didn't know how to find the right person. Fortuitously (things happen when they are supposed to), an old friend had read a WWII military memoir called *Descending from the Clouds* and had communicated with the coauthor, Gayle Wurst, who runs a literary agency. He arranged a telephone meeting for us, and she agreed to evaluate the manuscript. By now it was in its fifth or so revision, late in 2011. She read it and sent me a full evaluation with suggested alterations. The main one was to "put more of your own story in it." I was reticent to do this. In my opinion, this was Dad's story and, by inference, Mom's—not mine. My own thoughts were limited to interspersed notes of explanation or "rest of the story" comments and appended travel notes from the trip. I found myself to be quite shy and unlike my father when asked to reveal my own emotions, to bare my soul.

As to the letters, Gayle demonstrated how to carefully edit them, yet retain Dad's style. With her encouragement and permission to make his writing more reader-friendly, I felt relieved and ready to proceed. I began the next rewrite and created an improved family edition. Recruiting a retired creative writing and language arts teacher (a dear friend, also), I learned how to improve structure and tense and to be more concise overall. This was the specific help I'd needed for so long. I was thankful that I had asked her to "grade my paper," red ink and all, and that she had done so with gusto.

Each revision has reduced the content by shaving repetition. I find that long breaks from the project help me better recognize redundant material each time I go back to the manuscript, as does outside help as to which of the repeated parts I should keep. I don't resent the delay of this "fits and starts" method.

I've tried not to give in to an eagerness to publish quickly, though the urgency is there. Mom is now 92, and I very much want her to be able to hold the finished book in her hands. She asks, "How much longer do I have to live in order to see this book in print?" I don't want to make the mistake of choosing the wrong publication route in haste and ignorance. I want this book to be exceptional—handsome to the eye, well-written, informative and helpful to others who also wish to preserve their family histories. This project has more to do with love than money or notoriety. (Mom, however, sees a movie in the future. She wants to be played by Catherine Zeta-Jones.)

I live in Rome, Georgia, and in my area (as in most of the country, I presume) there has been a frantic push to gather stories from WWII veterans and families on the home front. Many organizations are devoted to preserving these stories through video interviews and documentary filmmaking. Chapters of Rosie the Riveter continue to increase membership and promote education regarding women's roles in support of the war. More and more memoirs of the period are being published. I hope readers will enjoy exploring their own histories as much as I have mine, and find a way to capture their stories "for posterity," as Dad would say. Perhaps by describing my discoveries and subsequent efforts to preserve and share them in perpetuity, I will have motivated others to do the same for their own families and descendants.

In closing, there are two memories that I would like to share. One occurred six years before Dad died. My husband and I became involved in a community project to upgrade the gravesite of America's Known Soldier, Charles Graves, a young WWI private killed on the Hindenburg Line in 1918. In 1922, his remains were on the troopship *Cambria,* the last ship to carry American soldiers home for permanent interment after temporary burial in Europe. The president of the United States asked that one of these be designated to represent all of the known dead and be interred at Arlington next to the Tomb of the Unknown Soldier. A random run of a finger down the long list of heroic dead on their way home stopped at the name of Charles Graves of Rome, Georgia. But the boy's mother thwarted the president's plan. She wanted him buried at home. Therefore, the parade and ceremony for this boy who represented all of America's known fallen heroes were held in the small town of Rome, Georgia, with all of the pomp and circumstance that could be mustered.

In the year 2000, the Known Soldier gravesite in Myrtle Hill, a beautiful old cemetery in downtown Rome, was upgraded and expanded to include Veterans Plaza, designed to more comfortably accommodate attendees of the annual Veterans Day ceremony that has been held there since 1923. To help fund the project, brick pavers were sold for $50, each one honoring a veteran, living or dead. Our family bought several bricks. Honored there now are my dad and my father-in-law, both veterans of WWII, along with an uncle-in-law who was KIA on Okinawa. Also honored are my maternal grandfather who was a veteran of WWI, my brother-in-law, my husband and two Marines who served with him in Vietnam—one KIA there. Many of our regional veterans are honored and many wars are represented, up to and including the war on terror.

On the day of the dedication, November 11, 2000, our family and guests (two Marines who served with my husband, and the brother and sister-in-law of the Marine who died in Vietnam) gathered. My dad stood through the entire event, taking it all in. The ceremony featured a flyover by a vintage plane. When this occurred, the noise of the low-flying plane caused my dad to throw his hands over his head and say "No—No—No." I thought this reaction was exaggerated for effect, if not fake altogether. Now, having read Dad's firsthand accounts of defending against the Luftwaffe, I understand the reaction was a valid reflex.

Only recently I remembered this: when I was a freshman in college, away from home for the first time, my father handwrote me a letter every single day. Dad said he knew how it felt to have no mail and no news from home. He made it his mission to see that I always had something in hand. My mother would send me a couple of typed paragraphs weekly. I went to the mailroom in the student center once or twice daily. Almost every time there was at least one long envelope, thickened by the several folded pages within. I knew Dad's handwriting from a distance, even through the tiny glass window in the tiny brass door that opened to me with my very own combination of turns of the tiny brass knob. I would open each prize envelope and read and read and read, searching for some real news of interest. Most were full of mundane thoughts and happenings that I thought boring and without substance. Little did I know what an effort it took to find something to say every single day. His rambling repetition accomplished the goal of fattening up an envelope, but in my opinion was not satisfying to read. I did not save any of them. Shame on me!

While home at Christmas after that first semester, I made the remark that Dad's letters contained no real information. He never wrote to me again. Only now do I understand how stream-of-consciousness works and how well Dad understood the importance of staying connected over space and time. It seems I still have much to learn and understand. Wisdom is always a long time coming.

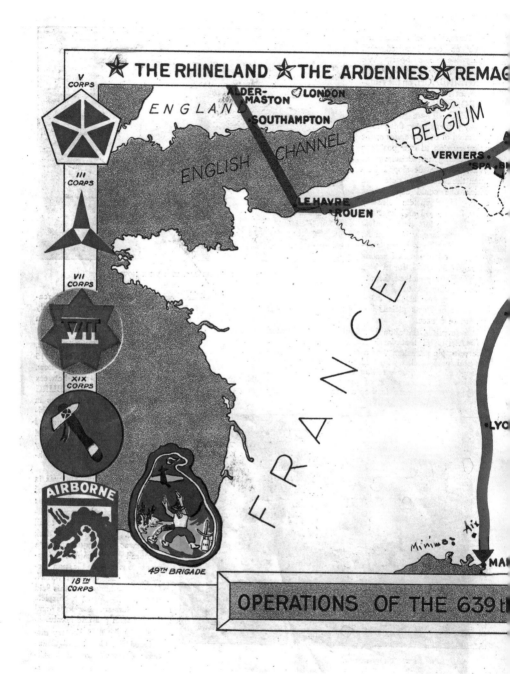

★ THE RHINELAND ★ THE ARDENNES ★ REMAG

V CORPS

III CORPS

VII CORPS

XIX CORPS

AIRBORNE

18TH CORPS

ENGLAND

ALDER-MASTON
LONDON
SOUTHAMPTON

ENGLISH CHANNEL

LE HAVRE
ROUEN

BELGIUM

VERVIERS
SPA B

FRANCE

LYO

Minimes
Ai
MA

49TH BRIGADE

OPERATIONS OF THE 639t